A Convergent Model of Renewal

A Convergent Model of Renewal

Remixing the Quaker Tradition in a Participatory Culture

C. WESS DANIELS

Foreword by Ben Pink Dandelion

☙PICKWICK *Publications* • Eugene, Oregon

A CONVERGENT MODEL OF RENEWAL
Remixing the Quaker Tradition in a Participatory Culture

Copyright © 2015 C. Wess Daniels. All rights reserved. Except for brief quotations in critical publications or reviews, no part of this book may be reproduced in any manner without prior written permission from the publisher. Write: Permissions, Wipf and Stock Publishers, 199 W. 8th Ave., Suite 3, Eugene, OR 97401.

Pickwick Publications
An Imprint of Wipf and Stock Publishers
199 W. 8th Ave., Suite 3
Eugene, OR 97401

www.wipfandstock.com

ISBN 13: 978-1-4982-0119-3

Cataloging-in-Publication data:

Daniels, C. Wess

A convergent model of renewal : remixing the Quaker tradition in a participatory culture / C. Wess Daniels.

xvi + 224 p. ; 23 cm. —Includes bibliographical references.

ISBN 13: 978-1-4982-0119-3

1. Church renewal. 2. Society of Friends. I. Title.

BV600.3 D25 2015

Manufactured in the U.S.A.   02/19/2015

To Stan Thornburg
A dear friend and Quaker minister who truly knew how to remix.

Contents

Foreword by Ben Pink Dandelion | ix
Acknowledgments | xiii
Abbreviations | xvi

Introduction | 1

CHAPTER 1
Alasdair MacIntyre and the Ongoing Nature of Tradition | 22

CHAPTER 2
Stephen Bevans and Mission: Developing the Synthetic Model | 43

CHAPTER 3
Henry Jenkins and Participatory Culture | 64

CHAPTER 4
A Convergent Model for Participatory Renewal | 101

CHAPTER 5
The Convergent Model and Early Quakerism | 119

CHAPTER 6
The Convergent Model and Freedom Friends Church | 162

Conclusion | 205

Afterword | 215
Bibliography | 217

Foreword

THIS IS A BOOK which claims to be about Quaker renewal but the insights Wess Daniels lays out here so clearly can be applied to the renewal of any faith tradition. Wess weaves a line between the dangers of anarchic individualistic resistance to the wisdom of the tradition and the strictures of abstracted doctrine held over and against the changing needs of communities in fresh contexts. I use "weaves" deliberately because this model is like a woven fabric, a quilt of many pieces laid out by many apprentices and sewn together in holy obedience to our present-day callings. Later the quilt will be reconfigured, subtracted from and added to, remixed, collectively re-sewn in a new and exciting a pattern and shape. This book is manifesto for faith renewal globally and in that, for greater cross-cultural cross-contextual dialogue and understandings. If we all authentically involve ourselves in the processes outlined here, we cannot but add to mutual understanding and world peace. For whilst the first motion is crisis, this is intrinsically a model of creative and constructive participation at its most communal level.

As Wess Daniels says:

> A model of this nature must take seriously all of the components of contextual theology: tradition, culture, dialogue and praxis. Building on these threads, the model developed here will be called a "convergent model of participatory renewal," convergent because the model is a synthesis of tradition and emergence of God's work in today's context, participatory because the model derives insights from culture studies' understanding of "participatory culture," an emerging culture that celebrates production over consumption, grassroots organizing, decentralized authority and collaboration as the means by which people are actively engaged with popular culture.

We engage with our own tradition, with what we are called to do, with the context we are embedded within, and with each other. Wess calls us to listen to the insights of MacIntyre, Bevans, and Jenkins and to find in faithful examples of church history those who have already modeled renewal for us along the way without knowledge of any book or theory. As is so often the case with good theory, it seems like common sense when it is pointed out to us and we start to see it everywhere.

MacIntyre's insights into the importance of tradition and, when working well, its self-generated renewal underpin convergent holiness, and help us understand the work of those who carry reflexive renewal forward, who struggle creatively with the quest for authenticity, who seek to cross the binary divides of the culture wars and internal fragmentation, who wish to return to essentials away from the propertied inertia of a task-oriented organization that has made a captive of tradition. We can see what we are not to do as well as what we can. We can hear the need to listen, to engage, to utilise, to fuse, to move from death to life, to resurrect our faith vehicle through complex synthesis. We are even given criteria to measure success:

> Has the tradition truly succeeded in overcoming a crisis? If it has, it will fulfill three exacting requirements.... The first requirement is that the newly enhanced scheme is able to systematically and coherently resolve the problems that the tradition initially found to be intractable. Second, it must be able to explain how and why the tradition, before the new concepts were adopted, became sterile and incoherent within its previous paradigm. Third, continuity between structures must be tended to carefully in these first two tasks.... Therefore, the three criteria could be summed up as (a) resolution of the previous problems, (b) explanation of what went wrong, and (c) continuity of some shared beliefs and practices with the tradition of enquiry.

We are not here to save Quakerism or any other tradition but to nurture our spiritual life as part of the people of God. This is a theme taken up on a wider platform by Douglas John Hall, Canadian theologian, who argues that the church needs prophecy rather than preservation. What is critical, he says, is not the context we find ourselves in but how we respond to it. Douglas John Hall argues that focusing on membership numbers for example is unimportant in the faith order of things, rekindling our spiritual essence is crucial to spiritual authenticity.

The work of Bevans offers us a model of post-colonial contextualisation that undercuts hierarchies of limited agency and arid theorisation based on notions and abstractions. It helps us challenge the individualism of the Enlightenment project, the way in which contract took over from covenant. It gives us agency again as everyday mystics, seeking to practice the Presence in the midst of the whole of life, in which we can start to live life as a prayer without ceasing. In this place and space (a practiced place), in Jenkins' term, we can be resolved as fans of God, participants in the creation of a culture of faith, co-creators in a bricolage of poaching. Here we remix and play, fools for God. Here agency and wisdom is extended beyond the faith elites, the professors, to us all. However, this is not then a free-for-all, a libertarian frenzy of freedom without responsibility, but a place to play within the parameters of the wisdom of the tradition, within the discernment of the community and the insights of the collective, our localised neighbourhood, our valley of love and delight, our holy syndicates.

In summary, Wess Daniels tells us:

> A convergent model for participatory renewal is based on the insights of MacIntyre, Bevans and Jenkins. The process is initiated when apprentices seek to overcome the confrontations, incoherences and break down of schemata that arise within their tradition. In order to bring about convergent renewal they must put in dialogue the original texts and interpretations of their tradition and current cultural artifacts and practices, putting them together (through same-saying and concept borrowing) in a way that (a) remixes the original texts of the tradition with new texts while maintaining their continuity—their uniqueness and complementarity; (b) as it resists a passive culture of consumerism in order to foster an authentic subjective experience; (c) and drawing on many voices forming an open work of shared power and knowledge; (d) and by doing so they will have created practices of an alternative participatory community that gives witness in the world.

It is model of covenantal renewal, of mutual open-ended promise-keeping and faithfulness. As I say, it can apply to all faiths. The first half is handbook for all of us.

For Quakers however, this book is timely and adds a further dimension. The compelling case studies of early Friends and Freedom Friends Church not only make original contributions to Quaker studies but also act as an affirmation of the many calls for convergence worldwide in Quakerism today. As I write this, British Friends are looking towards a new vision of Quakerism in exactly the ways described here, perceiving crisis and incoherence, dialoguing with the past and with the new context within and outwith Quakerism and working together to create a participatory community that can lend its hands to God.

This is an erudite but accessible volume. It is critically important in all that it unpacks for us. Significantly too, I feel the text walks the walk. It doesn't just profess the theory, the substance of faith, it possesses it. It shines as an example of the very theory it outlines. It adds to the fabric of renewal in an authentic way. It is part, an important part I believe, of the remix of retrieval and restoration, the collage of covenantal community. Now we need to act.

Ben Pink Dandelion
Woodbrooke Quaker Study Centre and
the Universities of Birmingham and Lancaster, England.

Acknowledgments

IF IT TAKES A village to raise a child, then it takes a multitude of villages to write a book. I am indebted to many people, many friendships and dialogue partners from many different "villages" throughout my lifetime. So many have helped me dream, think creatively and generate the ideas for this project. Here are the names of only few.

First, there is the community at Fuller Seminary. As strange as it might first appear as a Quaker wanting to ask specific questions about the Quaker tradition, Fuller Theological Seminary—which is not a Quaker school—was the perfect place for me to study. At Fuller I was encouraged to ask questions, read broadly, and take the risk of making connections that ultimately resulted in this book. My mentor, Ryan Bolger, was especially helpful in being generous with the space I needed to explore possible ideas and answers without pressing me into a mold. He helped me to think outside the box and constantly challenged my understanding of what the church can be in today's culture.

In Wilbert Shenk's course, "Missiological Perspectives on Contemporary Cultures," I had some of my first key insights that became the seeds of this project. His knowledge and insight into the importance of looking for God at work in culture helped open my eyes to new possibilities for Quakerism. "Ben" Pink Dandelion's long-distance mentorship, all the way from Birmingham, England, has been indispensable. First, in learning about Quakers from a Quaker scholar and second in pushing my thinking beyond the edges of what I knew coming from an evangelical background. He provided the convergence I needed to put my model to work. I am indebted to Nancey Murphy who not only introduced me to Alasdair MacIntyre, but she embodies the value of tradition and works constantly to innovate from that place.

Second, there are the various Quaker communities I have drawn inspiration from. The church I pastor, Camas Friends Church, has been tremendously supportive of my scholarship, giving me time to complete the majority of chapters that became the body of this work, allowing flexibility in my schedule for writing, studying and traveling where I have been able to present these ideas out in other Quaker communities and develop them accordingly. And they have been gracious enough to allow me to work out many ideas within our meeting there.

I give deep thanks to Freedom Friends Church for allowing me to study them, email them questions, for reading and making suggestions on edits of an earlier part of this research, and just letting me be a groupie. Peggy Morrison and Alivia Biko have mentored me, teaching me about what is possible within the Quaker tradition and giving me great optimism. Freedom Friends embodies the idea of what it means to be a convergent meeting and is an example to all of us. I can't say enough about T. Vail Palmer Jr.'s role in this project. Not only have we met for the past four years almost monthly to share questions and ideas as we both work on our books, but his work is a part of the very scaffolding of this project. Finally, Jaye Kismet's story was one that helped move me to a more generous place theologically and taught me about the importance of being authentic.

Those who are a part of convergent Friends deserve thanks as well. Many of the ideas here have been worked out in collaboration and friendship with those a part of convergent Friends. Robin Mohr has been a wonderful friend and partner in this work; she has taught me a lot about the Quaker faith, and invited me to lead workshops and co-write articles with her. She was the one who invited Emily and I to Quaker Heritage Day many years ago where the spark was lit for this project. Martin Kelley has been a great friend and collaborator as well. There are many others who are a part of convergent Friends who are carrying this work forward: Noah Baker Merrill, Zachary Moon, Christian Repoley, Chris Mohr, Ashley Wilcox, Chad Stephenson, Kathy Hyzy, Betsy Blake and all the women a part of Multwood.

Third are the family and friends who have supported me along the way. First and foremost is my mom, Jo Welden, who has been very supportive throughout my many years of college and grad-school. Others I'd like to thank are: Craig Miller and Ellen Strecker, Scott and Mary Daniels, Aaron Daniels, John Geib, Herbert Dymale, Jim Whisenant, Mark Lau Branson, Amy Kaherl, Kyle David Bennet, Susan Dow, Jamie Pitts, Chase

Roden, Brent Bill, Simon Latham, Jez Smith, Jade Souza, Seth Martin, Mark Condo, Joel Daniel Harris, Joel and Cherice Bock, Darla Samuelson, Jason Minnix, Emily Stewart, Dan McCracken, Carole Spencer, Jeff Dudiak, Mike Huber, Charles Martin and my very dear friend and mentor Stan Thornburg who we lost in the spring of 2014. My editors Janelle D'Alasandro, Alicia DK and Georgia Shaw. My outside reader MaryKate Morse. A very special thanks to Wally and Leslie Cole, Al and Sheri Hendrix, Rev. Jessie Vedanti, all of St. Anne's Episcopal Church in Washougal, and Pam and Jodi at Caffe Piccolo for providing writing space. And to Rev. Shelly Fayette, Aaron Scott, and Elena Vera many conversations with the three of you helped to shape the tone, ideas and outlook of this text.

I also want to thank Chris Spinks and the good folks at Pickwick who accepted this manuscript for publication and have labored to help this dream of publishing become a reality.

Finally, in keeping with Jesus' words about the last being first, I acknowledge my wife Emily for all of the time and the work that she put into this project. Not only did she work for a number of years to support our family while I was working on this research, but she's freed me up for time away to do the writing. Emily listened to these ideas and helped me refine them more than anyone else. She helped to keep me motivated to finished, even when motivation was lacking. She is the one who continues to inspire me to dream.

Abbreviations

DIY	Do It Yourself
FFC	Freedom Friends Church
FWCC	Friends World Committee for Consultation-Section of the Americas
KJV	King James Version
NRSV	New Revised Standard Version
NWYM	Northwest Yearly Meeting
NPYM	North Pacific Yearly Meeting

Introduction

> "I don't want to be an anti, against anybody. I simply want to be the builder of a great affirmation: the affirmation of God, who loves us and who wants to save us."
>
> —Oscar A. Romero, *The Violence of Love*

In 1970, Everett Cattell, Quaker missionary and ecumenicist, made a clarion call to Friends for the renewal of their church. His vision was that the Friends Church find a future not in simply retrieving the past, or accurately predicting the future, but rather as missionaries,

> Perhaps the call is now before us for a new seeking: a seeking to find where God's Spirit is actually at work in today's world and then a giving of ourselves to work with Him—whether within or without the framework of Friends. The future of Friends may be like the grain of wheat, which must fall to the ground and die. Perhaps this would be the way to a new harvest. (Cattell 1970: 5)

This renewal of the church through mission draws on both past and present, tradition and context. In other words, it is what Quakers have called in recent years: convergent. "Convergent" used in this context is a neologism, naming the interplay between a group being conservative—to the tradition—and emergent—within context.[1]

---

1. Robin Mohr, an unprogrammed Quaker from San Francisco, was the first to use this term in 2006, suggesting that this specialized meaning explained a growing movement within the North American Quaker context (Mohr, "Robinopedia").

QUAKERISM IN THE FACE OF OBSTACLE AND OPPORTUNITY

At the intersection of these two poles, the socially embodied community discerns the movements of God's Spirit and is renewed. Cattell's "model" is an early reference to what would later be called contextual theology. It is closest to Stephen Bevans' *synthetic model* of contextual theology, which I will develop later. Cattell was no Quaker apologist. He believed that renewal would happen "whether within or without the framework of Friends." While he hoped to see the Friends Church catch the missionary fervency that he believed early Quakers had—and had lost—the possibility included renouncing the institutions of Quakerism.

Following Cattell's cue, I argue that renewal is not only possible for Friends by finding God's Spirit at work in the present, but that it can— and already is—happening "within the framework of Friends." In fact, that framework, or as I prefer, "tradition," is itself the resource that makes this renewal possible. My task is to develop a model of renewal that contains within it Cattell's suggestion—*a la* Jesus—that renewal comes through a grain of wheat falling to the ground, or as I will later suggest, a remix of the tradition that at once pays homage to the original piece of art—the seed—while creating something new out of it—what is born out of the seed's "death." A model of this nature must take seriously all of the components of contextual theology: tradition, culture, dialogue and praxis. Building on these threads, the model developed here will be called a "convergent model of participatory renewal," convergent because the model is a synthesis of tradition and emergence of God's work in today's context, participatory because the model derives insights from culture studies' understanding of "participatory culture," an emerging culture that celebrates production over consumption, grassroots organizing, decentralized authority and collaboration as the means by which people are actively engaged with today's culture.

In hopes of giving some basic background, through this opening chapter I introduce the Friends and some of the internal difficulties they face as a faith tradition: brought on by internal separations in the nineteenth century, shifting demographics and changing contexts. Second, I briefly describe the three theoretical partners whose thought will be the framing of the convergent model. Rooted in the philosophy of Alasdair MacIntyre, Stephen Bevan's understanding of contextual theology and Henry Jenkins work in participatory culture, I develop an understanding of tradition and mission that has potential to lead to revitalization within Quakerism.

According to Michael Harkin, revitalization theory has become oriented around "deprivation" and the above example is true in this instance. Deprivation in "the typical case involves a group declining in political power, wealth, well-being, population, or, usually, a combination of these that develops a movement out of a bricolage of its own cultural materials, with the explicit purpose being to eliminate or at least exclude the threatening dominant group" (Harkin 2004: xxix).

However, deprivation is not enough to operate as the sole reason or diagnostic category for change within Quakerism because, as Harkin suggests, it is subject to "ethnographic interpretation" (ibid.). Thus, "enrichment" becomes a second category useful from revitalization theory. The "enrichment thesis" is where a movement builds on the richness of the resources (whether wealth, information, technology, and so on) available within ones own culture to produce something that is new within that context. Here "convergent Friends" (see later in this chapter) exemplify both a response to deprivation, as well as the enrichment thesis.

Third, I describe the work of convergent Friends as being both the inspiration and testing ground for the work that follows.

The Beginning of Quakerism

In the 1640s, England saw the beginnings of Quakerism, and by the 1660s there was close to 66,000 Quakers in Britain and Ireland (Dandelion 2007: 43).[2] The growth of the Quaker movement in Great Britain, into the Continent and the Colonies, was spurred on by an aggressive missionary impulse within the group. These early Quaker ministers and missionaries referred to themselves as "The First Publishers of Truth," publishing multitudes of pamphlets, tracts, epistles and books. This spread the Quaker message and drew attention to their radical understanding of Christianity (Russell 1979: 166–67).

Over against the control, hierarchy and inequality of the political and religious culture of seventeenth-century England, Quakerism was a fully participative and alternative social community. The history of Quaker origins is the story of a radical Christian movement that emerged

2. Dandelion suggests that during this period almost 1 percent of the British population was Quaker (*An Introduction to Quakerism*, 43).

during a tumultuous time in England in the 1650s. This Christian movement was radical because it was egalitarian, grassroots-oriented, and counter-cultural to the State and established church of the time. William Penn's "Primitive Christianity Revived," suggests that early Friends were self-aware of their attempt to go back to the root of the Christian tradition. Furthermore, early Quakerism was a movement that was inclusive, prophetic and participatory. It not only called the established church back to its roots, but it gathered together the dissenters, disinherited and the rejected of the church of their time and these became the folks who led the movement. Friends were also set apart because they rejected the necessity of clergy, the use of sacramental elements, held to a belief in the Inward Light of Christ in all people and embodied an eschatology that believed in the immediate and full presence of Christ.

Despite the random imprisonments Friends faced for producing or selling Quaker literature, they were very effective in their output (Russell 1942: 79). Elbert Russell acknowledges, "In the seven decades after 1653 there were 440 Quaker writers, who published 2,678 separate publications, varying from a single page tract to folios of nearly a thousand pages" (1942: 79). Adding to this fervor was the "Valiant Sixty," a group of Quaker missionaries went out two-by-two into the South of England and Wales in 1654. This was modeled after Luke 10:1 where Jesus' sent out seventy of his disciples. This mission succeeded in expanding the reach of the early movement all across England, especially in the south such as London (1942: 34).

The expansion of Friends continued with mainly female missionaries embarking westward across the ocean as early as 1656. Russell suggests that, "the first Quakers who came to America were almost wholly missionaries, impelled by the nascent enthusiasm of the Commonwealth period" (1942: 38). Mary Fisher Dyer and Anne Austin began the "Quaker invasion of Massachusetts" (Russell 39); Dyer was one of the first Quakers martyred on Colony soil. This and many other tragic actions against Quakers did little to stop the flood of Quaker missionaries. The concentration of Quaker missionaries increased to the point that after 1656, Barbados Island was referred to by Friends as the "Nursery of Truth." The Nursery of Truth, was a natural landing place after a long journey that served as a community, training ground, and distributing point for early Quaker missionaries (1942: 39).

By 1681, Quaker William Penn began his "Holy Experiment" in Pennsylvania. The goal was to create a moral settlement in the colonies, based on Quaker principles and practices that offered respite for religious dissenters under the banner of religious freedom and liberty of conscience (Dandelion 2007: 51). Quakers remained in control of the Pennsylvania Assembly until they began voluntarily withdrawing in 1756 over a refusal to participate in the French and Indian War (ibid., 52).[3]

By 1758, the Philadelphia Yearly Meeting "advised any Friend against holding any civil office which might involve compromise with Quaker principles" or marking a larger shift away from overall activity in the world that Quakers had been so successful in up until this point.[4] This withdrawal mirrored a growing sectarianism and eventual decline of the fervent mission activity that early Friends exhibited.

Nineteenth-Century Fragmentation

In the nineteenth century, the Quaker tradition underwent crisis. This was the outcome of the fragmenting forces of modernity which brought forth great transformations—and separations—within the American Quaker landscape (see Hamm 1992). Over time, Quakerism became three streams all finding their origins in that critical time period: evangelical (Gurneyite), "liberal-Liberal" (Hicksite),[5] and conservative (Wilburite).

---

3. See Yoder, Koontz, and Alexis-Baker, "Quakerism in Early American: The Holy Experiment" in *Christian Attitudes to War, Peace, and Revolution*. Where they suggest that the ultimate response of a pacifist run government would be to voluntarily bow out if the only other option was to take up the sword.

4. It would be too much of a caricature to say that there was a blanket withdrawal of all Friends. The charge of "Quietism" has come under scrutiny in Elaine Pryce's fine work "'Upon the Quakers and the Quietists': Quietism, Power and Authority in Late Seventeenth-Century France, and Its Relation to Quaker History and Theology" (Pryce, *Upon the Quakers*, 2010).

5. Dandelion writes: "For liberal-Liberal Friends, theology has become a story, God an option. Key parts of the tradition can be, and have been, questioned as new sets of individual experience/interpretations modify collective popular belief over time. The collective orthodoxy is reframed by each generation in a revised book of discipline. Liberal-Liberal Quakerism is one in which belief is pluralised, privatised, but also marginalised: it is not seen as important. This kind of Quakerism is held together by an adherence to form, by the way the group is religious, not by what it believes. There are Muslim, Hindu, Sikh, and Buddhist Quakers, theist and non-theist, agnostic and atheist" (Dandelion, *An Introduction to Quakerism*, 134). This group was formed by classic tenets of modernity such as the foundations of experience, cultural relevancy, new revelation, and adopted ideas of progressivism (ibid.). Interestingly, MacIntyre uses a similar designation: "Liberalism, as I have understood it in this book, does of course appear in contemporary debates in a number of guises and in so doing

There are two other ways these three groups are also identified. The first way is by their style of worship: programmed, unprogrammed and semi-programmed. A programmed Quaker meeting (evangelical) has a pastor and the worship will often, though not always, include silent worship,[6] along with singing, preaching, and prayers. An unprogrammed Quaker meeting (liberal and conservative Quakerism) has no pastor and participates exclusively in silent worship, waiting upon God to give rise to "vocal" ministry. The category of a semi-programmed meeting has emerged more recently and may or may not have a pastor and will have more emphasis on this silent or "waiting" worship with some level of programming. The second way is by the names of the three men who founded each particular strand of Quakerism, John Joseph Gurney, Elias Hicks and John Wilbur.

As I will suggest later, this crisis and the subsequent transformations parallel the emergence of modernity. Modernity is based on a philosophical system that is anti-tradition, foundationalist, and individualistic. It held deep implications not only for faith traditions but all of Western society. These three characteristics were adopted—mostly unconsciously but in some instances consciously—by the three branches of Quakerism and are still present within these organizations today. Anthony Giddens argues, "Inherent in the idea of modernity is a contrast with tradition" (Giddens 1990: 36). Part of the contrast is in how reflexivity is understood within modernity. Within tradition, interpretation is a "reflexive monitoring of action" rooted in a community (ibid., 37), whereas in modernity

---

is often successful in preempting the debate by reformulating quarrels and conflicts with liberalism, so that they appear to have become debates within liberalism, putting in question this or that particular set of attitudes or policies, but not the fundamental tenets of liberalism with respect to individuals and expressions of their preferences. The so-called conservatism and so-called radicalism in these contemporary guises are in general mere stalking-horses for liberalism: the contemporary debates within modern political systems are almost exclusively between conservative liberals, liberal liberals, and radical liberals. There is little place in such political systems for the criticism of the system itself, that is for putting liberalism in company" (MacIntyre, *Whose Justice?*, 392).

6. Within the broadly diverse Quaker world there are many names for worship done in silence: open, waiting, expectant or silent worship are a few names. What is at the heart of this practice of waiting worship is that the gathered community listens together in the silence for the Spirit to speak to individuals and prompt them to speak out of the silence to the rest of the group. For a fuller treatment of this subject see John Punshon's *Encounter with Silence*.

there is a narrowing of this field (social practices are constantly monitored) and a tightening of the feedback loop (based more in individual reason rather than communal interpretation) to the point that "thoughts and actions are constantly refracted back upon one another" (ibid., 38).

Present Day Quakers

What was once characterized as a prophetic and missionary movement has become pluralistic, fragmented and lacking a unified narrative. The "Great Separations" led inevitably to conflict between Quakers of different branches. Each newly formulated branch touts its own rival theories about the origins and core message of the Quaker tradition. Each polarization represents only a piece of the larger tradition. In the twentieth century, local meetings continued down this trajectory of fragmentation leading to a loss of identity, a break with the tradition, and a deepening pluralism among Friends. Dandelion succinctly puts the key differences this way:

> Evangelical Friends tend to find their identity in doctrine whereas Liberal Friends define themselves in terms of their 'behavioral creed,' the way they operate as a religious group. Liberal Friends will mention their form of worship as a defining characteristic rather than the theology underpinning it.[7] Experience is primary and sufficient for Liberal Friends as a source of spiritual authority. Conservative Friends require a blend of revelation and Scripture whereas Evangelical Friends emphasis Scripture above revelation. Liberal and Conservative Friends identify primarily as Quaker. For Evangelical Friends, they may see themselves as Christians primarily, who happen to be Quaker. (Dandelion 2007: 242)

In the twenty-first century, Quakers remain in this stagnant place, as witnessed by the decline of Quakers in the West as well as their dwindling social influence.[8] In a recent issue of *Friends Journal*, Robin Mohr, the executive secretary of Friends World Committee for Consultation-Section of the Americas (FWCC), noted that whereas there is growth among Friends in Asia, Europe and Africa, there is decline among Friends in

---

7. For a thorough treatment of how silent worship operates as a behavioral creed within liberal-Liberal Quakerism see Dandelion, *Liturgies of Quakerism*.

8. For instance, Quaker sociologist Pink Dandelion has predicted 2037 as the "death date" for Quakers in Britain.

North America. "FWCC has reported a decrease of about 10,000 over the past five years" (Mohr 2013: 28).

In Evangelical Friends churches in the US there is little numerical growth (Dandelion 2007: 248). Some of the largest of these churches have broken their connection to their Quaker past in hopes of competing in the American spiritual marketplace, while other Quakers—such as John Punshon in his *Reasons for Hope*—have issued a call to Evangelical Friends to return to the rich resources of their tradition to find meaningful renewal.

Each Quaker yearly meeting, monthly meeting and local church in the West wrestles with a way forward, hoping that revitalization will come through: (a) clinging to the tradition, (b) rejecting tradition in favor of being "biblical," "getting people saved," or other new methods of church growth, or (c) rejecting both Quaker tradition and the Bible in favor of a new pluralistic identity that reflects a growing fragmented cultural context. Often the aspects of tradition that get trimmed from Evangelical Friends are those practices that make Friends unique: silent worship, practice of discernment and consensus-based decision-making, and the "testimonies," which are practices rooted in nonviolence, equality, simplicity and truth-telling.

I argue, following Punshon and others, that the future of the Friends Church relies on its ability to draw on the distinctives of its tradition while continuing to contextualize those distinctives within today's participatory culture (Punshon 2001: 357–59). Simply put, if Quakers wish to remain Quaker the way forward includes reaching back; tradition is the only grounds for innovation. Only a revitalization that includes the mission and practices of the Quaker tradition will give reason for hope.

TRADITION, MISSION AND PARTICIPATORY CULTURE

In the previous section, background information was provided to explain the development of Quakerism as it stands today in America. Given the fragmentation and loss of identity, the tradition is in crisis. The way out of this crisis involves apprentices within the tradition retrieving resources within their tradition and reinterpreting them within today's context.

I argue that this retrieval and reinterpretation is the responsibility of the apprentices, or those who have been steeped in the narrative and practices of their tradition, and are consequently the ones most affected not only by the demise of their particular movement, but by the problems associated with their context that create the need for reinterpretation. Therefore, the model constructed is convergent in that it builds on the importance of both tradition and context, while recognizing the essential character of renewal is a participative engagement of its apprentices.

The first pole within the convergent model is tradition. The church's relationship to the past is an essential part of what it means to be the church; biblical faith is rooted in a narrative-based tradition. For the church, tradition is something that is alive and passed down to new generations. As Jaroslav Pelikan puts it: "Tradition is the living faith of the dead, traditionalism is the dead faith of the living" (Pelikan 1971: 9). However, the Enlightenment led to anti-tradition sentiments within the Western church that continues to inform Christianity today.

I experienced this anti-tradition influence first-hand as a young college student at a Friends' college. My initial experience of Friends churches and my education at a Friends college began from the perspective of what is known as the Gurneyite branch of Quakerism.[9] This branch finds its origins in the work of nineteenth-century Friend John Joseph Gurney (1788–1847). Gurney was drawn towards evangelicalism in his theology and understanding of mission. While Gurney was in many ways a traditional Quaker—for instance, he held the traditional Quaker view on the sacraments—his teachings opened the door to newer anti-tradition innovations within the church.

Today, Gurneyite Friends have pastors, sing during worship, and often have little to no silence during their gathered worship time. Some, such as those in Evangelical Friends Church Southwest, allow the use of physical sacraments in their meetings for worship. Others have all but stopped the practice of silence as central to their worship. More importantly, Evangelical "Friends" often differentiate themselves from "Quakers" (or those they see as more socially and theologically liberal, who worship in silence and generally identify more with the Quaker tradition). It is not unusual for these Friends to see "tradition"—and what Pelikan would call traditionalism—as a distraction from how they understand and present the gospel. In many of these colleges and Friends Churches, a connection to their history is seen as a liability to attracting new members, or is simply forgotten due to a devaluing of tradition and history within our

---

9. Part of the ethos of that school at the time was that any public knowledge of its Quaker tradition would make it less appealing to a broad range of students, so this part was downplayed (Oliver, Cherry, and Cherry, *Founded by Friends*, 203ff).

churches today. Added all together, these elements reveal anti-tradition strands of the Enlightenment within Friends churches.

George Marsden (1991), Nancey Murphy (1996), and Mark Noll (1994, 2002) have all done work to show the connections between the Enlightenment and the historical roots of Evangelicalism. For instance, Mark Noll argues that Commonsense philosophy heavily influenced the Revolutionary generation and helped that generation overcome some of their greatest challenges:

> First to justify the break with Great Britain. Second was to establish principles of social order for a new nation that was repudiating autocratic government, hierarchical political assumptions, and automatic deference to tradition. The third task, for evangelicals, was to preserve the hereditary position of Christianity in a culture that denied absolute sovereignty to any authority and that was turning against the structures of traditional religion (like the political episcopate or the establishment of congregation churches in New England) as actively as it was turning against other inherited authorities. (Noll 1994: 87–88)

According to Noll, the best place to look for influences of the Enlightenment on evangelicals is on their use of the Bible (ibid., 96). Prior to 1790, the Bible was something that people had less access to; it was something they would read together while gathered together during their meetings for worship. Leading up to 1790 there were only twenty-two editions of the Bible available in the Western World.

However, in 1790, copyright law changed, allowing for the increase in printing Bibles. From that point on, editions increased dramatically until slowing between 1830–1865 (ibid., 38). This was a remarkable shift and one that allowed for the Bible to become a book read primarily by individuals rather than communities. Noll also remarks that during this period "Trust in the Bible was religious analogue to political trust in the constitution and the analogy was sometimes drawn explicitly" (ibid., 372). These are just some of the examples of the ways in which evangelicalism followed the Enlightenment in being anti-tradition.

Evangelical Friends are not the only ones guilty of distancing themselves from their tradition. In *Liturgies of Quakerism*, Dandelion argues that "Liberal-liberal" Quakerism has become post-Christian and usurped the Bible. Much of the theological language has been lost, and as a result has drifted away from its "realized" eschatological outlook. In Douglas Gwyn's *Apocalypse of the Word* he argues that the force of George Fox's

(1650s) earliest message is that he believed that Christ had once again returned, was "in time" and manifest in the Quaker movement. This realized eschatology created an apocalyptic fervor among early Friends (Gwyn 1986).

In these Quaker meetings, Christ's role is often obscured and the historical figure of Jesus disavowed. Those who find centrality in Christ are often marginalized in their experience and convictions. Many "Christ-centered" Friends in unprogrammed meetings feel they are not safe using more explicitly Christian language. Consequently, the narrative which once held early Quakerism together has eroded and been replaced with a new one:

> It is argued that the understanding of liturgy mirrors in part the change in understanding of God. As God has become humanised and internalised in the twentieth century, so this 'liturgy of silence' is seen to be an individual event pointing not to an intimate transcendence but to an intimate immanence, or even, in some cases, self-divinity. Quakers in this framework have also moved 'out of time,' though not because of the imminent end of historical time, only the present is real or can be trusted. The future is no longer colliding with the present, rather it has ceased to exist. (Dandelion 2005: 6)

Instead, Dandelion argues these groups are held together by a "behavioral creed." A behavioral creed is the "form" of Quakerism—worshiping in silence or practicing consensus—that holds these individuals together without the need for any deeper sense of the Christian narrative and convictions that formed these practices explain (see Dandelion 2009).

In both instances, evangelical and liberal, these groups fail to grasp the essential nature of tradition. This failure to thrive results from what MacIntyre calls an epistemological crisis within a tradition. A crisis of this nature is one in which certain trusted forms of establishing rationality within a tradition are no longer viable. He suggests that the movement towards a solution follows at least three steps, which I discuss further in chapter 1.

> The solution to a genuine epistemological crisis requires the invention or discovery of new concepts and the framing of some new type or types of theory which meet three highly exacting requirements. First, this in some ways radically new and conceptually enriched scheme, if it is to put an end to epistemological

crisis, must furnish a solution to the problems, which had previously proved intractable in a systematic and coherent way. Second, it must also provide an explanation of just what it was which rendered the tradition, before it had acquired these new resources, sterile or incoherent or both. And third, these first two tasks must be carried out in a way which exhibits some fundamental continuity of the new conceptual and theoretical structures with the shared beliefs in terms of which the tradition of enquiry had been defined up to this point. (MacIntyre 1988: 362)

Thus, MacIntyre is an essential dialogue partner when it comes to developing a model of renewal that intends to take tradition seriously. The failings of these groups to renew tradition offers concrete evidence to MacIntyre's argument that modern individualism is "a self that can have no history" (MacIntyre 1984: 221). According to MacIntyre, the modern-self believes: "I am what I myself choose to be. I can always, if I wish to, put in question what are taken to be the merely contingent social features of my existence." This is true at the individual level, but it holds true at the community level as well. Over against this view MacIntyre argues that tradition is an unavoidable reality:

> What I am, therefore, is in key part what I inherit, a specific past that is present to some degree in my present. I find myself part of a history and that is generally to say, whether I like it or not, whether I recognize it or not, one of the bearers of tradition. (Ibid.)

In MacIntyre's view, the only way for a tradition to progress is by first having the adherents, or apprentices, develop a self-awareness of the problems within their tradition and begin to discover the resources within their tradition for overcoming the crisis. This self-awareness is essential:

> A tradition of enquiry is more than a coherent movement of thought. It is such a movement in the course of which those engaging in that movement become aware of it and of its direction and in self-aware fashion attempt to engage in its debates and to carry its enquiries forward. (Ibid., 326)

For MacIntyre, tradition is the means through which renewal can be brought about within a community, abandoning tradition will not bring about the kind of revitalization called for here.

Following this, the second pole of the convergent model is context. Drawing on a missiological perspective enables one to study the surrounding culture that influences a tradition, the history of that tradition, and provides a sociological look what gave rise to the movements under consideration. In the West, sacred and secular have become a dominant binary that leads the church into an increasingly isolated, inward-focused and stuck place. Too often only focused on what is considered "sacred," that deemed secular has been treated with suspicion or avoided altogether. Missiology reclaims the reality that the church is a church-in-mission and cannot be separated out from its context. Missiology reminds the church that essential to its very ecclesiology is to be in dialogue with cultural forces, looking for where God is already at work within the world. Second, missiology is ultimately concerned with God's past, present and future interactions in the world. As Johannes Verkyl puts it:

> Missiology is the study of the salvation activities of the Father, Son and Holy Spirit through the world geared toward bringing the kingdom of God into existence. . . . [It is] the study of the world-wide church's divine mandate to be ready to serve this God who is aiming his saving acts toward this world. Missiology's task in every age is to investigate scientifically and critically the presuppositions, motives, structures, methods, patterns of cooperation and leadership, which the churches bring to their mandate. (Verkyl 1978: 4)

In the last fifty years contextual theology has spurred on even further developments in missiological study, enabling a corrective to earlier dominate understandings of culture. Contextual theology is the recognition of the subjectivity of experience and theology. All theology is rooted within particular traditions, contexts, and human experiences. As Stephen Bevans puts it "There is not theology as such, only contextual theology," (Bevans 2002: 3). Quakers have done little to recognize or engage contextual theology today. The majority of writings available on Quakerism are either original texts of Quaker ancestors, histories about the Quaker tradition, or popular Quaker spiritual writings. Therefore, I am convinced that missiology is a necessary dialogue partner when it comes to considering the path forward for the church in this present moment. A number of years ago I had the experience of walking into a Quaker library and seeing the astonishing amount of Quaker history and original texts available, yet this collection led me to wonder if the tradition was already dead. With so much history, so much looking back, one might think there was nothing left to learn from culture today.

If the first problem we are confronted with in these post-Enlightenment times is a problem of tradition, the second can be classified as contextual inasmuch as the church operates out of a classical understanding of theology, neglecting the subjective turn theology has taken in recent years (Bevans 2002: 4–5). Because missiology is concerned with the interpretation of the Christian tradition within today's context, contextual theology is an essential component to my convergent model of renewal. For this reason, missiologist Stephen Bevans is the second dialogue partner for the model under development. Where are the adherents who are trying to progress the tradition, carry its enquiries forward, and interpreting the texts of the tradition into new contexts? Is a contextual Quaker theology possible for today, and what might it look like when it is embodied in the community? What resources are already present within the tradition and culture that might bring about a renewed community? These are only a few questions that begin to stimulate missiological reflection in light of one's tradition and context. As I demonstrate in Chapter 2, Bevans' Synthetic model provides the contours for how tradition, culture, dialogue and praxis all come together in a way that creates the possibility for a new contextual theology to arise.

This interplay hints at Bevans' model of contextual theology referred to as the "Synthetic" model which,

> tries to preserve the importance of the gospel message and the heritage of traditional doctrinal formulations while at the same time acknowledging the vital role that context has played and can play in theology, even to the setting of the theological agenda. In addition, the synthesis will include the importance of reflective and intelligent action for the development of a theology that does not ignore the complexities of social and culture change. (Ibid., 89)

Finally, the third pole of the convergent model of renewal is participatory culture.[10] If MacIntyre and Bevans are key to developing a deeper

---

10. There are different methodological approaches to the question of revitalization and problems that plague congregations. As a missiologist, I have chosen to focus strictly on the dialogue between tradition and culture. There are many other areas I could have focused this project, such as: Freidman's family therapy model (Friedman, *A Failure of Nerve*); appreciative inquiry (Branson, *Memories, Hopes, and Conversations*); social movements theory (Snow, Soule, and Kriesi, *The Blackwell Companion to*

understanding of *convergence*, then Henry Jenkins' work in the area of what is known as "participatory culture" names the specific context in which Quakers now find themselves working. Participatory culture not only names a dominant aspect of today's global context, but it also offers practices that might bring about a renewed tradition. As will become clearer throughout, I believe that Quakerism is aptly suited to thrive within "participatory" culture, because the tradition itself is at its core a participatory movement.

Participatory culture names the space within contemporary society where "older notions of passive media spectatorship" have been challenged by a new culture where participants produce the kind of media they wish to consume (Jenkins 2006: 3). "Convergence" is also a term used within participatory culture to name the intersection where old and new media collide. Henry Jenkins argues that the transition between older and new media often creates conflict, as is the case with remix culture. Complications with copyright infringement have dramatically increased since the advent of the Internet and websites like YouTube.

Another key term that Jenkins draws heavily on is poaching. Poaching—a term first used in this context by philosopher Michel de Certeau—describes an active reading strategy where the "fans" poach texts, appropriating them within their own contexts, for their own needs, and according to their own skills (de Certeau 1984). Often poaching is done in ways that break with bourgeois interpretive strategies. Poaching is an example of using texts in new ways that bring new life and new meaning to those texts. Fans who poach are treated within participatory culture similarly to the way apprentices are within MacIntyre's philosophy, and as insiders or practitioners are within the missiology of Stephen Bevans. They are all active participants who are deeply invested in their texts, practices and community and participate in the "construction and circulation of textual meanings" (Jenkins 1992: 24).

Social Movements), and participative models of change such as world café, open space technology and others (Cady, Steven, Devane, and Holman, *The Change Handbook*). Instead, I have delimited my research to the area of change that takes into account three factors: large scale traditions as it is described by Alasdair MacIntyre, contextual theology that comes out of the field of missiology, and cultural studies rooted in participatory culture. The goal of this project is to create a model that demonstrates how missiology and tradition are not antithetical to one another and how participation is a necessary dialogue partner that can bring these two poles together. The model I have created is flexible enough to work in conjunction with other models mentioned above.

There are five practices that take place within participatory culture that will be explored in more detail in chapter 3: authentic resistance, remix, cultural production, collective intelligence, and decentralized authority. Engaging in these kinds of practices often results in the formation of a sixth element: an alternative social community of resistance. This is what I will later refer to as a *renewed participatory community*. Participatory culture gives insight into how renewal takes place within today's culture through a community of participants working together.

CONVERGENT FRIENDS AND "NEW" QUAKERISM

One Quaker group has already begun this process of wrestling with revitalization within Quakerism today: convergent Friends. Convergent, in the way these Quakers intend to use it, is a hybrid of conservative and emergent.[11] They seek to hold together both tradition and mission. Convergent was also meant to name an impulse already happening among some Friends. Robin Mohr, the Quaker who coined the term, writes:

> It describes Friends who are seeking a deeper understanding of our Quaker heritage and a more authentic life in the kingdom of God on Earth, radically inclusive of all who seek to live this life. It includes, among others, Friends from the politically liberal end of the evangelical branch, the Christian end of the unprogrammed branch, and the more outgoing end of the Conservative branch. It includes folks who aren't sure what they believe about Jesus and Christ, but who aren't afraid to wrestle with this question. It includes people who think that a lot of Quaker anachronisms are silly but who are willing to experiment to see which are spiritual disciplines that still hold life and power to transform and improve us. . . . Linguistically, it alludes to an affinity for both Conservative Friends and the Emergent Church. (Mohr 2006)

This term has since become very well-known in Quaker circles and synonymous with bringing different Friends together for dialogue, experimentation of worship, and renewal.

Convergent Friends are, in MacIntyrean language, apprentices who have "become aware [of their tradition] and of its direction and in

---

11. Initially, some of the inspiration and understanding for renewal was drawn from what is called the "emerging church" though the understanding has developed beyond that particular meaning (Gibbs and Bolger, *Emerging Churches*).

self-aware fashion attempt to engage in its debates and to carry its enquiries forward" (MacIntyre 1988: 326). It could be said that convergent Friends signal the emergence of a new Quakerism that transgresses the boundaries of any one Quaker group. Convergent Friends might be better identified as hybrid Quakerism, driven towards a more holistic expression of faith as it is rooted in tradition, while seeking to faithfully live out that tradition in today's context. Convergent Quakerism rejects the binaries propounded by Evangelical, Conservative and Liberal-liberal Quaker streams of Quakerism (Daniels 2011: 87). Because dialogue with tradition and culture are central, Convergent Friends embodies the features of today's participatory culture in that it resists the categories available within Quakerism, bypassing institutional hierarchy and bias through grassroots organizing, largely empowered through the internet and social media (ibid.). It is a decentralized group that produces new material through their blogs and local gatherings. They remix Quaker texts by applying them to their lives in new and creative ways. They display collective intelligence through the free sharing of information, ideas, and understandings of the Quaker tradition.

The core features of convergent Friends can be summarized in terms of three impulses: tradition, mission and dialogue. First, they have, as MacIntyre puts it *"an adequate sense of tradition,"* which includes a commitment to the tradition as a whole (MacIntyre 1984: 223). Thus, convergent Friends share an affinity with the "Conservative" branch of Quakers.[12] Second, convergent Friends have a contemporary cultural—or emergent—impulse inasmuch as they seek to translate and contextualize their tradition into new contexts through a variety of means. For instance, many convergent Friends use blogging as a forum for expression and making public their faith. This gives new meaning to the old idea of Friends as "Publishers of Truth."

There are six practices that I have identified within the convergent Friends community that blend tradition and mission: practice holism rather than adopt a dualistic faith; take seriously the need to have a public presence within society; meet and worship in whatever space is available; seek to incorporate fresh ideas of what it means to be the church in the twenty-first century by offering contextual examples of Quaker practices;

---

12. "Conservative" here is a self-designation that this group of Quaker use to identify their sense of seeking to conserve tradition. Often these Friends wear plain dress, use plain speech, and worship without pastors in old Quaker meetinghouses, such as the historic one in Barnesville, Ohio.

work within the structures while not being contained or determined by them; place emphasis on friendships and hospitality (Daniels 2010).

There are also many Quakers who were involved with the Occupy movements in the United States and Great Britain. They drew support for this work by collecting financial support, writing minutes, teaching Occupy how to do consensus business models, calling for public silent worship, and by participating in these grassroots communities (Smith 2012). Third, through dialogue they seek an empathetic listening with diverse Quakers. Thus, there is what we might call an ecumenical or "cross-branch" impulse. Dialogue helps convergent Friends become aware of and draw on the resources available within the tradition as a whole. The goal for convergent Friends is to help form, join, and create timely worship, as well as to make their tradition meaningful in the present (Daniels 2010b).

The model or renewal developed here is convergent inasmuch as it participates in a dialogue between tradition and context in ways that are fully engaged with the practices of today's culture. The goal of the model is to aid in renewal for any faith tradition that seeks to be both convergent and participatory. It is also convergent in that it draws on the language, experience and inspiration of convergent Friends as a participatory renewal movement.

In 1970, a conference of Friends convened in St. Louis for a dialogue on the "Future of Friends." At that conference twenty-four American Quaker Yearly Meetings were present and 135 people in attendance. Everett Cattell was one of the keynote speakers for the event. In 1971, an edited book by T. Canby Jones was published containing a collection of essays birthed out of the conference.[13] In that book was this query:

13. Since the time of the great separations in the United States there have been Friends working to bring about change and renewal to the movement. In fact, both the Gurneyite and Wilburite movements can be seen as attempts to progress the Quaker tradition; Gurneyites emphasized innovation, whereas Wilburites emphasized tradition. Beyond this, the Manchester Conference in 1895 was one early attempt to bring leaders and academics together to think about the future of Quakerism. The Manchester conference spurred on the influential career of Rufus Jones who focused much of his work on the task of reinterpreting the Quaker tradition within Modern-Liberalism. Lewis Benson's "Catholic Quakerism" was an attempt to reclaim the prophetic roots of Quakerism. Out of Benson's work the New Foundation Fellowship was born. This group believes that seventeenth-century Quakerism is the one true expression of the tradition and every stream since them fails to live up to that original vision (Abbott, *The A to Z of Friends*, 193). Elton Trueblood attempted to bring about spiritual renewal through the work of small groups of people committed to discipline.

What is the purpose of the Faith and Life movement among American Friends? (a) To come into unity through agreeing in a collective statement of our common faith? (b) To reconstruct the theology or find again the spirit of early Quakers? (c) To know the present state of our Society through what might be called "comparative Quakerism": a study of the various theological types and points of view to be found in our Yearly Meetings and associations? (d) To seek through meeting together and dialogue between the various strands of current Quakerdom new life and light under the leading of the Holy Spirit–something that might be called "convergent" or "emergent" Quakerism? (Jones 1971)

This project stands within these earlier attempts hoping to usher in a new "convergent" Quakerism, which has only in recent years begun to gain momentum. The convergent model of participatory renewal developed here is my contribution to this work.

CONCLUSION

The overall goal of this project is to construct a convergent model of participatory renewal rooted in the insights of Alasdair MacIntyre, Stephen Bevans, and Henry Jenkins. In order to do this, the chapters are structured as such.

In chapter 1, I address the topic of tradition by introducing a number of central features of MacIntyre's philosophy. MacIntyre is essential for developing a robust understanding of the ongoing nature of tradition and the Enlightenment's impact on our understanding of tradition today. In fact, the MacIntyrean perspective is that tradition is the only grounds for innovation. Therefore, I explain what it means to think of tradition as a historically extended argument and a socially embodied community. I discuss the role of virtues and practices within that community and their impact on the adherents or apprentices within these communities. Finally, I delve into the process through which traditions overcome what

---

The Yokefellows, as they were called, became a prison-oriented ministry that is now a national organization (cf. chapter 6 in Trueblood's, *While it is Day*). There have been many other attempts to bring about revitalization, from the New Meetings Project of Friends General Conference, to Quaker Quest that comes out of Britain Yearly Meeting and is meant to be an outreach program for liberal Quakers. Over the last century there has been much work done, both large and small, to carry the Quaker tradition into the future.

MacIntyre calls an "epistemological crisis," which is instructive for the model of renewal under development.

In chapter 2, I turn to the subject of contextual theology and the impact of the Enlightenment on the church's understanding of mission. The Enlightenment initiated a split in the church's understanding of evangelism and social action. This split, also found within the divisions of Quakerism, is overcome through the emergence of contextual theology. Contextual theology offers a way of understanding not only how to bypass these modern bifurcations, but also the process of how new theology is developed while honoring both tradition and context. In this chapter, I specifically draw on Bevan's synthetic model, which offers supporting framework for my convergent model. Synthesis is an attractive model to replicate because it contains within the ability to draw on a plethora of sources: tradition, context, dialogue and praxis. If tradition is the grounds for innovation, changing context is the impetus for innovation within a tradition.

In chapter 3, my emphasis turns to participatory culture. Participatory culture is the contextual backdrop and dialogue partner for thinking about how renewal takes place in today's culture. The first task will be to describe what participatory culture is and some of the key aspects of this new global phenomenon. Then I describe the six key practices within participatory culture: authentic resistance, remix, cultural production, collective intelligence, decentralized authority, and alternative social community. These practices are the final pieces necessary to construct the model.

In chapter 4, I bring the previous three chapters together into a unified model. Building on MacIntyre, Bevans, and Jenkins, I argue that my convergent model of participatory renewal is capable of revealing insights about historical and as well as contemporary renewal movements.

In chapter 5, I test the model historically by turning to the early Quaker movement. In the process what is revealed is that Quakerism as a movement is highly participative and mission-oriented. Early Quakers were creative in the way that they read the Bible, produced new practices and theology within Christianity, and built an open-ended ecclesiology based on communal discernment.

In chapter 6, I test the model out on a contemporary Quaker meeting called Freedom Friends Church. Freedom Friends Church in Salem, Oregon is a new meeting that seeks to be faithful to the tradition of Quakerism while also being a creative expression of something new. Freedom

Friends fits the convergent model well, bringing practices and theology from different Quaker groups together in one meeting. They produce a new space within Quakerism where people who normally would not find themselves in church have found a home. And this space is distilled down into a Faith and Practice, which the community wrote together. Finally, they are open to change and adaptation by their practice of a renewed understanding of Gospel Order.

In the Conclusion, I present the findings of the research and outline questions for further research.

CHAPTER 1

Alasdair MacIntyre and the Ongoing Nature of Tradition

QUAKERISM GOT ITS START as an energetic and radically alternative Christian community in seventeeth-century England, but over time the early radicalism began to wane. Practices and theology transformed in light of the shifting cultural milieu. From where Friends stand today, more than three hundred and fifty years later, it is easy to see how far surviving Quaker practices have come from their original expressions. While Quakers today certainly resemble earlier Friends, in many ways today's Quakerism is a vastly different movement than it was in the seventeeth century. The next two chapters address the interplay between tradition, context and change.

Inside and outside the church today, "tradition" is often used pejoratively as something "old" or "the way things used to be." For Jaroslav Pelikan this is more rightly named "traditionalism," or the "dead faith of the living." For our purposes, tradition is living. The interpretations and practices that first gave rise to the tradition can evolve over time and can adapt to new contexts. In order to develop a thorough understanding of tradition we turn to the work of philosopher Alasdair MacIntyre.[1]

---

1. Bringing a Catholic philosopher's conception of a tradition into dialogue with Quakerism may seem at first to be like running a fool's errand, yet this is not the first time it has been done. In *Reasons for Hope,* Quaker theologian John Punshon draws on MacIntyre to develop his conception of virtues and practices. However, Punshon is the only Quaker thinker to have engaged MacIntyre at any length. MacIntyre's thought has been heavily used by a number of Anabaptist or Anabaptist-minded theologians such as Stanely Hauerwas, Nancey Murphy, James Wm. McClendon Jr., Chris K. Huebner,

MacIntyre's thought demonstrates how a renewed understanding of tradition can help communities move beyond the impasses of modernity. Therefore, any model that takes tradition as a necessary resource in the process of change must take into account MacIntyre's conception of tradition, virtues and practices, and the socially embodied community.

TRADITION AND MODERNITY

As with many faith traditions today, modernity has impacted the Quaker tradition. In the opening chapter, I offered only a cursory account of the earliest parts of the Friends narrative. There were disagreements and rival interpretations in the beginning of the Quaker movement, but on a small scale compared to what took place in the nineteenth century during the great schisms.[2] Today, fragmentation marks the landscape of Quakerism. MacIntyre's understanding of the narrative of traditions offers guidance as to how this fragmentation may have come about within Quakerism and the appropriate course of action to take. But first, we must gain a general understanding of modernity and how it has negatively impacted our understanding of tradition.

Modernity is marked by the rationality of the individual as the centerpiece of authority, the detachment from any overarching *telos,* and the deficiency of common language to help adjudicate between rival moral claims. MacIntyre argues that today's morality, and by extension the traditions that propagate it, is only a simulacra of what once was:

> What we possess, if this view is true, are the fragments of a conceptual scheme, parts which now lack those context from which their significance derived. We possess indeed a simulacra of morality, we continue to use many of the key expressions. But we have—very largely, if not entirely—lost our comprehension, both theoretical and practical, of morality. (MacIntyre 1984: 2)

The symptoms of this loss are most clearly seen in the three examples of philosophy in modernity that MacIntyre offers: perspectivist, emotivist, and relativist. The emotivist believes that "there are and can be no valid rational justification for any claims that objective and impersonal moral standards exist and hence that there are no such standards"

---

and Bryan Stone to name a few.

2. For an in-depth account of the schisms see Hamm, *The Transformation of American Quakerism.*

(MacIntyre 1984: 19). This "emotivist-self," as MacIntyre calls it, is the truly modern, truly separated, and absolutely autonomous subject, isolated from any objective standard of rationality (ibid., 31, 34). It is a self that is rooted in personal preference and expression (ibid., 12). The relativist and perspectivist hold slightly different positions to rationality than the emotivist: "The relativist challenge rests upon a denial that rational choice among rival traditions is possible; the perspectivist challenge puts in question the possibility of making truth-claims from within any one tradition" (MacIntyre 1988: 352).

Each of these expressions can be found within the Quaker community today. Once a bastion of Radical Reformation Christianity, Quakerism today is thwarted by rampant pluralism; from Evangelicals to "Liberal-liberals," non-theists to Conservatives, Quakers have the theological and political spectrum covered. If the individual is the center of authority and there is a loss of *telos* then the difficulty of adjudicating between rival claims about the meaning of Quakerism is further evidence of modernity's effects on the tradition. This level of disagreement has made communication among Friends fraught with difficulty. Some of MacIntyre's core themes are essential to helping move beyond this fragmentation. We will cover them in turn: tradition as historically extended arguments and socially embodied communities.

TRADITIONS AS HISTORICALLY EXTENDED ARGUMENTS

In *After Virtue*, MacIntyre argues that a tradition is a historically extended argument about the interpretation of its most important and authoritative texts and how the apprentices within the tradition articulate the pursuit of the good:

> A living tradition then is an historically extended, socially embodied argument, and an argument precisely in part about the goods which constitute that tradition. Within a tradition the pursuit of goods extends through generations, sometimes through many generations. (1984: 222)

He argues that "fundamental agreements" are formed over time as the interpretations and arguments over the meaning of central texts coalesce. Conflict plays an essential role in this process; it aids both in the refinement of the arguments, as well as the definition of the terms of debate, and is what leads to a tradition's progress (ibid., 86). Further, conflicts arise within particular traditions and between adherents of one tradition and outside traditions.

The formation of a tradition proceeds through "a number of well-defined types of stages" (MacIntyre 1988: 354).[3] First, every tradition is always in a state of change based upon the texts and voices it has deemed worthy of interpreting:

> Every such form of enquiry begins in and from some condition of pure historical contingency, from the beliefs, institutions, and practices of some particular community which constitute a given. Within such a community authority will have been conferred upon certain texts and certain voices. Bards, priests, prophets, kings, and, on occasion, fools and jesters will all be heard. (Ibid.)

In this place of enquiry, changing and wrestling with primary texts is where tradition begins and it continues in a similar state from this point forward. Any belief that there are some traditions or cultures that are able to remain neutral or unchanged is misguided by the deceptions of modernity; everything is born out of "historical contingency." The stages of development are determined by the success or inability of a tradition to interpret texts in light of these contingencies, rival claims, and competing or incompatible interpretations of those same texts. The first stage in development is characteristically marked by a kind of "internalizing of the law," where what is presented by the interpretive community, its "beliefs, utterances, texts and persons taken to be authoritative" are received unquestioningly.

To move from this stage into the second, a tradition must enter into a stage where there is a breakdown in schemata; this confrontation reveals the vulnerability and incoherences of earlier claims. Consequently, "Authoritative texts or utterances may be shown to be susceptible to, by actually receiving, alternative and incompatible interpretations, enjoying perhaps alternative and incompatible courses of action" (ibid., 354–55).

3. For instance, MacIntyre writes: "For a prerequisite for understanding the present disordered state of the imaginary world was to understand its history, a history that had to be written in three distinct states. The first stage was that in which the natural sciences flourished, the second that in which they suffered catastrophe and the third that in which they were restored but in damaged and disordered form. Notice that this history, being one of decline and fall, is informed by standards. It is not an evaluatively neutral chronicle. The form of the narrative, the division into stages, presuppose stands of achievement and failure, of order and disorder" (MacIntyre, *After Virtue*, 3).

MacIntyre suggests that the cause of the breakdown and realization of potential alternative interpretations stems from a confrontation of new contexts, questions and situations that "reveal within established practices and beliefs a lack of resources for offering or for justifying answers to these new questions" (ibid., 355). This breakdown leads to the possibility of a new hybridity of thought and action where something new emerges out of the old: "The coming together of two previously separate communities, each with its own well-established institutions, practices, and beliefs, either by migration or by conquest, may open up new alternative possibilities" (ibid.). Successfully passing through this transitional stage and overcoming conflicts is essential for the progress and development of an interpretive community.

A community's ability to respond well to the re-defining of their beliefs and practices depends "not only upon what stock of reasons and of questioning and reasoning abilities they already possess but also upon their inventiveness" (ibid.). This inventiveness will "determine the possible range of outcomes in the rejection, emendation, and reformulation of beliefs, the reevaluation of authorities, the reinterpretation of texts, the emergence of new forms of authority, and the production of new texts" (ibid.). The second stage is the conflict that confronts the tradition with its own incompatibilities. As the original texts are read in light of new challenges, previous interpretive arguments may need to be refashioned or done away with. Ability to adjust and enter into the creative act of reformulations and reevaluations is a central aspect of extending a tradition historically. A successful transition will be able to show how it remains connected to its history despite the ruptures; "Shared belief, constitutive of allegiance to the tradition, has to survive every rupture" (ibid., 356); while being caught in one stage of development shows signs of degeneration (ibid., 146). If a tradition arrives at this new place, having made sense of its past, overcome the conflicts, and successfully engaged in reformulating their basic interpretations it has entered the third stage..

TRADITIONS AS EMBODIED COMMUNITY

Thus far, I have described a tradition as a "historically extended argument" that draws on its original texts and interpretations and develops through three stages. Another feature of a tradition is that it is a socially embodied community. A tradition's interpretation of key texts are always socially embodied within communities, and it is these communities that test and define how interpretations are implemented in their context. The core characteristics of these embodied communities are shaped by the virtues and practices that result from interpretations and reformulations of their original texts.

Understanding Virtues

MacIntyre argues that virtues are dispositions that are formed within the apprentices of a tradition and guide the direction of their community toward the good. They are "Not only to act in particular ways, but also to feel in particular ways. To act virtuously is not, as Kant was later to think, to act against inclination; it is to act from inclination formed by the cultivation of virtues" (1984: 150). For MacIntyre, virtues help individuals discern between perceived goods and actual goods. In order to apprehend the latter, the capacity to judge between competing goods is required. This is to know how "to do the right thing in the right place in the right way." This cannot be acquired by simply applying universal rules to particular situations, instead "a virtue is an acquired human quality, the possession and exercise of which tends to enable us to achieve those goods which are internal to practices and the lack of which effectively prevents us from achieving any such goods" (ibid., 191).

Therefore, achieving the virtues is necessarily interrelated to a person's convictions about the *telos* or the "good life."[4] Human life has directedness; yet, this directedness has rival possibilities. Disagreement over interpretation of original texts and the *telos* of human life are key points of competition between traditions. How a tradition answers questions such as: "What is the goal of human life?" and "What goods ought the community pursue?" will aid in determining what the good life is. The virtues of any particular tradition are what make possible the achieving of that end in life. Consider a community that wishes to create a utopia, there are certain qualities and dispositions the individuals in this community will need to embody for their vision of utopia to be fulfilled. This is in accordance with how the New Testament understands virtues as "a

---

4. In this sense every tradition must also grapple with what it means to die. To learn how to die well is to know how to live well. The *telos* of a human life rightly orients an individual's life within a holistic framework that accounts for the reality and transformative capabilities of death within a community (ibid., 40).

quality the exercise of which leads to the achievement of the human *telos*" (ibid., 184).

MacIntyre explains in *Dependent Rational Animals* that in order to achieve one's *telos*, human beings are dependent on one another to develop the right kinds of moral behaviors—he later refers to this as the virtue of acknowledged dependence. Therefore, the communities of practice are like communities of apprentices, made up of people who collectively aid in the development of the virtues necessary for excelling in their community.

> Just as the virtues are exercised in the whole range of our activities, so they are learned in the same range of activities, in those contexts of practice in which we learn from others how to discharge our roles and functions first as members of a family and household, then in the task of schoolwork, and later on as farm-workers or carpenters or teachers or members of a fishing crew or a strong quartet. For to be instructed in the virtues together with the relevant skills is nothing other than to learn how to discharge those roles and functions well rather than badly. (MacIntyre 1999: 88–89)

Therefore, a community's ability to flourish is directly related to the apprentices within its tradition who have learned how to master the virtues and are able to guide others into their formation.

Within the concept of virtues, MacIntyre names three layers that are essential for understanding how virtues function within the embodied community. These three layers are: practices, "narrative order of a single human life," and the tradition itself, which gives context to the practice and understanding of the virtues.

Practices

A MacIntyrean practice roots the abstract principles of virtues into the lived social characteristics of the embodied community. For MacIntyre, practices are:

> Any coherent and complex form of socially established cooperative human activity through which goods internal to that form of activity are realized in the course of trying to achieve those standards of excellence which are appropriate to, and partially definite of, that form of activity, with the result that

human powers to achieve excellence, and human conceptions of the ends and goods involved, are systematically extended. (1984: 187)

Brad Kallenberg has broken this complex definition down into four parts (Kallenberg, Murphy, and Nation 1997: 21). First, practices are participative and foster a social cooperation among members of the community. They are directed toward an end purpose and are necessarily done in cooperation with other people. As I mentioned above, human beings are dependent on one another to develop the right kinds of moral behaviors. In other words, the ability of a community to flourish is interdependent upon the apprentices of that same community cooperating together within their tradition, and learning how to master the virtues necessary for the progress of their tradition.[5]

Second, all practices are made up of internal goods inherent to those practices. They are internal in two ways: first these goods can only be described within the context and terms of that particular practice, or practices similar to it, and second they are recognizable only by those who have participated in the practice (MacIntyre 1984: 188–89).

Third, practices have developed their own rules, apart from which the goods of that practice cannot fully be accessed. Participants, assuming the tradition's role as authority in their lives, submit themselves to the practices in order to learn their rules.[6] Taking on the role of apprentice, participants of a tradition submit themselves to the historical nature of that traditions' practices. "To enter into a practice is to enter into a

---

5. It is apropos to the discussion of practices and their relation to cooperation within a community that one considers MacIntyre's words on practices and institutions. Practices are not the same as institutions, but practices cannot survive without the sustaining power of institutions (ibid., 194). Practices and the institutions that form in relationship to those practices "form a single causal order in which the ideals and the creativity of the practice are always vulnerable to the acquisitiveness of the institution, in which the cooperative care for common goods of the practice is always vulnerable to the competitiveness of the institution" (ibid.).

6. Rules are important within a practice because they help guide the participants toward the standards of excellence necessary to achieve the goods of that practice. "To enter into a practice is to accept the authority of those standards and the inadequacy of my own performance as judged by them. It is to subject my own attitudes, choices, preferences and tastes to the standards, which currently and partially define the practice. Practices of course . . . have a history: games, sciences and arts all have histories. Thus, the standards are not themselves immune from criticism, but nonetheless we cannot be initiated into a practice without accepting the authority of the best standards realized so far" (ibid., 190).

relationship not only with its contemporary practicioners, but also with those who have preceded us in the practice, particularly those whose achievements extended the reach of the practice to its present point" (ibid., 194). In this way, apprentices learn from and build on the achievements internal to the practices of that tradition (ibid.).

In order for one to become an apprentice, some authority has to be accepted within the practices. "To enter into a practice is to accept the authority of those standards and the inadequacy of my own performance as judged by them. It is to subject my own attitudes, choices, preferences and tastes to the standards, which currently and partially define the practice" (190). To be initiated into a practice is not to assume the practices are availed of any criticism, rather it is to accept the "best standards realized so far" as the starting point (ibid.). The example MacIntyre offers of this is that of listening to music. If one does not first learn the standards of basic judgment within the musical community, and accept his or her own "incapacity to judge correctly," it will be impossible to appreciate or even to recognize something as masterful as Bartok's last quartets (ibid.). Thus, there are standards by which practitioners must be informed in order to perform that practice well, but also to be formed appropriately by that same practice. "In the realm of practices the authority of both goods and standards operates in such a way as to rule out all subjectivity and activist analyses of judgment" (ibid.).

And finally, practices have histories; they have narratives that can be told. Insofar as a community participates in their practices, they develop and change overtime, and often the apprentices become better at those practices. The practice, mentioned above, of individual and corporate discernment within Quakerism is case-in-point. Kallenberg writes, "Doctors were no doubt sincere when they once treated fevers with leeches, but contemporary physicians possess skills that far surpass those of their predecessors. Yet the dependence of contemporary practitioners upon their predecessors is unquestionable" (1997: 22). However, it is not only the practices that develop and change, but the apprentices' understanding of what goods ought to be pursued. This is apparent in the way MacIntyre describes the shifting of goals and historical nature of practices:

> Prayers never have a goal or goals fixed for all time—painting has no such goal nor has physics—but the goals themselves are transmuted by the history of the activity. It therefore turns out not to be accidental that every practice has its own history and

> a history which is more and other than that of the improvement of the relevant technical skills. (1984: 193–94)

The crucial point here is that practices can, and in the best cases do, develop over time, not simply in working to improve technical skill, but in the very ends which they seek to achieve. This narratival core of practices leaves them flexible enough to adjust with the relevant contexts, yet rigid enough to have an identifiable history. On the other hand, this is not to say that every historical advance is as faithful to its historical roots.

Development of "Testimony" as Practice

Within the Quaker tradtition, one obvious practice that not only clearly identifies with MacIntyre's "embodied community," but is also an example of a practice that has developed over time is that of the 'testimony' of nonviolence. In the earliest manifestation of the tradition, unity had not yet emerged around the practice of nonviolence. First, a number of Cromwell's men joined the Quaker movement early on, and secondly, there was arguably a Quaker "military wing" led by James Nayler (Dandelion 2007: 44), even though there was, from the beginning, contention with miliary involvement. Gerard Guiton cites the removal of a number of Quakers from the army because they were "argumentative and insubordinate" after following George Fox's suggestion to cease paying the compulsory tithe that Cromwell himself had promised to abolish (Guiton 2005: 80).[7] There were other leading Friends who believed that the "better state" was a non-violent one:

> Generally, leading Friends believed—as Penington's writing would shortly confirm—that those whom God had drawn out of the Fall should not be required to fight, that they be acknowledged instead as 'chosen to be an example of meekness and peaceableness in the places where they live.' The assumption being that when peace so 'chosen' had covered the earth fighting would naturally cease." (Ibid., 87)

George Fox embodied nonviolence in his life, responding to his repeated "physical beatings without retaliation" (ibid., 100) and refusing

---

7. In another instance, Richard Hubberthorne, another early Quaker leader, "advocated the use of the 'Civil and Military sword' for justice's sake, but he opposed the propagation of religion by means of the 'material sword'" (Gwyn, *The Covenant Crucified*, 165).

the position offered him as captain in Cromwell's Army in the 1650s because as he said: "I told them I lived in the virtue of that life and power that took away the occasion of all wars, and I knew from whence all wars did rise, from the lust according to James' doctrine [James 4:1]" (Fox et al. 1985: 65). By 1661, Fox along with eleven other leading Friends of the time, signed a document that restated Margaret Fell's 1660 arguments written to Charles II outling the peaceableness of Friends and said that they believed in a warfare based in a spiritual not carnal reality (Dandelion 2007: 44). This practice of nonviolence developed into the 'testimony against outward warring,' and while there have been some Quakers that have joined armed forces throughout its history, "few have questioned the corporate holding of the testimony" (ibid.).[8]

The Testimony against War Historically Extended

By the 1750s, this "testimony against war" was developed further within the context of the French and Indian War and early Abolitionist work of John Woolman and other Friends. As Barbour and Frost state:

> John Woolman and others who tried to rethink Friends' role in society and resist the norms of most colonial Americans made creative innovations modifying inherited Testimonies. Friends decided that slavery was an immoral institution. They expanded the meaning of the Peace Testimony, grappled with the conflict between holding government power and obedience to God, and debated war taxes." (Barbour and Frost 1988: 7)

Further development of this particular testimony occurred in the late nineteenth and early twentieth century as modern-liberalism began to influence the Quaker tradition. Dandelion argues in "Testimonies as Consequence, Not Value" that Quaker testimonies shifted from being understood in terms of "consequence" to now being understood in terms of "values." In the earlier part of the Quaker tradition, testimonies were rooted in the spiritual life of the community and were not "discrete" as Dandelion says. In other words, testimonies were the convictions of the

---

8. Cf. Guiton's (*The Growth and Development*) chapter 4 "For the Kingdom of Christ: Violence, Carnal Weaponry and Early Quaker Testimony" for a more in-depth look at the development of early Quaker testimony around nonviolence.

embodied community; "everything is testimony that comes from God" (Dandelion 2007b: 3).⁹

Today, these same testimonies have shifted further, moving towards individualistic values and preferences. What was once called the "testimony against outward warring" is now called the "Peace Testimony." The 'testimony against outward warring,' which offers a great case study showing how a MacIntyrean reading can be done within Quakerism, has changed over time as the community has developed through different historical periods and contexts. Part of this development is due to how the participants understand what goods ought to be pursued. Today the practice of nonviolence is often rendered in indvidiualistic and private terms and in many ways has lost its initial radical Chrsitian meaning. This shift has made room for more pluralistic expressions within Quakerism. Being for peace is less specific than being "against outward warring." One might support bombing as a mode to greater peace in a war-torn area, while the latter leaves less room for interpretation. These changes signal deeper change within the tradition. Dandelion argues four things are lost in this shift from consequence to value: there is a lack of specificity to how it can be applied, there is no singular faith tradition needed to root the expression, they are less prescribed for the whole community, and therefore, they are less enforced within the community.

Virtues and Narrative Unity of a Single Life and a Tradition

For MacIntyre, context is essential for the development of virtues. Drawing on Aristotle he shows that the virtues were once lived out within the context of the *polis*. The shape and goal of the virtues was to achieve the *telos* of any particular *polis*. Therefore, virtues are embedded within a

---

9. Dandelion says that "testimony [was] the term used to describe the expression of the collective experience of Quaker faith, the experience of the group as it tries to remain faithful. In some ways then, it is similar to the way 'testimony' is used in evangelical churches when the converted relate their stories. It is about proof. For Quakers, the words have always been less important than the life and the story of faith comes out in practical and, paradoxically (for Quakerism is based on an interiorised spirituality), outward forms. So the words reflect the experience. The words may act as aspiration but they are primarily a reflection, not a rule or a doctrine. For example, there is no 'testimony to the earth' in Britain because as yet it is not the experience of Friends here to live in that way. Thus, in one sense, Quaker testimony is the whole of the way we live our lives as Quakers, everything about it that is visible to ourselves or others" (Dandelion, "Testimony as Consequence," 1).

context and cannot be understood apart from that context. Today, instead of the *polis*, it is the narrative unity of a single life that is the context for understanding virtues: "Human beings, like the members of all other species, have a specific nature; and that nature is such that they have certain aims and goals, such that they move by nature towards a specific *telos*" (MacIntyre 1984: 148). For MacIntyre, all human activities, questions, practices are directed toward some good, a good that can be understood as directed toward a final goal (ibid.). In order for the virtues to develop in our contemporary lives, especially given the fragmentation that has taken place in the West, we need to recover the "understanding of human life as a whole" (ibid., 204). This fragmentation is evident in the progression and development of the testimony mentioned above. As the meaning behind a practice shifts away from original text and conviction of a community and into private spheres of life, the characterization of the virtues and practices moves towards a more fragmented and individualized expression.

Human life has been segregated into components "so work is divided from leisure, private life from public, the corporate from the personal. So both childhood and old age have been wrenched away from the rest of human life and made over into distinct realms" (ibid.). Human life located within this fragmentation is problematic for individuals' formation of virtues. For instance, to be a good "committee man" is not—typically—to be virtuous but effective. Each sphere of life requires different responses, some virtuous, some not; some require seeking ends that rival one another.

To counter these effects, MacIntyre argues for a "concept of a self whose unity resides in the unity of a narrative which links birth to life to death as narrative beginning to middle to end" (1984: 205). MacIntyre uses the example of a gardener to illustrate how easy it can be to divorce action from context. The initial question arises: what is the gardener doing in the garden and why? Is the gardener out pulling weeds in the garden for love, is he preparing for winter, is he simply trying to please his wife, or maybe he is out to get a little exercise? These questions illuminate that we do not know what the character is doing until we know the backstory and context (ibid., 207). "There is no such thing as 'behavior,' to be identified prior to and independently of intentions, beliefs and settings" (ibid., 208). This "historicist-holist" account shows that human life is not composed of detached components, but is rather to be understood as a narrative whole: "Man in his actions and practice, as well as in his fictions, is essentially a story-telling animal" (ibid., 216).

Building on this, the unity of an individual's narrative is found within the "unity of a narrative quest" (ibid., 219). This "quest" has three features: first, the quest is at least in part formed by some "conception of the final *telos* [or] there could not be any beginning to the quest;" second, the quest itself is a good, "A quest is always an education both as to the character of that which is sought and in self-knowledge" (ibid.). Third, the end-goal as well as the purpose of the quest is "always embedded in the story of those communities from which I derive my identity. I am born with a past; and to try and cut myself off from that past, in the individualist mode, is to deform my present relationship" (ibid., 221). Thus, the narrative unity of a human life is always embedded within some inherited historical setting and transmitted through the practices of generations: "What I am, therefore, is in key part what I inherit, a specific past that is present to some degree in my present. I find myself part of a history and that is generally to say . . . one of the bearers of tradition" (ibid.). Similarly to the way that a human life is unified in its quest for the good life, tradition is unified in that same pursuit by the emobodied community seeking a shared good. Thus, we now have a fuller picture of a tradition that is made up of three essential and inseparable parts: traditions are historically extended arguments, socially embodied within a community, and unified by the narrative quest of what its practitioners understand to be the good of human life.

TRADITIONS AND EPISTEMOLOGICAL CRISES

In this final section, I want to discuss MacIntyre's understanding of epistemological crises, which offers a detailed way of understanding how traditions progress through conflict and change. An epistemological crisis happens when either individuals, communities, or whole traditions cease to progress, owing to the unresolved problems of rival claims, or "when certain trusted forms of establishing rationality within a tradition are no longer viable" or can "no longer be sustained" (1988: 361, 364). Epistemological crises are often only recognized in retrospect (ibid., 363).

To use MacIntyre's example from quantum physics, "Boltzmann's 1890 derivation of paradoxes from accounts of thermal energy framed in terms of classical mechanics produced an epistemological crisis within physics which was only to be resolved by Bohr's theory of the internal structure of the atom" (ibid., 363). But in the time between the lives of these two men, the crisis went undetected by the majority of physicists. When a tradition faces this kind "dissolution of historically founded certitudes," and without the invention, discovery, or framing of new concepts or theory (ibid.), the tradition in question becomes degenerate and ceases to make progress (ibid., 362).

The Two Stages in Overcoming a Crisis

When a conflict arises between two rival traditions or competing claims in which one or both traditions are unable to progress this is due to the fact that there is no neutral way to adjudicate between rival claims; each standpoint has "its own mode of characterizing the relevant subject matter" (ibid., 166). Therefore, overcoming an epistemological crisis is not guaranteed (ibid., 356). However, if two rivals wish to proceed and attempt to work through their contentions, MacIntyre suggests two stages. The initial stage is characterized by *same-saying*:

> The first is that in which each characterizes the contentions of its rival in its own terms, making explicit the grounds for rejecting what is incompatible with is own point of view and in the light of its own standards of judgment its rival has something to teach it on marginal and subordinate questions. (Ibid., 166)

Here, adherents of each rival tradition catalogue the contentions in ways that translate into their schemata. This process of same-saying enables the first tradition to reject what is incompatible and learn from what is adaptable from the second tradition (ibid.). The second stage is characterized by *concept borrowing*:

> A second stage is reached if and when the protagonists of each tradition, having considered in what ways their own tradition has by its own standards of achievement in enquiry found it difficult to develop its enquires beyond a certain point, or has produced in some area insoluble antinomies. (Ibid., 166–67)

It is possible in this stage that the rival tradition may afford new resources to the floundering tradition. Through the process of concept borrowing, the rival tradition may "be able to provide resources to characterize and to explain the failings and defects of their own tradition more adequately than they, using the resources of that tradition, have been able to do" (ibid.,167). What is most difficult about this step is that it is innovative and relies on the:

> Rare gift of empathy as well as of intellectual insight for the protagonists of such a tradition to be able to understand these arguments and concepts of their rival in such a way that they are able to view themselves from such an alien standpoint and to recharacterize their own beliefs in an appropriate manner from the alien perspective of the rival tradition." (Ibid., 167; 1990: 120)

If the tradition in crisis is able to stand within an alien paradigm and discover the necessary insights, that will help the tradition overcome its internal crises. Through the use of same saying, the tradition may again begin to progress. MacIntyre calls the ability to do this a "rare gift of empathy" and shows that the apprentices have become like poets in their work of translation: "Knowing how to go on and go further in the use of the expression of a language is that part of the ability of every language-user which is poetic" (1988: 382).

The reason why these stages are important is because translation is an essential part of the solution in overcoming an epistemological crisis. The formative texts of a tradition were often written in cultures and languages much different than their contemporary settings. Thus, every tradition:

> Is embodied in some particular set of utterances and actions and thereby in all the particulars of some specific language and culture. The invention, elaboration, and modification of the concepts through which both those who found and those who inherit a tradition understand it are inescapably concepts which have been framed in one language rather than another. (Ibid., 271–72)

Therefore, these stages of same-saying and concept borrowing name the work of translation. In a similar fashion to an anthropologist, apprentices of one tradition work to become a native of the other tradition. These adherents will work to learn the other tradition's language as a "second first language" (ibid., 374) so that they "go to live in the society of the other culture and transform themselves, so far as is possible, into native inhabitants" (ibid.). This is the exact opposite of what modernity does to language, which universalizes and loses particularity:

> The condition which I have described as that characteristic of the late twentieth century language of internationalized modernity is perhaps best understood as an ideal type, a condition to which the actual language of the metropolitan centers of modernity approximate in varying and increasing degrees, especially among the more affluent. And the social and cultural condition of those who speak that kind of language, a certain type of rootless cosmopolitanism, the condition of those who aspiring to be at home anywhere—expect that is, of course, in what they regard as the backyard, outmoded, undeveloped cultures of traditions—are therefore in an important way citizens of nowhere is also ideal-typical. It is the fate toward which modernity moves precisely insofar as it successfully modernizes itself and others by emancipating itself from social, cultural, and linguistic particularity and so from tradition. (Ibid., 388)

Thus, even the act of translation that moves towards linguistic particularity, rather than universal generalization, is a counter move to modernity.

Consider, for example, Thomas Aquinas's own masterwork the *Summa Theologiae*.[10] Aquinas was able to translate (both in language and in historical setting) his predecessors, Aristotle and Augustine, in new and compelling ways. Both Augustinian and Aristotelian traditions were, until Aquinas proved otherwise, at a stand-still, both holding incommensurate positions. And yet the brilliance of the *Summa* is that Aquinas was able to reinterpret both contending traditions and integrate them into a newly "dialectical synthesis which had the capacity for directing enquiry still further beyond itself" (MacIntyre 1990: 165).

The contentions between the two traditions were at least three-fold: epistemological, truth, and the will (ibid., 109–11). For Aristotle, the mind was capable of achieving knowledge, whereas for Augustine it was incapable of this on its own apart from divine aid (ibid., 109–110). Truth posed another problem. For Aristotle, truth is found "in the relationship of the mind to its objects" while Augustine's again is situated theologically. All finite objects find their truth fully and in their relationship to God (ibid., 110). Finally, the intellect is always within the possibility of defect

---

10. MacIntyre notes four important features of Aquinas's Summa: he took the arguments as far as they needed to go and then left it open for further development later, it was systematic in a way that surpassed his predecessors, he wrote in a way that integrated and synthesized two positions into one mode of thought, and it was done with a singleness of purpose (MacIntyre, *Whose Justice?*, 164–65).

and error (because it is liable of being misled by the will). Therefore it is untrustworthy according to Augustine, it is always apt to fall into error, while Aristotle's perspective contrasts by supposing that "the intellect is fully competent to arrive at both theoretical and practical truth" (ibid., 111).

Aquinas's task, according to MacIntyre, was to help reconcile these two traditions by immersing himself into both and making their central problems his own (ibid., 115):

> Aquinas's strategy . . . was to enable Augustinians to understand how, by their own standards, they confronted problems for the adequate treatment of which, so long as they remained within the confines of their own system, they lacked the necessary resources; and in a parallel way to provide the same kind of understanding for Averroistic Aristotelians. (Ibid., 172)

He was successful in not only synthesizing these two contending standpoints, but he also demonstrated that it was possible to develop his own standpoint in ways not possible prior to the synthesis of these two positions. Drawing on these insights, I will further develop synthesis as it pertains to the renewal of traditions in the following chapter.

Criteria for Reconstruction

One main question that arises from a newly reconstructed tradition after an epistemological crisis concerns continuity. How, after all the same-saying, the concept borrowing, the linguistic innovation, and the reformulations and reinterpretations, does a tradition remain the same? If it is the same, how is it similar and different from what it once was? And when does it become a different tradition altogether? These questions have been raised within Quaker circles regularly since the schisms of the nineteenth century.

Part of, Quaker philosopher, Rufus Jones's work in the late nineteenth and early twentieth century was an attempt not only to prepare Quakerism to adapt to findings within higher criticism and modern scientific innovations, but also to help reintegrate various strands of the Quaker tradition that had developed in the nineteenth century. Elias Hicks, Joseph John Gurney, and John Wilbur were all precursors to Rufus Jones. Each of these men have been vilified or hailed as heroes depending on one's standpoint, but each of them were innovators in their time.

They each responded to cultural and philosophical shifts and each attempted to reformulate Quakerism in light of rival data. Today the labels "Hicksite," "Gurneyite," and "Wilburite" identify the three main Quaker streams. Each hoped to find their origins in their respective founders who pioneered new revisions within Quakerism in their own time (the decades of the 1820–1850s).

The way forward has been difficult, owing in large part to questions about the criterion of continuity. MacIntyre suggests three resources for sorting out such questions. First, there is the question of success: Has the tradition truly succeeded in overcoming a crisis? If it has, it will fulfill three exacting requirements (1988: 362). The first requirement is that the newly enhanced scheme is able to systematically and coherently resolve the problems that the tradition initially found to be intractable. Second, it must be able to explain how and why the tradition, before the new concepts were adopted, became sterile and incoherent within its previous paradigm. Third, continuity between structures must be tended to carefully in these first two tasks. It must be able to demonstrate "some fundamental continuity of the new conceptual and theoretical structures with the shared beliefs in terms of which the tradition of enquiry had been defined up to this point" (ibid.). Therefore, the three criteria could be summed up as (a) resolution of the previous problems, (b) explanation of what went wrong, and (c) continuity of some shared beliefs and practices with the tradition of enquiry.

One important example that MacIntyre gives of a tradition progressing through epistemological crises involves John Henry Newman's work (ibid., 362–63). Newman argued that the fourth century debate over doctrinal understanding of the Trinity was resolved "by a use of philosophical and theological concepts whose understanding had itself issued from debates rationally unresolved up to that point" (ibid., 362).

Finally, once a tradition has passed through these three stages, apprentices are able to re-write a history that takes into account the continuities that survived the transition but in a more clear and insightful way "identify more accurately that structure of justification which underpins whatever claims to truth are made within it" (ibid., 363). This revised history involves responding to the above three elements. Further, it can always be called back into question again by a later interpretation or rival claim.

> The most we can claim is that this is the best account which anyone has been able to give so far, and that our beliefs about what the marks of "a best account so far" are [sic] will themselves change in what are at present unpredictable ways. (MacIntyre 1980: 57)

Apprentices must accept that a tradition's newly rewritten history is provisional and remains open to be built upon, and challenged at a later time—just as in the earlier example of Aquinas's *Summa*.

CONCLUSION

In this chapter I discussed MacIntyre's understanding of tradition to create a fuller picture of how the Quaker tradition might be conceived. MacIntyre's conception was broken down into four characteristics: tradition as extended history, tradition as socially embodied community, tradition as virtues and practices, and tradition that progresses through epistemological crises. Each of these are part of the whole of MacIntyre's philosophy of tradition-constituted rationality.

There are a number of key elements taken from MacIntyre's thought that can be carried into the convergent model of renewal. First, MacIntyre demonstrates that tradition is a living and a historically extended concept, and therefore—if it is a successful tradition—it indeed has the resources within it to overcome the challenges and confrontations of rival claims. Within modernity the church has been quick to see tradition as a liability and as something to be distanced from. MacIntyre's thought demonstrates that even this is a tradition and that everyone has a place from which they stand.

Second, renewal within this context necessarily involves apprentices within a given tradition who submit themselves to the formation of their original texts, virtues and practices, and the socially embodied community of that tradition. The only way forward is to draw on the resources found within their tradition, and therefore they must be able to speak it as a kind of second-first language. They must also be creative and empathetic so that they can practice translation through same-saying and concept-borrowing within their changing contexts. Renewal must come from the insiders of the movement, those for whom the loss of tradition will be a tragic loss of their own way of life.

Third, crisis initiates change. MacIntyre suggests that there are three stages that a tradition goes through in its development: internalizing the law in an unquestioning way, experiencing conflict and incoherence in a disorienting way, and finally, a reformulation of the tradition through the innovation, creativity and empathy of its apprentices. A progressive tradition will pass through these stages and be able to narrate the development. A tradition that is around long enough will go through this process more than once.

Finally, there are criteria for a newly reconstructed tradition that can help those within the tradition know if they have been faithful in their attempts at renewal. This renewed tradition can: resolve the problems that were initially intractable, explain how and why the tradition became sterile in the previous paradigm, and can demonstrate a fundamental continuity of some shared beliefs and practices between the new and older structures.

CHAPTER 2

Stephen Bevans and Mission
Developing the Synthetic Model

MACINTYRE'S PHILOSOPHY IS THOROUGH in regards to how a tradition forms, progresses, declines and reinterprets its origins, and it is especially helpful in today's context where modernity has led to a culture that is anti-tradition. While MacIntyre clearly accepts the importance of context when developing his understanding of virtues and practices his philosophy only goes so far when it comes to the church in dialogue with culture. In fact, in the church today tradition and mission are often pitted against one another; this is especially true within both liberalism and evangelicalism where modernity has exercised profound influence.

Within Quakerism, those who are Evangelical Friends are less likely to draw on the resources of their tradition or to exercise the "virtue of having an adequate sense of the tradition to which one belongs." Whereas within liberal Quakers, there is a rejection of tradition as it relates to the Christian narrative. In this chapter we will look at how the Enlightenment has not only impacted the church's relationship to the past, but also how it relates to culture in its practice of mission. In order to do this, three areas are addressed: how the Enlightenment has affected the relationship between mission and tradition; the emergence of contextual theology as a response to the "objective" (or anti-tradition) theology of the Enlightenment; and models of contextual theology that may incorporate tradition and mission in a way that could aid in the church's renewal.

MISSION AND THE ENLIGHTENMENT

The Enlightenment caused the break between Christian mission and tradition. As John R. Stott argues in his book *Christian Missions in the Modern World*, there are two extremes views of mission today. On the one hand there is the "witness" or "evangelism" approach. In this view, the caricature of the missionary is set forth as the exotic, paternalistic preacher who wears native dress and preaches to convert the lost souls (Stott 2008: 26). On the other hand, Stott believes that the opposite extreme is one that sees the *missio Dei* as the establishment of shalom in the world. A reference to what Stott sees as liberal Christianity's primary understanding of mission as social action (ibid., 30–32).

Early Friends did hold that shalom is a central part of God's mission, referring to this as "new creation" and "gospel order," but in a way that he misses altogether. However, his basic concern that there is a focus on social action without any spiritual component is a critique worthy of reflection, especially within liberal Quaker Yearly Meetings. For instance, on Britain Yearly Meeting's website one can find the statement: "We do not share a fixed set of beliefs and you do not need to be a Quaker to worship with us at one of our meetings. Quaker faith is expressed through action and we are most widely known for our work for peace" (Britain Yearly Meeting 2012).

However, this false dichotomy reveals the effects of the Enlightenment upon the church's understanding of mission. "Word" and "deed" need not be bifurcated in the life of the church. Wibert Shenk acknowledges that:

> In the twentieth century the content of the gospel has often been described in terms of a dualism: word and deed, or proclamation and service. This would have impressed earlier generations as a strange construction. The Bible, for example, contains no discussion of strategies of "social service" or "evangelistic preaching." Nor is there any attempt to contrast one with the other or to establish the primacy of one over the other. We moderns have managed to introduce into our reading of the Bible a distinctively twentieth-century problem. (1999: 20)

This dualism is a new problem and consequence of the Enlightenment; "No area of life in the west has been exempted from its influence" (ibid., 21). But how is it that the Enlightenment led to this discrepancy between social service and proclamation? The dualism in mission is largely due to the dominance of human reason and the promotion of the scientific method as the foundational authority for truth.

Nancey Murphy argues that this bifurcation came about due to the philosophy of foundationalism. Foundationalism,

> is specifically about how knowledge claims can be justified. When we seek to justify a belief, we do so by relating it to (basing it upon, deriving it from) other beliefs. If these other beliefs are called into question, then they too must to be justified. Foundationalists insist that this chain of justifications must stop somewhere; it must not be circular or constitute an infinite regress. Thus, the regress must end in a "foundation" of beliefs that cannot themselves be called into question. (Murphy 1996: 12)

Foundationalism became the epistemological grounding for the Enlightenment, thus shaping not only the approach of the scientific method, but the church's response to science. As Murphy says, this created essentially a "two-party system: liberal and conservative" (ibid., 1). Thus, there was a forcing of the hand to choose which side one was on. For liberal Protestantism, the challenge was to incorporate scientific evidence into theology. This gave birth to the Higher Critical method and a social-action program that was based on an "evolutionary vision of the kingdom of God that was being established in the world" (Shenk 1999: 22). On the other hand, while conservative Christians may or may not have been willing to concede science's mastery in some matters, they certainly were not willing to "concede authority in the religious realm to science" (ibid.). According to Murphy, this bifurcation was motivated by a search for "indubitable foundations for theology" (Murphy 1996: 28):

> Thus, we see that there are two distinct strategies for satisfying the demand for indubitable foundations for theology. The Scriptures themselves are understood differently by proponents of the two strategies. Conservatives emphasize that these books are the result of acts of God, not of human discovery, and emphasize as well the factual character of their contents. The Scriptures provides precise and true accounts of supernatural realities. Liberals see the Christian Scriptures as belonging to a class of writings that express, with different degrees of aptitude, insights regarding God and human life that arise from religious experience. So, according to Liberals, the Christian Scriptures may be especially authoritative for Christians, but they differ from other religious writings in degree, not in kind. Here the emphasis is on adequacy of expression or ability to engender

religious experience rather than on factuality or precision or accurate presentation of state of affairs.

Shenk and Murphy spell out deep-seated theological disagreements that have been observed within the narrative of Protestant Christianity since the eigtheenth century (see Bosch 2005: 262). In MacIntyrean terms, the Enlightenment challenged Christianity with rival claims to truth around the authority of tradition. Inevitably this split has shaped the church's understanding of mission and its reliance upon tradition in building lasting communities of faith in around the world.

Effects of the Enlightenment on Christian Tradition

Missiologist David Bosch offers insight into how the Enlightenment shaped the Protestant missionary paradigm. For one, the Enlightenment marked the shift away from a "divinely constituted order of things" towards the *Age of Science* (ibid., 263). In this period, the church no longer validated the structure of reality as it once did. For instance, the Enlightenment made possible questioning God's existence. "God was largely eliminated from society's validation structure. People discovered, somewhat to their surprise at first, that they could ignore God and the church, yet be none the worse for it" (ibid.). Validation for humanity now came from below, rather than from above (ibid.). Murphy refers to the difference here as being inside out vs. outside in epistemology (1996: 28–35).

Bosch argues that this period marked a revolution where the power of "kings and nobles" was destroyed. "The ordinary people now saw themselves as being, in some measure, related to God directly, no longer by way of king or nobility or church" (ibid.). This dismantling mirrors the Quaker challenges within religion, where in secular society it was the kings and nobles whose power was destroyed, the Quakers sought to uproot the power of the clergy. People no longer needed a mediator to get to God, now in some way there was, in the words of George Fox, "that of God in everyone."

It was inevitable, then, that the Enlightenment changed the church's relationship to tradition. Bosch argues that this happened in at least three ways: elimination of purpose, belief in objectivity of scientific knowledge (and preference for it), and the autonomy of humankind. First, teleology was central to the ancient world. "Ancient Greek and medieval scientific reflection believed in an animated causality and took purpose as a category of explanation in physics" (Bosch 2005: 265).

The Enlightenment eliminated the connection between purpose and scientific questions. Bosch argues that science was no longer interested in questions related to the universe and why and by whom it was created. Instead, it focused on "simple mechanistic, billiard-ball-type causality. The cause determines the effect. The effect thus becomes explicable, if not predictable" (ibid.). For Bosch, this determinism removes any teleological connections to God or tradition.

Second, the Enlightenment could be characterized as holding facts of science as objective, value-free or neutral. In the Enlightenment, "Facts have a life of their own, independent of the observer. They are 'objectively' true" (ibid., 266). There is no room for opposing perspectives, objectivity is central to scientific claims of the Enlightenment. This kind of objectivity is exemplified in Karl Popper's[1] statement, "(It) . . . is totally independent of anybody's claims to knowledge: it is also independent of anybody's belief . . . knowledge in the objective sense is knowledge without a knower; it is knowledge without a knowing subject" (ibid.). From the viewpoint of science, anything that cannot claim objectivity in this sense is opinion or belief. From the theological side of this debate, theology must justify how it is trustworthy knowledge or it must attempt to only make "objective" truth claims. This need to have indubitable truth-claims gives rise to the epistemology of foundationalism.

Third, Bosch argues that the Enlightenment has created autonomous individuals, emancipated from the confines of community (ibid., 267). Prior to the Enlightenment the community took precedence over the individual. It was not until the Reformation that individuals, while not emancipated, were of importance and could stand in relation to God. The Enlightenment ushered in a challenge to this way of thinking by placing the emphasis on individuality. Bosch argues that the Enlightenment's

> progress was assured by the free competition of individuals pursuing their happiness. The free and 'natural' human being was infinitely perfectible and should be allowed to evolve along the lines of his or her own choice. (Ibid., 267)

Following Bosch's arguments, modernity ushers in a series of breaks within society that have an immediate impact on the church's mission.

---

1. Karl Popper is regarded as one of the greatest philosophers of science of the twentieth century.

From a loss of teleology, to claims of objectivity, and a rejection of the co-dependence on community and tradition, the Enlightenment challenges some of the core features not only of the Christian tradition, but the Quaker tradition as well. In the Enlightenment,

> The individual experienced himself or herself as liberated from the tutelage of God and church, who were no longer needed to legitimize specific titles, classes, and prerogatives. There were, in principle, no longer any privileged persons and classes. All were born equal and had equal rights. These were, however, not derived from religion, but from "nature." Thus human beings were, on the one hand, more important than God; on the other hand, however, they were not fundamentally different from animals and plants. (Ibid., 267)

Thus, the Enlightenment signals a loss of reference to God, uprooting of individuals from community and tradition, and a loss of teleology.

Effects of the Enlightenment on Christian Mission

The Enlightenment has not only changed the West's relationship to tradition, it has drastically effected how the church understands and practices mission in the world. Bosch's perspective sheds light on how mission-theology ended up with a split between word and deed. However, beyond this, mission in the modern period has often developed in contradiction to tradition. This has happened in at least three ways.

First, a loss of teleology can be seen in missionary approaches in the conversion of individuals over against development and care for the society as a whole. In the loss of *telos*, Christian mission is either broken down into the primary goal of converting individuals or bettering society. Not only does the former betray a preference for the individual over the community, it reveals a loss of larger, more universal *telos* and societal focus that more traditional expressions of Christianity may have held; while the latter betrays an objectivity that favors the concrete over religious experience. For instance, the ushering in of the Kingdom of God, or the nurturing of the "New Creation"—as Paul calls—stand as more universal callings that deal with structures and societal patterns and includes repentance and conversion to a new way of life that is often lost when the end goal of Christian mission is focused on the conversion of individual "lost souls."

Second, the objectivity and universalizing tendency of the Enlightenment is most clearly seen in the rise of colonialism propagated by modern missionaries. One of the main critiques, and there are many, of colonialism is that it is an objectification and universalization of Western culture and theology (ibid., 302). Shenk writes:

> The charge that has been brought against the modern missionary movement is that it has been but another attempt to universalize something that was profoundly particular and parochial, namely Western civilization. And this is experienced as the ultimate effrontery: that one culture or people arrogate to itself the role of determining and maintaining the destinies of other people. (1999: 74)

In colonialism "the missionaries became pioneers of Western imperialistic expansion" (Bosch 2005: 305) because there was a belief that Western society was objectively more superior and more civilized than other cultures. Bosch argues that they were "blind to their own ethnocentrism." These advocates of mission;

> Confused their middle-class ideals and values with the tenets of Christianity. Their views about morality, respectability, order, efficiency, individualism, professionalism, work, and technological progress, having been baptized long before, were without compunction exported to the ends of the earth. (Ibid., 294)

Christendom contributed to this idea that Western culture was superior and objective and therefore should be universalized. This is why,

> Colonialism fostered a feeling among those who were colonized that anything that was really good and worthwhile was something that originated in the colonizing country and that what was in the colony was sketchy, of poor quality, only an imitation of the real thing. (Bevans 2002: 11)

Finally, the breaking free of autonomous individuals may have been a necessary historical move that liberated people from the domination of a church-state monopoly in the West, but in the long run it led to uprooting people from concern for community and tradition. Authority based on human rationality, which favored progress and new insight, no longer needed the authority of tradition passed down from generations before (Bosch 2005: 269).

The Enlightenment has similarly impacted mission insofar as it leads to an uprooting of Christian theology and practice from tradition. Thus, the "gospel" becomes a matter of individual salvation, and stripped of any of its cultural or traditional understandings. In the Enlightenment model of mission, the gospel is thought of as pure, objective, and isolated from culture. This personal evangelism is aimed at individuals rather than social transformation, and does little to bring disciples—or apprentices—into the tradition.

Being a convert in this context is separate from participating in the practices and virtues of the missionary's tradition of origin. This is because tradition has often been seen as a liability for communicating the gospel clearly and effectively in foreign contexts. However, Bosch argues, "the gospel always comes to people in cultural robes. There is no such thing as a 'pure' Gospel, isolated from culture" (ibid., 297). The same is true for the gospel and tradition; there is no place outside of tradition in which the gospel can be understood or communicated.

Given the various issues mentioned in this section related to the Enlightenment and mission in today's world, we need a model of renewal that overcomes the challenges of colonialism, questions of authority and the loss of community, not to mention the other issues brought on by the Enlightenment. This model must work to learn where God is already at work within one's context, while also being in dialogue with her or his tradition. Because of these factors, I argue that contextual theology offers the best approach to developing a convergent model of renewal.

THE RISE OF CONTEXTUAL THEOLOGY

The rise of contextual theology in the twentieth century was a breakthrough for understanding the church's mission. Shenk suggests that there have been three stages in the development of a Protestant understanding of mission: replication, indigenization, and contextualization. The seventeenth and eighteenth centuries used the replication model, which held the assumption of Christendom in the background. In this stage the focus of the missionary was "to replicate or reproduce a church in another culture patterned carefully after that of the church from which the missionary originated" (Shenk 1999: 51). The replication model had "precritical" understanding of culture, one that was ethnocentric and understood Western ways of existing as superior to those in other cultures (ibid.). The main role for the gospel is to bring people into this superior culture (ibid., 52), which can only be ensured through "careful tutelage by a representative of Christendom" (ibid., 53).

Indigenization is the second stage in development and is a process by which Christendom will be reproduced "by drawing on the people and materials of the other culture, but the script is provided from outside [that culture]" (ibid., 53). In this stage of mission, the missionary is still central to the communication and translation of the gospel in other cultures. In terms of its understanding of culture, Shenk suggests that this position holds a view of culture that ranges from "primitive to most highly developed (or 'civilized'). Culture is evolving" (ibid., 53). It is different from the replication model insofar as it sought to find "functional equivalents" in the other cultures. "Whereas the replication approach focused on the correct reproduction of the 'original,' indigenization emphasized finding the functional equivalent within the other culture of the 'original.' That is to say, the goal of indigenization was to find the symbols and forms in the host culture through which the Christendom view of religious life might be expressed" (ibid., 55).

Contextualization is different from the previous two inasmuch as "the responsibility for contextualizing the message of the gospel no longer was seen as resting with individuals from outside the culture; rather, that responsibility lay with the church and its leaders from within the culture" (ibid., 56). Not only is contextualization a far more present and dynamic understanding of how God works within culture, but it also undercuts the pretensions of Christendom and the allure of colonialism. This is because it is an insider movement and draws on many voices, thus emphasizing the participatory role of those native to the context. Contextualization seeks an authentic Christianity within each context that is driven by the "adherents" of that culture. It is far more sophisticated in its understanding of culture than the models influenced by the Enlightenment. As Shenk argues, "Culture is understood to be a dynamic and evolving system of values, patterns of behavior, and a matrix shaping the life of the members of that society" (ibid., 56).

What is Contextual Theology?

Stephen Bevans argues that "there is no such thing as 'theology'; there is only contextual theology: feminist theology, black theology, liberation theology, Filipino theology, Asian-American theology, African theology, and so forth" (Bevans 2002: 3); and to that we might add Quaker theology. In keeping with a MacIntyrean perspective on mission, contextual theology recognizes that there is no place to do theology outside of tradition and context. Contextual theology holds both "traditional" and the "radically new" contexts. Thus, it stands in opposition to what Bevans calls "classical" theology, or the theology of the Enlightenment that understands "theology as a kind of objective science of faith" (ibid.). This sort of objective theology is foundationalist in its epistemology; it draws on Scripture, or tradition, or human experience as the indubitable foundations of truth. From this perspective, the content of whatever foundation the faithful draw on is unchanging and stands outside of culture and human history (ibid., 4).

Bevans argues that there are at least four external factors for why objective theology is not a suitable option for the church. First, classical theology does not fit with the many shifts and changes that have taken place in theology, culture, and science. "Any kind of understanding of theology as an unchanging, already finished *theologia perennis* is being challenged in the First World in the name of relevance" (ibid., 9). Second, older classical approaches are oppressive in nature. Classical theology has ignored the experiences of those who were not white and male, and often of privilege. "United States black theologian James Cone has pointed out repeatedly in his works how traditional theology ignores the black experience and makes blacks invisible and inaudible" (ibid., 10). Third, helping local churches mature in their identity requires a robust contextual theology (ibid., 10). "When a person or nation or culture comes to a clear realization of its identity, no other person, nation, or culture can use it, oppress it, or foist any unwanted or destructive thing upon it" (ibid., 11). In the words José Rizal, "there are no tyrants where there are no slaves." Colonialism is the consequence of classical theology superimposed onto other non-Westerners, devaluing the people, their practices and culture. The fourth factor reflects how the social sciences and cultural studies have changed how we understand what culture is. This change has challenged the "universal and permanent" character of classical understandings of culture. Today culture can be defined as "a set of meanings and values that inform a way of life" and there are no limits to the possibilities that arise from this (ibid.).

Instead, contextual theology is "subjective" in its approach, incorporating all of these elements together in a non-foundationalist way. It is theology of a certain time and place, concrete and connected to the history of a particular people and related to their specific concerns. As "Henri Bouillard once said a theology that is not up-to-date (French: *actuelle*) is a false theology" (ibid., 5). Thus, subjective or contextual theology recognizes, as does MacIntyrean philosophy, the narrative shape of human life:

> By subjective, however, I do not mean relative or private or anything like that but the fact that the human person or human society, culturally and historically bound as it is, is the source of reality, not a supposed value- and culture-free objectivity "already out there now real." (Ibid., 4)

By incorporating human experience as an essential element in the construction of theology and understanding of human thought, the whole equation is changed (ibid., 5).

Bevans' articulation of contextual theology fits an approach to culture that is faithful to tradition because it holds as essential these two components: "First, it takes into account the faith experience of the *past* that is recorded in Scripture and kept alive, preserved, defended and perhaps even neglected or suppressed—in tradition.... Second, contextual theology takes into account the experience of the present, the *context*" (ibid.). Context is that which combines several features: personal life (family, deaths, relationships, births tragedies and successes); these personal and communal experiences unfold within a culture or system "of inherited conceptions expressed in symbolic forms by means of which people communicate, perpetuate, and develop their knowledge about attitudes toward life" (ibid., 6); one's social location, position to power and privilege; and finally, context includes social change where all cultures experience decline, growth or improvement (ibid.).

Finally, Bevans argues that contextual theology develops in relation to its own context in one of two ways: creation-centered or redemption-centered. These two poles represent a continuum along with how traditions interact with the world. First, a creation-centered orientation to theology:

> Sees the world, creation, as sacramental: the world is the place where God reveals Godself; revelation does not happen in set-apart, particularly holy places, in strange, unworldly circumstances, or in words that are spoken in a stilted voice; it comes

> in daily life, in ordinary words, through ordinary people. (Ibid., 21)

This is an analogical approach; based on "spirit or imagination," it recognizes the basic goodness of all things created, and trusts that God is at work within creation and culture, regardless of whether the church is a part of that process or not.

On the other hand, the redemption-centered orientation to theology is rooted in a theology that comes from the outside. It can be:

> Characterized by the conviction that culture and human experience are either in need of a radical transformation or in need of total replacement. In this perspective, grace cannot build on or perfect nature because nature is something that is corrupt. In a real sense, therefore; grace replaces nature rather than being a vehicle for God's presence. The world distorts God's reality and rebels against it. Rather than a culture being already holy with the presence of God, Christ must be brought to a culture for that culture to have any saving meaning whatsoever. (Ibid., 21–22)

Rather than the analogical approach of the prior orientation, Bevans sees the redemption building on the dialectical imagination, calling culture beyond itself to a synthesis with the gospel. Here, the stress is upon creation's need for redemption, the lack of goodness of people and the call the gospel places on humanity for reconciliation with Christ.

While Quakerism, in different times and in difference places, has modeled both of these approaches, the creation-centered approach is closest to what is most natural to the practices of the tradition. Given convictions such as the inward covenant of Light—where Friends believe that everyone has been given some measure of Christ's Light (John 1:9), any contextual model for Quakerism will be required to see the world and approach it at least somewhat positively (ibid., 22). In other words, a model of renewal that takes seriously contextual theology and the creation-centered approach will draw from resources not only from within its tradition, but from within the surrounding culture, building on where God is already at work.

Six Models of Contextual Theology

In *Models of Contextual Theology*, Stephen Bevans develops six different models for understanding how the church interacts with culture and the gospel. These models move from creation-centered to redemption-centered and are: anthropological, transcendental, praxis, synthetic, translation, countercultural. The *anthropological* model is among the most radically creation-centered because its view of cultural identity is such that it is emphasized over and above Scripture or tradition (ibid., 31). The *transcendental* focuses on the subject that is transformed in the encounter with Christ. Here the subjective experience is what matters most; the content of the contextual theology is secondary (ibid., 32). *Praxis* is action-oriented, committed above all to the need for justice and social change within a particular culture. The *synthetic* model seeks to hold a balance between context, tradition, dialogue and praxis. The *translation* model places primary importance on Scripture or tradition and how it is brought to and translated within a new culture. Lastly, the *countercultural* model is the most conservative of the six and works from a place of distrust concerning the "sanctity and revelational power" of context (ibid., 31).

In the 1600s, early Friends drew on a mixture of these models. The mixture is different today depending on which branch of Quakerism is under discussion. However, given the differences of today, among early Quakerism there are common threads. For instance, they can be seen as having what might be called a *praxis-oriented transcendentalism*, a strong desire to encounter Jesus Christ inwardly and be radically renewed internally. But this transcendentalism had this-worldly consequences and was rooted in a program of social transformation that left a lasting impact on Western society.

The renewal was not limited to internal change; it manifested itself in how Friends engaged the world publicly. And yet, there was also a strong taste for countercultural mistrust of those in power. While they believed that everyone had access to the Inward Covenant of Light, it seems that they were more likely to trust Christ's revelation to individuals and small groups of people than to hierarchical systems of politics or religion. Further study could prove beneficial in looking at different early Friends to investigate which models each preferred and find if there was any collective model that was agreed upon as a standard approach. However, for the task of building a convergent model of renewal, I want to suggest a more appropriate model for today, building on the insights from MacIntyre's understanding of tradition and the variety of differences among Quakers, the synthetic model offers a necessary framework for bringing about renewal in a way that draws on tradition while engaging today's context.

Framing Convergent Renewal: The Synthetic Model

The model best suited for developing a contextual Quaker theology today is what Bevans calls the synthetic model. Christian mission is to be anchored both in fidelity to the past and challenged to fidelity in the present, and this is where Quakerism has floundered in recent times. Adherents must preserve, defend and proclaim the *constants* of their church's tradition while at the same time responding creatively and boldly to the *contexts* in which they finds themselves (Bevans and Schroeder 2004: 1). Holding these two aspects in tension is the goal of the synthetic model, enabling it to overcome at least some of the problems inherent in the modernity. The goal of this model is to synthesize one's tradition and context; it not only draws on the resources from its own context and tradition but "it makes creative use of whatever is at hand" (Bevans 2002: 88).[2]

To illustrate how this process works, Bevans offers the example of the diary of José P. Laurel written during World War II. Laurel, who was incarcerated at Sugamo prison, managed to write his journal entries in the margins and white space of a Western book he had found. Historian Horacio de la Costa said that this act was "oddly symbolic because it reveals something very meaningful about the Filipino condition and presents a kind of model for the construction of Filipino thought." Costa remarks, "We, as a nation, have received a rich intellectual legacy from the West: our religious faith from Spain, our democratic institutions from America. But this legacy, rich as it is, has blank spaces which, in the providence of God, we are meant to fill" (ibid.). This example is helpful in understanding how a model of synthesis can hold a variety of elements together while remaining faithful and committed to its own history and tradition. It is as Bevans calls it a "both/and" approach.[3]

---

2. Elsewhere, I have referred to this process—drawing on philosopher Peter Rollins' thought—as a faithful betrayal. Where one rooted within the tradition is so committed to the tradition that they are able to play with it, subvert it, and betray it for its own good (Daniels, "New Quakers" 2010).

3. Another helpful example of synthesis that Bevans offers is the formation of books of the Bible. "The Bible came about gradually, through a collection of individual books, each of which was formed within the context of present concerns interacting with contemporary culture, neighboring cultures, and ancient traditions" (Bevans,

In Bevans' *Models of Contextual Theology*, the word "synthetic" describes a process of bringing four different threads together into a new contextual theology: tradition, culture, dialogue and praxis. First, Bevans says that "synthesis" is made up of the other five models discussed above. "It tries to preserve the importance of the gospel message and the heritage of traditional doctrinal formulations, while at the same time acknowledging the vital role that context has played and can play in theology, even to the setting of the theological agenda" (ibid., 89). This synthesis also encourages reflection on the complexities of social change and how these various threads work to bring about changed cultures.

Second, in this model traditions borrow resources, whether theological or cultural, from outside itself to aid in the reformulations of theology. Bevans argues that every culture is a composite made up of common elements and elements that are unique to that particular context (ibid., 90). Practitioners of the synthetic model attempt to emphasize both aspects: the complementarity and the uniqueness. This is because "one's identity emerges in a dialogue that includes both" (ibid.). This model works from the conviction that there is something of God in every culture, something to be borrowed from, learned from, and drawn on. One culture can learn from another without giving into cultural domination.

Third, the model brings together various points in a *dialectic* that is acceptable to multiple standpoints. It could also be called the "dialogical model" because of its constant use of dialogue and analogical imagination (ibid., 90). For Bevans, not only is dialogue what nurtures "true human growth," it is also participatory, involving the practitioners within the community:

> Each participant in a context has something to give to the other, and each context has something from which it needs to be exorcised. As men and women read literature, philosophy, and history produced by people with different experience, from different ages, from other cultures, and from other social locations, and when they can come together in some form of conversation, each person will recognize her or his uniqueness. (Ibid., 91)

This gives the practitioners of the synthetic model the experience that God is not only in their tradition, context and community, but is revealed in and through other traditions and contexts. MacIntyres use of same-saying and concept borrowing are appropriate here and reveal

---

Models of Contextual Theology, 88).

that in this practice expands the opportunity for encounter and growth in Christ through the "other" but also enlarges the possibility for a deeper and more contextual theology from within their own tradition.

I would suggest a fourth feature to this model, which Bevans does not explicitly name, in that the synthesis model is orientated towards *praxis*. Praxis is related to understanding social change in the present experience and working together to understand how to interact with it:

> The praxis model is a way of doing theology that is formed by knowledge at its most intense level—the level of reflective action. It is also about discerning the meaning and contributing to the course of social change, and so it takes its inspiration from neither classic texts nor classic behavior but form present realities and future possibilities. (Ibid., 70)

For the praxis side of the synthetic model, there is a drawing on knowledge that is not just about a history of ideas or the authority of ortho-doxy theology, but instead finds that reflection is born out of orthopraxy. Praxis, "in its most profound sense is understood as the unity of knowledge as activity and knowledge as content" (ibid., 72). In this way, practitioners become apprentices of the tradition and culture of which they are a part.

> At one point traditional practices might need to be cultivated. Perhaps in another set of circumstances they need to be resisted. To use our horticultural example, the synthetic sees the need and value of cross-pollination so that new and sturdier plants might be developed to be better suited to a particular environment. (Ibid., 92)

"Cross-pollination" is about sharing of ideas and conservation that is often difficult:

> Conversation is a game with some hard rules: say only what you mean; say it as accurately as you can; listen to and respect what the other says, however different or other; be willing to correct or defend your opinions if challenged by the conservation partner; be willing to argue if necessary, to confront if demanded, to endure necessary conflict, to change your mind if the evidence. (Ibid., 94)

Synthesis is not possible without adherents who are engaged in the practices of the communities they find themselves in.

While I have outlined the basic model and its features, how synthesis happens is rather complex; it is done "on the go" and is process-oriented. This is no step-one, step-two formula. It is more like an artist constructing her masterful work of art. To an outside observer the process may look haphazard or incomplete, but the artist addresses each line, coloring, and object, as they are needed. Furthermore, an observer may comment on the artwork, they may even add to it in some way, but the artist alone can make the piece. In a similar way, a missionary has only a small part to play in helping to construct a local theology, while the major "work of inculturation can only be done by cultural subjects," just as in MacIntyre's framework, where the apprentices of the tradition are ultimately responsible for the translation of that tradition within new contexts. While synthesis allows for, even stresses the importance of dialogue with outside cultural resources, it is the native participants who decide how and in what ways those resources are employed within their own paradigm. Thus, this makes the process far more like "producing a work of art than following a rigid set of directions" (ibid., 92).

Critiques of Contextual Theology

Bevans suggests that there are at least two possible critiques that may be leveled at the synthetic model: making the tradition too open or too weak. As the synthetic model is based in postmodern philosophy, it counters the correspondence theory of truth by drawing on dialogue and openness to truth from more than one point of view. The critique of openness is a critique from those operating under the correspondence model of truth:

> Contemporary postmodern thinking . . . is moving away from this correspondence understanding of truth and understanding truth more in terms of relation, conversation, and dialogue. It is encouraged in this regard by the radical pluralism and multicultural consciousness that is emerging, at least implicitly everywhere. Truth in this scheme of things is understood not so much as something "out there" but as a reality that emerges in true conversation between authentic women and men when they "allow questioning to take over." (Ibid., 93)

In this way, dialogue keeps the contextual theology that arises from this model open-ended and constantly in process. It is never a finished product but one that is on-going (ibid.). It is what might be called an "open work" just as with MacIntyre's tradition.[4] This leads to a Christian faith that is in some sense universal, because it is convinced that "every person in every context can learn from every other person and the fact that the present can continue to learn from the past points to the reality of 'something,' however elementary or however preconceptual" (ibid., 94)

While the synthetic model can be troubling for those working under an Enlightenment model of truth, where objectivity of "facts" is still an illusion, the critique of openness and fear of dialogue within that tradition need not be accepted. Many philosophers, including MacIntyre, have refuted the correspondence theory and the presuppositions that it is based on:

> But facts, like telescopes and wigs for gentlemen, were a seventeenth-century invention. In the sixteenth century and earlier "fact" in English was usually a rendering of the Latin "factum," a deed, an action, and sometimes in Scholastic Latin an event or an occasion. It was only in the seventeenth century that "fact" was first used in the way in which later philosophers such as Russell, Wittgenstein, and Ramsey were to use it. It is of course and always was harmless, philosophically and otherwise, to use the word "fact" of what a judgment states. What is and was not harmless, but highly misleading, was to conceive of a realm of facts independent of judgment or of any other form of linguistic expression, so that judgments or statements or sentences could be paired off with facts, truth or falsity being the alleged relationship between such paired items. (MacIntyre 1988: 357)

A second critique of this model is that the theology that comes out of the synthesis model is "too weak, too wishy-washy" (Bevans 2002: 95). Even if the formation of a dialectic theology where all sides agree upon the newly constructed theology is possible, is it desirable? This is a problem that was foreseen by one Quaker missionary in the mid-part of the twentieth century, Everett Cattell. Cattell, also influenced by Hegelian philosophy, raised a similar question in a 1971 article titled, "What Future for Friends." It is there that Cattell argues that identifying the structural and decorative differences can help Friends know where they stand, and possibly help them take a step forward. Decorative differences are of little consequence; they are not where real divisions lay. The real issues lay within disagreement over substantive issues, like "Jesus Christ is Lord":

---

4. Cf. MacIntyre's comments on Aquinas' *Summa Theologia* above in chapter 2.

> It is important to note that these structural polarizations of Friends do not correspond to, and indeed cut right down through, some of our organizational structures. I would emphasize that these groupings around ideas have an organic unity and are real entities as much or more than is true of our organizational structures. (Cattell 1971: 32)

One possible way of dealing with these issues is through what Cattell calls a "synthetic" approach. However, according to Cattell, this approach does not go deep enough into dealing with the structural differences. His synthetic approach is "produced by artificial processes" and is what many Friends have used for a long time. This process was most evident at the turn of the century (1900–1902) when a number of Hicksite and General Conference Friends joined together over shared concerns without creating a legislative body or bringing together the yearly meetings (ibid., 33). They made decorative changes, but did not adjust structures.

Synthesis also happened when Friends World Committee for Consultation was created and the Five Years Meeting merged into one. The latter has the binding powers of a legislative body, yet even so, it has not fully realized its vision and "remains in reality a federation because of the heterogeneity of its elements" (ibid., 34). These examples have not succeeded to the level originally hoped. This is most likely because "the basis for our effort has been too synthetic, too artificial, too much a putting together of things which do not belong together in any natural sense" (ibid.).

From Cattell's perspective, synthesis is undesirable for Friends because it does not go to the level of change that is needed if Quakerism is to be renewed. If he had a chance to learn from Bevans approach, he may have realized that synthesis can bring structural change within a tradition. While it is clear that Cattell is not discussing the intricacies of contextual theology, and Bevans' model is far more robust than Cattell's version, Cattell makes a helpful point when he suggests that there can be the creation of something "too artificial." This concern is less about the *process* of the synthetic model and more about the *results* of the process. Finally, Cattell's concern betrays his own philosophical assumptions, which may be uncomfortable with more postmodern approaches; in either case it reflects a concern that is still alive within the Society of Friends.

A model of synthesis that follows MacIntyre's understanding of how a tradition is reformulated during and after an epistemological crisis will be less susceptible to these criticisms. Following MacIntyre, there are requirements for a successful reconstitution or synthesis of traditions, just as there is within contextual theology. Following José de Mesa and Lode Wostyn, Bevans suggests there are three criteria the new contextual theology should meet: First, it "should be oriented in the same direction as other 'successful' or approved formulations" (2002: 23). In other words, the basic intentions of Christianity should be left intact. Second, it should be rooted in Christian orthopraxis. Any theology that appears Christian at first but leads to non-Christian practices is not "orthodox." While, conversely, a theology that may at first appear to be non-Christian but leads to clearly Christian oriented practices is justifiable. Finally, the newly formulated theology should receive a proper reception and be acceptable to the whole community it represents (ibid.). In other words, there should be some process of consensus through which the new theology is appropriated into the community.

CONCLUSION

Bevans' understanding of contextual theology, and his model of synthesis provide a paradigm that demonstrates how an embodied community can be both faithful to its tradition, while at the same time respond creatively to new contexts. For much of the past century and a half, Quakers have divided very much along these lines as though the choices were between faithfulness to the Quaker tradition and adjusting to the times. Within the Enlightenment there is a false dichotomy that frames mission today. Bevans' model of contextual theology is the perfect companion to MacIntyre and demonstrates how a model for renewal can be constructed that takes into account tradition and context while overcoming the crisis brought on by the Enlightenment.

I have suggested that there are four basic characteristics included in Bevans synthetic model that consequently also work well with MacIntyre's philosophy. These qualities are (a) the inescapable quality of tradition, (b) the necessity of responding to and drawing resources from the immediate context, (c) the importance of dialogue with other practitioners and (d) the centrality of practices (or praxis in Bevans' language) for the ongoing identity of a community. These four qualities must be synthesized by apprentices of that particular tradition and culture; it is essential to both MacIntyre and Bevans that insiders are the key proponents of reconstruction.

Finally, MacIntyre's criteria for reconstruction is helpful in offering guidance for how a new synthesis of two cultures or traditions might both be faithful to their past, while at the same time new in useful ways.

CHAPTER 3

Henry Jenkins and Participatory Culture

IN THIS CHAPTER, I aim to build on insights gleaned from what is known as fan studies or participatory culture. This chapter consists of two parts: a description of what fan studies consists of, and a description of six elements of participatory culture. If Bevans' synthesis model suggests that the missionary must listen and dialogue with one's present culture in order to discover what might be translatable from one's tradition (*a la* MacIntyre), then our next task is to look more closely at one very significant and increasingly global cultural dynamic: participatory culture.

Fandom is a specific type of participatory culture in which fans draw meaning from and produce new material on existing artifacts. Convergence culture is also another way of talking specifically about certain aspects within participatory culture. Jenkins' book *Convergence Culture* (2006a) describes the shift away from the scandalous category of 'fan' to the culture of today where the fan (or active audiences) has become "central to how culture operates" (Jenkins 2006b: 1).

He writes in *Fans, Bloggers and Gamers: Exploring Participatory Culture* that the "New technologies are enabling average consumers to archive, annotate, appropriate, and recirculate media content. Powerful institutions and practices (law, religion, education, advertising, and politics among them) are being redefined by a growing recognition of what is to be gained through fostering—or at least tolerating—participatory cultures (ibid.).

FANDOM AND PARTICIPATORY CULTURE

The word "fan," derived from Latin word "fanaticus"—once meant "of belonging to the temple, a temple servant, a devotee," but has evolved to take on more negative aspects, "Of persons inspired by orgiastic rites and enthusiastic frenzy"—and has often been used derisively within pop culture to refer to an almost cult-like reverence for a person or other fan-artifact (Jenkins 1992: 12). Henry Jenkins has challenged earlier characterizations of fans by constructing an alternative narrative about what fandom stands for in society now:

> To speak of a fan is to accept what has been labeled a subordinated position within the cultural hierarchy, to accept an identity constantly belittled or criticized by institutional authorities. Yet it is also to speak from a position of collective identity, to forge an alliance with a community of others in defense of tastes which, as a result, cannot be read as totally aberrant or idiosyncratic. (Ibid., 23)

Fan, in this context, takes on new meaning: an individual who moves from bystander to active participant in (ibid., 55) the "construction and circulation of textual meanings" (ibid., 24) and in doing so create an alternative social community of cultural resistance. By studying fandom, not as a scandalous category within society, but as alternative community, Jenkins and others have demonstrated how fans create a participatory space that resists the consumptive nature of popular culture and moves into a new spaces of creative production.

Fandom and Cultural Studies

Study of fandom emerged as an aspect of cultural studies—following the tradition of cultural studies of Birmingham, England—inspired by Michel de Certeau's *The Practice of Everyday Life* (1984). De Certeau insisted that the everyday practices of the disempowered operate as "tactics" of meaning-making and popular resistance within popular culture (1984: xx). As de Certeau argues, "A tactic is an art of the weak" (ibid., 37). Many within society do not have the economic or the social capital to participate in the dominant forms of cultural production, and those marginalized voices were thought to be little more than automatons within a hegemonic meaning-making system. Nevertheless, de Certeau documents "not the strategies employed by this hegemonic power to restrict the circulation of popular meaning or to marginalize oppositional voices but rather to theorize the various tactics of popular resistance" (Jenkins 1992: 26).

De Certeau set the stage within cultural studies to prove there was cause to "reconsider the place of popular response, of personal speculations and non-authorized meanings in the reception of artworks and to overcome professional training that prepares us to reject meanings falling outside our frame of reference or interpretive practice" (de Certeau 1984). These responses of the "subordinate classes" stem from a resistance derived from re-appropriation of popular "texts" that give way to authentic meaning-making and true creativity. These individuals and communities clearly exhibit meaning-making in creating alternative "spatial grids" (cf. Johnson et al. 2004: 112) or "free-space."[1] Cultural Theorist Stephen Duncombe writes that cultural resistance can provide a "free space" where new practices and theory can be developed,

> Freed from the limits and constraints of the dominant culture, you can experiment with new ways of seeing and being and develop tools and resources for resistance. And as culture is usually something shared, it becomes a focal point around which to build a community. (Duncombe 2002: 5–6)[2]

---

1. This idea that a free space can be created through cultural resistance is reminiscent of Mikhail Bakhtin's notion of the "carnival"—from the Middle Ages and the Renaissance—as a "popular production of subversion." The carnival offered a "world inside out" where "The fool was made king and the king a fool, the sacred ceremonies and rigid strictures of Church and State were defiled and ridiculed" (Duncombe, *Dream: Re-Imagining*, 83). Bakhtin writes that the rituals and festivities of these carnivals "had an important place in the life of medieval man. . . . They offered a completely different, nonofficial, extraecclesiastical and extrapolitical aspect of the world, of man, and of human relations; they built a second world and a second life outside officialdom, a world in which all medieval people participated more or less, in which they lived during a time of the year" (Bakhtin, "Rabelais and His World," 84). And again this resistance in the form of carnival "celebrated temporary liberation from the prevailing truth and from the established order; it marked the suspension of all hierarchical rank, privileges, norms and prohibitions. Carnival was the true feast of time, the feast of becoming, change, and renewal. It was hostile to all that was immortalized and completed" (Bakhtin, "Rabelais and His World," 87).

2. "Free-space" operates as cultural resistance and understood as ideological—a place where new language, new meaning, new future can be configured—as well as materially—networks, organizational models that challenge dominant models and new forms of community (Duncombe, *Dream: Re-Imagining*, 8).

Following this, early fandom sought to "construct an alternative image of fan cultures," building upon de Certeau, demonstrating that fans were not dupes but active participants in creating a new and alternative culture of resistance.

Textual Poachers

Henry Jenkins, a pioneer in the field of fan studies, has written extensively on the subject of fandom and participatory culture. Two central works are *Textual Poachers: Television Fans and Participatory Culture* (Jenkins 1992)[3] and *Convergence Culture: Where Old and New Media Collide* (Jenkins 2006). In both, Jenkins outlines features of a culture that fosters participation in and resistance to consumer culture. Each book turns on a main theme he develops throughout: poaching and convergence. Because both "poaching" and "convergence" are central to Jenkins' understanding of participatory culture, I will describe them below.

In *Textual Poachers*, Jenkins argues that the primary practice of fans is "poaching," Michel de Certeau's term for this active reading strategy (Jenkins 1992: 19). Poaching can be described as a kind of cultural bricolage where pop cultural texts are appropriated in ways that challenge bourgeois interpretive strategies. Poaching takes a cultural text and appropriates it in a way that makes sense of the fan's life, social and emotional experiences. It is a:

> Series of "advances and retreats, tactics and games played with the text," as a type of cultural bricolage through which readers fragment texts and reassemble the broken shards according to their own blueprints, salvaging bits and pieces of the found material in making sense of their own social experience. (Ibid., 26)

3. Textual Poachers was Henry Jenkins' first book on participatory culture and has since shaped all fandom research (Jenkins, *Textual Poachers*, 1992). One of the initial purposes of the study was to show a sympathetic side to fan culture that countered stereotypes and myths surrounding media fandom. Because of the deterritorialized nature of media fandom and the diversity of "fan objects," fan communities are fluid, not fixed by a particular identity, and are characterized by instability: fans are always located within "other forms of cultural production and other social identities" (ibid., 3). Yet, this does not mean that there is no solidity to this community, instead Jenkins' book outlines five distinct dimensions of this fan culture: "its particular mode of reception; its role in encouraging viewer activism; its function as an interpretive community; its particular traditions of cultural production; and its status as an alternative society" (ibid., 2).

This form of cultural bricolage allows for the fan to not only make sense of his or her life based on contemporary experience, but creates a sense of freedom of voice and expression. The production of "fan fiction" demonstrates that:

> . . .Fans enthusiastically embrace favored texts and attempt to integrate media representation into their own social experience. Unimpressed by institutional authority and expertise, the fans assert their own right to form interpretations, to offer evaluations, and to construct cultural canons. (Ibid., 18)

> Fans have produced countless spin-offs, reinterpretations, and alternative storylines over the years, often met by contempt of the original writers and actors. (Ibid., 30)

Poaching challenges the authorized meanings and sanctioned interpretations of particular texts by making way for multiple voices, readings and interpretations.[4] Often fan fiction blurs the lines between fact and fiction "[speaking] of characters as if they had an existence apart from their textual manifestations" (ibid., 18), meaning that fans appropriate popular texts and reread them in new and often unsanctioned ways. Thus, a Star Wars fan might write a short story that challenges gender roles within one of the films or "circulate erotic stories that expressed their desires and fantasies about the characters" even as the producer, George Lucas, may try to force those alternative readings underground (ibid., 32). It is this act of poaching that transforms the spectator into the participant: "Fans as readers who appropriate popular texts and reread them in a fashion that serves different interests, as spectators who transform the experience of watching television into a rich and complex participatory culture" (ibid., 23).

While the fan and the producer may have a tenuous relationship at best, this theory of appropriation should not be mistaken for a theory of "misreading" the texts. Misreading is itself an evaluative category that suggests one person, interpretation or community is in a "neutral" place to adjudicate properly the intended meanings of a given text. "The term 'misreading' is necessarily evaluative and preserves the traditional hierarchy bestowing privileged status to authorial meanings over reader's meanings" (ibid., 33). Instead, poaching is open-ended and fluid, allowing for a multiplicity of valid, yet competing interpretations. It challenges

---

4. It is not insignificant from this perspective that early fandom was dominated by women (Jenkins, *Convergence Culture*, 1).

those readings of the text that are based on "institutional power" and argue for a singularity of meaning (ibid., 33.). It is fluid insofar as it recognizes that popular meanings are not fixed, they are formed through a process that is not in isolation from other social factors (ibid., 34).[5]

Finally, Jenkins argues that poaching must be understood as a communal practice. "Fan reading . . . is a social process through which individual interpretations are shaped and reinforced through ongoing discussions with other readers. Such discussions expand the experience of the text beyond its initial consumption" (ibid., 45). Meanings that emerge through this communal process are not simply for the moment but take on an instructive feature for the community. "These previously poached meanings provide a foundation for future encounters with the fiction, shaping how it will be perceived, defining how it will be used" (ibid.). Thus, meaning within fandom is constructed dialectically; the participant is reader and writer, interpreter and originator of meaning. "Fandom does not preserve a radical separation between readers and writers. Fans do not simply consume reproduced stories, they manufacture their own fanzine stories and novels, art prints, songs, videos, performances, etc" (ibid.). Poaching describes how fandom rejects one-sided consumptive media practices but is instead a participatory culture that creates not only new texts, but an entirely new community to go along with them (ibid.).

Convergence Culture

If in *Textual Poachers* Jenkins was acting apologist for fandom, in *Convergence Culture,* he shows how fans "have become central to how culture operates" (2006a: 1). What was once a controversial and scandalous category is now taken for granted within the new media landscape. What Jenkins calls convergence culture is rooted in new technologies that have created an entirely more fluid, "convergent," experience between platform, content and audience:

> By convergence, I mean the flow of content across multiple media platforms, the cooperation between multiple media industries, and the migratory behavior of media audiences who

---

5. For de Certeau, "the reader's meanings originate in response to immediate concerns and are discarded when they are no longer useful" (Jenkins, *Textual Poachers,* 44).

will go almost anywhere in search of the kinds of entertainment experiences they want. Convergence is a word that manages to describe technological, industrial, cultural, and social changes depending on who's speaking and what they think they are talking about. (Jenkins 2006a: 2–3)

Today's convergence, or participatory culture, marks an even greater shift in consumptive media where consumers "are encouraged to seek out new information and make connections among dispersed media context" (Jenkins 2006a: 3). In other words, from Jenkins' view, popular culture has finally caught up with the participatory nature of fandom. There are three characteristics of this culture I name below: active, collective and a convergence of old and new forms of media.

This new convergence culture is active. The consumer is no longer deviant nor is she passive. Now mass media relies on fans to add content to websites such as YouTube or update their live newsfeeds via websites such as Twitter. Gone are days when fans produce texts relegated to the catacombs of sub-culture. Fans are now in the driver's seat of pop culture. For instance, in the spring of 2008, the London-based band, Radiohead, put convergence culture to use for the release of the single "Nude" off their record *In Rainbows*, when they announced a remix contest for their fans (Kreps 2008). As a part of the contest, Radiohead released separate "stems" or isolated tracks of the bass, drums, vocals and guitar tracks from "Nude" and sold each stem through Apple's iTunes music store.

Fans and musicians alike remixed the tracks and uploaded them to the website radioheadremix.com (Radiohead 2008). The band then listened to the mixes and allowed fans to vote for their favorite. In all, the group received 2,254 remixes of "Nude," had 274,181 votes, and 2,522,031 unique visitors to the site (Richardson 2012).[6] Radiohead's invitation to intentionally "poach" one of their songs reveals a major shift in consumer culture. Where once an artist would protect his or her "original artwork" from deviations, today's participatory culture is one that:

---

6. Taking this one-step further, James Houston shows another aspect of convergence culture (see below) where old and new media collide. Houston remixed "Nude" by "program[ing] a roomful of outdated hard drives and other office equipment to play the song orchestra-like" (Baldwin, "Machinery Nostalgia") and then filmed a video of the song and retitled it "Big Ideas: Don't Get Any." Between the views on YouTube (http://youtu.be/pmfHHLfbjNQ) and Vimeo (http://vimeo.com/1109226) the video has been video more than 1.7 million times.

Requires media companies to rethink old assumptions about what it means to consume media, assumptions that shape both programming and marketing decisions. If old consumers were assumed to be passive, the new consumers are active. If old consumers were predictable and stayed where you told them to stay, then new consumers are migratory, showing a declining loyalty to networks or media. If old consumers were isolated individuals, the new consumers are more socially connected. If the work of media consumers were once silent and invisible, the new consumers are now noisy and public. (Jenkins 2006b: 18–19)

Convergence names a new level of participation within today's culture that works from the top down as well as the bottom up (ibid. 18).

Not only is convergence based on active participants who produce the products they wish to consume, it is also done collectively. Jenkins uses the term "collective intelligence," drawing on the French "cybertheorist" Pierre Lévy who describes collective intelligence as a:

> Form of universally distributed intelligence, constantly enhanced, coordinated in real time, and resulting in the effective mobilization of skills. . . . The basis and goal of collective intelligence is the mutual recognition and enrichment of individuals rather than the cult of fetishized or hypostatized communities. (Lévy 1997:13)

The faster and bigger our global information culture grows, the more difficult it becomes to make sense of our everyday lives. Collective intelligence recognizes that there is too much for any one person to take in and process, thus the sharing of specializations and the rise of dialogue between consumers becomes essential: "None of us can know everything, each of us knows something; and we can put the pieces together if we pool our resources and combine our skills" (Jenkins 2006b: 4).

Collective intelligence has ushered in new "knowledge communities" and a period of apprenticeship, where new skills for navigating today's work are taught and learned (ibid., 27–29). Lévy writes:

> Through our relationship to others, mediated by process of initiation and transmission, we bring knowledge to life. Skill, understanding, and knowledge (which can all refer to the same objects) are three complementary modes of cognitive transaction and continuously interpenetrate one another. Each activity, each act of communication, each human relation implies an *apprenticeship*. (Emphasis mine: Lévy 1997: 11)

Therefore, these new communities create a "circuit of exchange" in which knowledge, skill and understanding are passed on freely to other members of the knowledge community (ibid., 11). This form of apprenticeship is open-ended and mutual; it mediates relationships and forms new identities within these emerging communities (ibid., 11–12). Further, it is this exchange of knowledge and practice that holds these communities together:

> And these new communities are "defined through voluntary, temporary, and tactical affiliations, reaffirmed through common intellectual enterprises and emotional investments. Members may shift from one group to another as their interests and needs change, and they may belong to more than one community at the same time. These communities, however, are held together through the mutual production and reciprocal exchange of knowledge. (Jenkins 2006b: 27)

These knowledge communities show that how community is understood, embodied and mediated is shifting within convergence culture.

One helpful example of a new knowledge community surrounds the fan fiction of the *Harry Potter* children's book series (ibid., 169–205). Jenkins writes about how a thirteen year old girl named Heather Lawver began a *Harry Potter* fan website called *The Daily Prophet* (ibid., 171). That online publication—as of the time Jenkins book was published in 2006—had one hundred and two youth staffing the website from all over the world. The main goal of the website was to promote literacy and get children writing. Heather, the managing editor, hires "columnists" to write about recent Quidditch matches and other events pertaining to the fictional world of *Harry Potter* (ibid., 171–72).

Beyond helping children enter into the imaginary space and create fictional identities where they can live out the very real connections they feel with the characters in *Harry Potter*, they are able to work out in the safety of this new "knowledge community" the difficulties of the ones they may be experiencing "back home."

> Heather has suggested that many kids come to *The Daily Prophet* because their schools and families have failed them in some way; they use the new school community to work through their feelings about some traumatic event or to compensate for their estrangement from kids in their neighborhoods. . . . Children use stories to escape from or reaffirm aspects of their real lives. (Ibid., 174)

Finally, convergence culture brings along those new to the culture and helps them find their way through mutual apprenticeship (ibid., 178). For instance, the practice of "Beta Reading" is a built in peer-review process that helps children improve writing not through editing, but through making suggestions and by giving the same children the opportunity to do their own critical analyses of others' writings (ibid., 180). Just as in the practice of poaching, they learn by appropriating existing cultural material into their own words, creating a "remix" of something original based out of something already there. This kind of re-writing, "copying" and appropriation of *Harry Potter* should be thought of as apprenticeship.

> Historically, young artists learned from established masters, sometimes contributing to the older artists' works, often following their patterns, before they developed their own styles and techniques . . . these young artists learn what they can from the stories and images that are most familiar to them. Building their first efforts upon existing cultural materials allows them to focus their energies elsewhere, mastering their craft, perfecting their skills, and communicate their ideas. (Ibid., 182)

This community of youngsters is only one example of the many ways that *collective* intelligence fosters new communities of shared skills and knowledge and builds upon mutual apprenticeship.

One last feature of convergence culture is that when old and new media collide, old media never dies, it is only the delivery technologies that change (ibid., 13). Jenkins defines media that operates on two levels:

> On the first, a medium is a technology that enables communication; on the second, a medium is a set of associated 'protocols' or social and cultural practices that have grown up around technology. Delivery systems are simply and only technologies; media are also cultural systems. Delivery technologies come and go all the time, but media persist as layers within an ever more complicated information and entertainment stratum. (Ibid., 13–14)

Convergence accepts the instability of culture while all the time working for constant unity (ibid., 11). It does this in part by rejecting the idea that old media is automatically absorbed into newer media (ibid., 5). In other words, within *convergence* culture, there is a rejection of the ideology that new is always better; all devices do not converge into one "universal" device (2006a: 15).[7] "Old media are not being displaced.

---

7. The online video sharing website YouTube is a perfect example of old and new

Rather, their functions and status are shifted by the introduction of new technologies" (ibid., 14). This sustainability, or at the very least, residue, of older mediums points at just how impossible it is to have a complete break from older mediums even if it becomes increasingly complex and many-layered.[8]

Conclusion

In this first section, I have outlined the development of fan studies as stemming from the work of de Certeau's conception of practices that demonstrate how subordinate classes resist dominant culture. When applied to fandom, this view reveals tactics and strategies developed to forge new "knowledge identities" and "knowledge communities" as Pierre Lévy calls it. Rather than fans simply being thought of as fanatics or dupes of consumer culture, I have demonstrated, building on the work of Henry Jenkins, that fandom is highly participatory. Jenkins' work has been central to fan studies since the publication of his book *Textual Poachers* in 1992, and his subsequent book *Convergence Culture* shows an evolution both in the acceptance of the fan category within today's culture, as well as the technologies that undergird these participatory practices. Of special interest are two of Jenkins' key terms: poaching and convergence. Poaching reveals how fans, or adherents of a particular fan tradition, appropriate existing cultural material and make it their own by extending those texts, challenging their sanctioned meaning and reinterpreting them in the context of their everyday lives.

Convergence reveals how culture has begun to reflect the active participation of fandom. It also reflects a collectivity that emerges from

---

media colliding. In describing YouTube Jean Burgess argues that what is unique about YouTube is its scalability; it is able to be formed from the "bottom-up by the 'users en mass' via consumption, evaluation, and entrepreneurial activities" (Burgess and Green, *YouTube*, 5). While it is a site of participatory culture it is also a business model that puts on display how bottom-up and top-down models might work together in economic and cultural rearrangement (ibid., 10). In this way YouTube itself is a convergence of the old and new, a "co-evolution and uneasy co-existence of 'old' and 'new' media industries, forms and practices" (ibid., 14).

8. Caroline Bassett argues that this new global information narrative "is a vital element of contemporary culture, lying at the heart of the process through which humans make sense of their experiences in everyday lives that are, by virtue of mediation through and across information, increasingly multi-layered and complex both temporally and spatially" (Bassett, *The Arc and the Machine*, 2–3).

within these fan communities that rejects expert knowledge, drawing instead on the expertise of individuals as their communities are shaped through mutual apprenticeship. Finally, convergence names the use of old media within new contexts. Fans demonstrate that so long as old media speaks to the core of human condition, there is some way that it can be appropriated within a new context.

THE SIX FEATURES OF PARTICIPATORY CULTURE

Thus far I have outlined the basic concepts and contours of participatory culture as they have been developed through fan studies. Participatory culture is best understood as communities of fans who engage in the practice of poaching "texts" from popular culture and adapting them in ways that make sense of their everyday lives—often in resistance to dominant culture. In this way, participatory culture is a kind of bricolage for the masses. Today's participatory culture is also a culture of convergence inasmuch as consumers are now embraced, at least tentatively, by more dominant modes of production. Consumers are now thought of as being capable of producing the content they want to consume. Participatory culture is not a niche culture within Western society; it is a widespread global information phenomenon:

> Participatory culture is anything but fringe or underground today. Fan fiction can be accessed in astonishing quantities and diversities by anyone who knows how to Google. Media producers monitor the Web forums such as 'Television Without Pity,' planting trial balloons to test viewer response, measuring reaction to controversial plot twists. Game companies give the public access to their design tools, publicize the best results, and hire the top amateur programmers. The amateur subtitling and circulation of anime arguably helped to open the market for Asian cultural imports. And meetup.com formed as a way for collectors to trade Beanie Babies; its impact was first demonstrated by X-Philes as they lobbied to keep their show on the air; but it became a central resource in the 2004 presidential campaign. News stories appear regularly about media companies suing their consumers, trying to beat them back into submission, and the blogging community continues to challenge the mainstream news media and shake up the political parties. (Jenkins 2006b: 2)

Building on what has already been argued, as well as other cultural theorists, the following section organizes into six elements the dominant features of this participatory culture. The six elements of participatory culture are: authentic resistance, remix, cultural producers, collective intelligence, decentralized or networked authority, and alternative social community.

Authentic Resistance

The first element of participatory culture is both to dismantle and build a free space where meaning can be constructed outside the purview of authorized meanings and dominant culture. This is best described as an authentic resistance. Authentic because fans show high levels of emotional investment and ownership in relation to their fan-objects and are known for assimilating cultural artifacts into their lives in order to create meaning out of those artifacts. Resistance because what is produced is often—though not necessarily always—in tension with the sanctioned meanings, authorial intent or even outdated "intellectual property rights" crafted at the turn of the twentieth century (Lessig 2008: 25).[9] Fan communities emerged as the marginalized—in terms of gender, race, orientation, skill level or education, political viewpoints, religion—sought to retain power by creating meaning through reinterpretation.

In describing fandom through the lens of "the politics of alternative culture," Stephen Duncombe turns to the helpful example of "Zinesters." Zinesters are those who produce "zines" or independently produce and publish magazines that go "against a society predicated on consumption, zinesters privilege the ethic of DIY, do-it-yourself: make your own culture and stop consuming that which is made for you" (Duncombe 1997: 2). Zines, a self-published and early form of blogging, represent a "true culture of resistance" and "vernacular radicalism" (ibid., 3). As Duncombe writes, "the interpretations they give to the circumstances and conditions that surround them, and the ideals and character traits they possess," is a powerful weapon (ibid., 20).

Sociologically speaking, Zinesters were often outcasts of society, people labeled losers by mass culture, who set out to redefine what it

---

9. Fan communities who emerged as the marginalized—in terms of gender, race, orientation, skill level or education, political viewpoints, religion, etc.—sought to retain power by creating meaning through reinterpretation.

meant to be a loser: they turned "a deficit into an asset" (ibid., 20). This was done through the creation of a new identity, a manufacturing of the self and/or community that surrounded the zine. For instance, in the zine *Cool Loser*, "losers" were extolled as role models forming a new identity that subverted the cultural expectations they faced. These zinesters turn a "negative label [into] a positive one" (ibid.). Duncombe describes this authentic resistance when he says, "Zines foster a community of losers within a society that celebrates winners" (ibid., 43).

The motivation for this kind of active investment and creation of meaning is a desire for all of life to be thoroughly personal and authentic. Duncombe argues that the draw for zinesters is the authenticity and personal nature of what they write about. The "perzine," a homemade printed version of today's "personal weblog," is written in a way that shares the details of intimate everyday life with others. Because no permission is needed and no editor is relied upon, non-experts are permitted to write about what is most personal to them (ibid., 22). Zines operate under the assumption that "politics is personal."

This connection between the personal and political mirrors an earlier form of "zines" found in another form of underground media known as pamphlets. Pamphlets were small booklets—usually only a few pages long and unbound—often used to voice dissenting opinion from groups such as the Quakers. Thomas Paine's famous *Common Sense* was another such response (ibid., 27). Zines use a personal voice about every issue, which means that they take writing a step further than these earlier pamphlet writers, who often abstracted themselves from their own political and theological discourse (ibid., 28).

Authentic resistance, as in the context of zine culture, cuts through all the "spin, promotion, public relations and pseudo-events," and gets back to a reality that is rooted in what they know and personally believe (ibid., 32):

> Zinesters believe that authenticity can be found only in a person *unshackled by the contrivances of society*. An authentic individual, therefore, is one who cuts through the conventions of manners, norms, and communication and connects to his or her "real" self. More than anything else, this search *to live without artifice, without hypocrisy*, defines the politics of underground culture. (Ibid., italics added)

This is why zine writers go into self-publishing; they can be themselves and express what is most important to them (ibid., 33). "Even if you're not out to change the world . . . self-publishing allows you to be yourself and express your real thoughts. Your real feelings" (ibid.).[10]

As fans attempt to create meaning out of life, they remove the obstacles necessary to form new identities and create communities of authentic resistance that are more personal and meaningful than the dominant culture they are subordinate to. Therefore, authenticity is as much about assimilating cultural products in a meaningful way as it is about stripping back all contrivances, making way for the authentic "real" self beyond society's norms and expectations.

Remix

The second characteristic of participatory culture names a practice that follows as a result of the first; fans poach, or remix, existing cultural material in a way that not only transgresses the text's original intent and blends it with other popular or traditional "texts," but also brings an authentic, self-expression to that material. I see Jenkins earlier term "poaching" being related to, if not synonymous with, the term "remix." Poaching as has been suggested derives from Michel de Certeau's *The Practice of Everyday Life*. Poaching, like remix, is a kind of interpretive, playful reading of texts, which fosters an interplay between popular culture and one's own "texts." According to Jenkins poaching can be thought of as, "'advances and retreats, tactics and games played with the text,' as a type of cultural bricolage through which readers fragment texts and reassemble the broken shared according to their own blueprints, salvaging bits and pieces of the found material making sense of their social experience" (Jenkins 1992: 26). And just like poaching, these newly remixed versions of texts or media challenge "the sanctioned expert interpretations and readings of the text" (ibid., 25).

---

10. One interesting example of this "politics of authenticity" can be found in Bob Dylan's practice of the "stutter style." Counterculture social critic Michael Harrington argues that Dylan and others from the Students for a Democratic Society practiced the stutter style because it "assumed that any show of logic or rhetorical style was prima facie proof of hypocrisy and dishonesty, the mark of the manipulative. The sincere man was therefore supposed to be confused and half articulate and anguished in his self-revelation" (Duncombe, *Notes from the Underground*, 35).

Lawrence Lessig argues that, "Whether text or beyond text, remix is collage; it comes from combining elements of [Read Only] culture; it succeeds by leveraging the meaning created by the reference to build something new" (Lessig 2008: 76). It sees creating derivative work out of original material as a legitimate form of creativity.

In his book *Remix: Making Art and Commerce Thrive in the Hybrid Economy*, Lessig relates remix to a fan-art installation of John Lennon's solo work called *Working Class Hero (A Portrait of John Lennon)* (ibid., 6). The installation was made up of twenty-five Lennon fans who each sang a different song from the album *John Lennon/Plastic Ono Band*. Each person "conveyed an extraordinary and contagious emotion. They were not fantastic singers...but you could see that this music and its creator were among the most important thing in these people's lives" (ibid.). These fans appropriated, or remixed, Lennon's work in a new way that not only celebrated Lennon but the "lives Lennon had touched" (ibid.).

In contrast to the analog age, the digital era has greatly increased the accessibility of remixing.[11] On the one hand the Internet has made media widely available (ibid., 69), while the digital era and consumer technology has made it easier to remix media (ibid.,36–37). Seen in this light, remix is a celebration of what Lessig describes as *amateur culture* or a cultural production that is not limited to the elites of society (ibid., 25).

On the other hand, in today's digital era, these two cultures are colliding: Read/Only (copy-right protected) and Read/Write (copy-right free).[12] This extendibility of digital media has created many legal issues over copy-right for R/O and R/W culture. R/O culture was one whose "business model [has] depended upon controlling the distribution of copies of culture" (ibid., 37). Over against this, Lessig sees R/W culture as a free-culture where what is essentially at stake is the "right to quote" (ibid.). Therefore remix, "is a critical expression of creative freedom that

---

11. The practice of "remix" is not exclusive to the digital age. It can be found throughout human history. I argue that the Hebrew practice of Midrash is a form of remix. Jesus' statements in Matthew "You have heard it said . . . but I say to you" is another form of remix. Negro Spirituals that drew on the biblical text and applied them within new contexts is yet another. As I will demonstrate in chapter 5, Quakers too practiced a form of remix that is referred to as "empathetic Bible reading." The difference for today is that remix is more widely accepted and ubiquitous.

12. A non-profit organization known as "Creative Commons" has provided free legal tools to encourage sharing and creative distribution, editing and modifying a artist's content. The Creative Commons license allows artists to specifically tailor their copy-write to their unique needs and requirements (Wikipedia, "Roots of Remix").

in a broad range of contexts, no free society should restrict. Remix is an essential act of R/W creativity. It is the expression of a freedom to take 'the songs of the day or the old songs' and create with them (ibid., 56). Lessig argues that in order for a new generation of creativity to emerge, the right to remix—the right to innovate and amateur culture—needs to be protected.

Remixers, like poachers, do not simply "read" the original texts, but go on to write and re-write those "texts" in ways that reflects their own authentic-self through the newly constructed media. In remix culture there is always a push to move from reading (RO) to writing (RW) (ibid., 87). Remixers, "add to the culture they read by creating and re-creating the culture around them" (ibid., 28). Lessig sees the differences between those who read and those who remix/poach as the same as those who passively and actively learn: "One emphasizes learning. The other emphasizes learning by speaking. One preserves its integrity. The other teaches integrity. One emphasizes a hierarchy. The other hides the hierarchy" (ibid., 87).

A remixer chooses to build upon specific cultural references, images, or sounds –in a practice not unlike Bevan's *synthesis*—adapting them to new contexts and leveraging their meanings in powerful, if sometimes paradoxical, ways. Speaking of the newly created "tokens" Lessig argues:

> Their meaning comes not from the content of what they say; it comes from the reference, which is expressible only if it is the original that gets used. Images or sounds collected from real-world examples become "paint on a palette." And it is this "cultural reference . . . has emotional meaning to people. . . . When you hear four notes of the Beatles' "Revolution," it means "something." When you "mix these symbolic things together" with something new, you create. . .something new that didn't exist before. (Ibid., 74–75)

Hip hop, the birth mother of American remix, is a prime example of mixing symbolic elements that do not normally fit together, in order to make new meaning.[13] Rapper Jay-Z describes how remix culture works within hip hop:

---

13. Hip hop finds its origins in Jamaican reggae of the 1960s and early 70s. The first rapper, Coke La Rock, was from Jamaica, and so were three most important deejays to the birth of hip hop in the United States: "Grandmaster Flash, who invented 'turntablism' concept before it had a name, to Afrika Bambaataa, the 'God father of hip hop' who's of Barbadian and Jamaican lineage, to hip hop's founding father, Jamaican born

Part of how contradictions are reconciled in rap comes from the nature of the music. I've rapped over bhangra, electronica, soup samples, classic rock, alternative rock, indie rock, the blues, doo-wop, bolero, jazz, Afrobeat, gypsy ballads, Luciano Pavarotti, and the theme song of a Broadway musical. That's hip-hop: Anything can work—there are no laws, no rules. Hip-hop created a space where all kinds of music could meet, without contradiction. (Jay-Z 2010: 240)

Jay-Z points to how remix culture "re-writes" texts to create new meaning when he refers to the "theme song of a Broadway musical." That theme song he refers to is from the musical *Annie* and his remixed version called "Hard Knock Life (Ghetto Anthem)."

In the remixed version of the song, Jay-Z samples the chorus of the Broadway version, "It's a hard knock life for us / It's a hard knock life for us for us / 'Stead of treating / we get tricked / 'Stead of kisses / we get kicked / It's a hard knock life," while adding drum beats and his own lyrics about growing up in the ghettos of Brooklyn overtop. Jay-Z wrote "Hard Knock Life" based on *Annie's* theme song because it resonated with his own life and was a cultural reference that already had meaning within pop culture. "'When the TV version [of Annie] came on, I was drawn to it,' he says. 'It was the struggle of this poor kid in this environment and how her life changed. . . . It immediately resonated'" (Gross 2010). Because it resonated with him, he decided to remix it, adapting it to his own context. In building upon the old Broadway song, Jay-Z purposefully remixed in a way that added to the imagery and meaning of *Annie*:

> I wasn't worried about the clash between the hard lyrics *(where all my nigga with the rubber grips, buck shots)* and the image of redheaded Annie. Instead, I found the mirror between the two stories—that Annie's story was mine, and mine was hers, and the song was the place where our experiences weren't

---

DJ Kool Herc, the culture's first acknowledged deejay. Without Herc there is no hip hop" (Higgins, *Hip Hop World*, 23). The term "sampling" is specific type of remix used in hip hop to refer to using elements from one song to create something new. According to Higgins sampling began in the 1960s not in hip hop, but in early pop bands such as the Beach Boys who sampled Chuck Berry's "Sweet Little Sixteen" to create their hit song "Surfin' USA" (ibid., 42). Hip hoppers took this one step further, "by using inexpensive digital technology they borrowed fragments of old Rand B records and re-tooled them by combing these sounds with modern ones. . . . To some, sampling is a way of paying homage to legendary music masters who might otherwise have been forgotten" (ibid.). In participatory culture, one cannot be expect to be celebrated without being appropriated (Jenkins, *Fans, Bloggers, and Gamers*, 149).

> contradictions, just different dimensions of the same reality. . . . I felt like the chorus to that song perfectly captured what little kids in the ghetto felt every day "'Stead of kisses, we get kicked." We might not all have literally been orphans, but a whole generation of us had basically raised ourselves in the streets. (Jay-Z 2010: 240)

Jay-Z's recording not only brought an old song back into popularity again—it would become one of his biggest hits—but by blending the original material and meaning of the song with his experience of growing up as a young African American, he breathed new significance into a song that long since lost relevance. In the same way that highly skilled DJs, artists, or remixers, draw on many layers of meaning available within the palate of existing cultural material, Jay-Z's "Hard Knock Life" threaded together a song that "poaches" meaning from the Broadway version and carries it forward in new and creative ways. Remix allows the artist to take the already-established meaning of a particular cultural artifact and compress that meaning—through image, repeated chorus, or another well-known reference—to make a new "recontextualized" creation even more meaningful.

Finally, Remix culture signals a shift in how fans, artists, and whole communities participate and appropriate texts by creating and circulating meanings even if they may be on the margins of popular culture (Jenkins 1992: 24). Just like poachers in fandom, hip hop is a remix community that challenges "the sanctioned expert interpretations and readings of the text" (ibid., 25), and struggles for control over the meaning of a text (ibid., 24). In this way then, remix encourages a democratized, unsanctioned approach to appropriating and internalizing older "texts." It is a communal practice that happens "within a community of remixers" (Lessig 2008: 77). Access to the resources themselves have become more *democratized* and are based more on one's "membership in some community, and not upon a special status or hierarchy within some company or government" (ibid., 141).

Remixing is not new; not only is it a practice communities have participated in long before the digital era began (82), it is a practice that can be used as a paradigm for understanding how tradition and innovation work together.

> The idea of an active engagement with culture—"talking back," "appropriating," or "rereading"—is nothing new. People have long made their own use of the cultural texts surrounding them,

fashioning them into formulas and relationships best suited to their needs and desires. (Duncombe 1997: 112)

The practice of forming communities around shared texts and their re-interpretations is an ongoing aspect of human history. It is also the process of synthesis I discussed above.

Remix reveals the interplay between the old and the new, between tradition (R/O) and innovation (R/W). Both need to co-exist, "In protecting R/O culture, we shouldn't kill off the potential for R/W" (Lessig 2008: 90). Thus, even within participatory culture there is the tension between what we might call an "antiquarianism of tradition" and the impulse to innovate at the expense of R/O culture. Instead, remix shows tradition and innovation working together to create something new; it shows how apprentices can pay homage to their tradition while also creating something original. The tension and its resolution could be summed up this way: (a) Free-for-all: Innovation over against tradition (a)contextualization that tends towards individualism); (b) R/O culture: Tradition over against any innovation (a conservatism that tends towards separatism) or; (c) Remix or R/W culture: tradition as grounds for innovation and imagination (a contextualization that borrows the language and resources of our community).

Cultural Producers

The third element of participatory culture is that it is active; convergence culture experiences a shift where the consumer becomes producer. Jenkins argues that the consumer engaged in cultural production contrasts with older spectator models of consumption: "Rather than talking about media producers and consumers as occupying separate roles, we might now see them as participants who interact with each other according to a new set of rules that none of us fully understand" (Jenkins 2006a: 3). This kind of active cultural creation is an expression of creativity and participation, as well as resistance to the passivity and deadness older forms of media fostered (Duncombe 1997: 124).

There are a growing number of ways in which a person can create his or her own culture. As mentioned above, early forms of participatory culture could be seen in the activism of pamphleteers, such as Thomas Paine (and Quakers), as well as the composers of African American spirituals (ibid., 112). Newer forms of cultural production range from blogging as a tool for political transformation (cf. Moulitsas Zuniga 2008); to using YouTube as a bottom-up platform for creating anything from home videos to mini-television series, music videos, and encouraging activism; to earlier forms of do-it-yourself publishing of the Zinesters. Participatory culture resists the passivity of consumerism, and thus do-it-yourself is born. "Doing it yourself is at once a critique of the dominant mode of passive consumer culture and something far more important: the active creation of an alternative culture. DIY is not just complaining about what is, but actually doing something different" (Duncombe 1997: 118).

Wherever participants resist passive consumption, they create a liberating space where the division between reading and writing, consuming and producing is circumvented:

> Having readers become writers and writers become readers circumvents a fundamental tent of the logic of consumer culture. This division is normally reinforced by the professionalization of *cultural creation,* which divides the world into those with the talent, skills, and authority to create, and those without. . . . Those inside the underground culture [of zines] cast aside these restrictions. (Ibid., 124; italics added)

Within participatory culture, a space where anyone who wants to can create something they feel is worth consuming or participating in; these producers become the "entertainer of themselves" (ibid., 105). Duncombe describes that within the zine culture of the 1970s and 80s this culture of production was liberating in that it no longer took a professional to create culture. "This Freedom from the 'specialness' or 'professionalism' that are supposed to accompany any creation of culture in our society is liberating. It asserts the possibility of a participatory and democratic culture" (ibid., 125).

Today's do-it-yourself ethic is about the *active creation of an alternative culture.* DIY is not just complaining about what is, but actually doing something different" (ibid., 118; italics added). Early zines like *Punk* were not just fanzines, offering the latest gossip, photos and news on favorite bands, but were meant "to convince their readers to go out and do it themselves" (ibid., 118). Many zine-articles appeared on subjects dealing with the DIY of bookmaking, silkscreening, publishing and other projects (ibid., 117).

One example of DIY culture at work today is the video website YouTube. YouTube, created in 2005, was the first website of its kind to host user-generated material, where as Burgess and Green argue, sharing was the basis of its business model (Burgess and Green 2009: 4). In other words, it has no content of its own. It only provides the platform for sharing content. Prior to YouTube, websites were more one-dimensional; the owner of the site was the one to upload the content. YouTube changed all of this by making the basis of its content the users' responsibility. In this model the customer is the co-creator, formed from the "bottom-up by the 'users en mass' via consumption, evaluation, and entrepreneurial activities" (ibid., 5). Bringing together a DIY sensibility, with new advancements in technology, YouTube embodies how participatory culture converges to allow everyday people to create the culture they want to consume.

YouTube becomes a community formed around particular practices. It is a convergence—rather than collision—of old and new media; it is a "co-evolution and uneasy co-existence of 'old' and 'new' media industries, forms and practices" (ibid., 14). In order to successfully use YouTube, "citizens" of the site need to draw on older skills—such as filming and video editing—as well as learn new skills in order to navigate, comment and respond, and use the site for their own needs (ibid., 70). Combining these skills in successful ways leads to some users to have highly interactive YouTube pages. These citizens come together to share and shape identities, share interests, and mobilize over the practice of making short videos (ibid., 77).

The "fake news" host Stephen Colbert of the *The Colbert Report* uses YouTube not just for distribution of his television show's content but to foster a community around his show that is based on discussion, response and interaction (ibid., 34). In the past, Colbert has solicited remixed material based on his "green screen challenges." Fans that choose to participate post their content on YouTube and Colbert selects some of them to present to his audience on *The Colbert Report* (Silverman 2009). The community mentors one another (Burgess and Green 2009: 65), helping users gain feedback on their work, nurture the skills necessary to be successful on the site (ibid., 70), and inspiring further innovation of content despite YouTube's limited architecture (ibid., 67).

Today it is not enough to consume media. People of all ages, skills and backgrounds are producing culture they wish to consume or believe is being neglected by those in power. From the early pamphleteers to African American Spirituals that appropriated the Exodus narrative into a story of hope that led them to freedom, to today's use of convergence culture, culture production is not limited to cultural elites, professionals or the specialists. Participatory culture circumvents divisions between consumer and producer and creates something different.

Collective Intelligence

The fourth element of the participatory rubric is *collective intelligence*. Pierre Lévy's *Collective Intelligence* has taken a key place among participatory cultural studies because of his insight into the contemporary information landscape (Lévy 1997). Collective intelligence is concerned with establishing "social relations" and "constructing society" (ibid., 10), where the new knowledge-culture is progressing toward an "achievable utopia." In contrast to earlier formulations of fandom as resistance to dominant culture, collective intelligence offers:

> A way of thinking about fandom not in terms of resistance but as a prototype or dress rehearsal for the way culture might operate in the future . . . an achievable utopia—not something that grows inevitably from the new configuration of technologies but rather something we must work toward and fight to achieve. (Jenkins 2006b: 134)

Thus for Jenkins, "fandom is one of those spaces where people are learning how to live and collaborate within a knowledge community" (ibid.). Knowledge, within this context, is not simply immaterial but participative, mutual and relational.

Collective intelligence fosters apprenticing communities, or communities of shared practice (see Bolger 2007) where adherents gain the skills necessary for the thriving of that community, as demonstrated by YouTube. In these communities: work is shared, participation is mutual, and authority is decentralized—no one, or better yet everyone, is an expert. "The basis and goal of collective intelligence is the mutual recognition and enrichment of individuals rather than the culture of fetishized or hypostatized communities" (Lévy 1997: 13). According to Lévy, the future of society is in "the renewal of the social bond through our relation to knowledge and collective intelligence itself" (ibid., 11). As participants relate to others in the knowledge community, they are apprenticed, and are mentored into the particular skills necessary for the thriving in that community:

> Through our interactions with things, we develop skills. Through our relation to signs and information, we acquire knowledge. Through our relationship to others, mediated by processes of initiation and transmission, we bring knowledge to life. Skill, understanding, and knowledge (which can all refer to the same objects) are three complementary modes of cognitive transaction and continuously interpenetrate one another. Each activity, each act of communication, each human relation implies an apprenticeship. By means of the skills and understanding that it envelops, a life can continuously feed a circuit of exchange, nourish a sociability of knowledge. We can explicitly establish, openly and publicly, mutual apprenticeship as a way of mediating relationships among individuals. Our identities would then become knowledge identities. (Ibid., 11–12)

In these communities mutual interactions of learning bring about new knowledge. These interactions entail a sharing of skill, understanding and knowledge. In order to maintain this kind of mutuality of learning and apprenticing, the very practices of the community must nourish this "circuit of exchange, [and] nourish a sociability of knowledge" (ibid.). This approach assumes there are some practices that do not, or no longer, nourish this kind of knowledge identity.

Collective intelligence names a collaboration and pooling of knowledge by all of the members of a community, broadening the horizon through which the entire community is able to operate:

> Lévy distinguishes between *shared knowledge* (which would refer to information known by all members of a community) and *collective intelligence* (which describes knowledge available to all members of a community). Collective intelligence expands a community's productive capacity because it frees individual members from limitations of their memory and enables the group to act upon a broader range of expertise. (Jenkins 2006b: 139)

This act of collaboration within participatory culture has become synonymous with the online encyclopedia Wikipedia. Wikipedia is a salient example of collective intelligence at work, where the collective knowledge extended through new media creates a consensus of information that is unparalleled in society. Jimmy Wales created the "wiki," "a platform [or software] that lets anyone write or edit in a common space ... It was originally intended to enable a team to work on a project collaboratively (Lessig 2008: 156). The creation of the wiki made possible an encyclopedia that hosted user-generated content, drawing on "wisdom of the crowds." Wikipedia embodies Lévy's point: "No one knows everything, everyone knows something, all knowledge resides in humanity" (Quoted in Jenkins 2006b: 139). Now presumably that knowledge also resides on Wikipedia, where there are more than four million entries in the English version alone.

Like collective intelligence more broadly speaking, Wikipedia is a knowledge community of shared practice. Lessig writes, "Wikipedia... is more than software. It is also a set of norms that were built into the practice of using that software. The objective was an encyclopedia. That meant articles were to be written from a 'neutral point of view'" (Lessig 2008: 157). The practices that emerged within this community are that: it is run by volunteers, there is no exclusive ownership over Wikipedia, it is not be ad-based, and the final rule was to "ignore all the rules." As Jimmy Wales explains it,

> "Ignore all rules" ... is not an invitation to chaos. It is really more an idea of saying, 'Look, whatever rules we have in Wikipedia, they ought to be, more or less, discernable by any normal, socially adept adult who thinks about what would be the ethical thing to do in this situation. That should be what the rule is.' It should be pretty intuitive. (Ibid.)

This ensures that Wikipedia is easy to use and self-manage, which is essential for a completely volunteer-based organization. Wikipedia has thousands of people who volunteer their time editing, formatting, reviewing and adding content to the website. No one is directed, people interact with the articles they know or care the most about, and decide upon the "chores" they engage in (ibid., 158). The community of "Wikipedians" are driven by the end goal of Wikipedia: "[To gather] together to build this resource that will be made available to all the people of the world for free. That's a goal that people can get behind" (ibid., 159).

This collaboration of knowledge around a common goal not only creates a community—that works together, argues together, and face controversy together—but it also accomplishes it in a way that reflects a consensus of what is known about the subject. As Wales suggests:

> One of the things that we are doing better, I think, is when we have a mass public event or story with breaking news.... Wikipedia does a very interesting thing ... which is a census of the news that's coming out. So, the way I present this is when you

> have a big event like this, you'll have ten, twenty, or thirty, or fifty reporters all there, on the scene gathering information. But they're each seeing only the piece that they can see and even if they're all absolutely excellent journalists who are doing their very best to get the whole story, they're each coming from a particular perspective and they're each interviewing particular people with particular views. And then that stuff goes out onto the Web where people can read all of it. (Ibid., 160)

Wikipedia "mass collaboration" is based on a consensus-making process that brings together the collective intelligence of the community and organizes it in a way that is surprisingly accurate and efficient (see Tapscott and Williams 2008). This mass collaboration allows for differentiation as Lévy describes it: "collectivity is not necessarily synonymous with solidity and uniformity. The development of cyberspace provides us the opportunity to experiment with collective methods of organization and regulation that dignify multiplicity and variety" (Lévy, 1997: 66). Similarly, Jenkins argues that bloggers are an example of a community of people who draw on collective intelligence but are not bound by uniformity. Instead they form "tactical alliances with other bloggers or with media producers to insure that important messages get more widely circulated" (Jenkins 2006b: 151). Therefore even blogging becomes both a creation of collective intelligence and the formation of new social bonds:

> The new proletariat will only free itself by uniting, by decategorizing itself, by forming alliances with those whose work is similar to its own (once again, nearly everyone), by bringing to the foreground the activities they have been practicing in shadow, by assuming responsibility—globally, centrally, explicitly—for the production of collective intelligence. (Ibid., 36)

Collective Intelligence names a cohesive, yet differentiated, community based on mutuality and participation rooted in dialogue and openness within participatory culture. These knowledge communities that emerge as a result are motivated by the goal of an achievable utopia, rooted in shared practice, mass collaboration and are symbiotic in their relationships.

Decentralized (System/Network/Paradigm) Authority

Decentralized authority is closely related to collective intelligence. Any community that practices collective intelligence will by necessity develop a decentralized or networked approach to authority. The collective intelligence the group values within participatory culture contrasts authority with modernity's "expert paradigm:"

> The expert paradigm requires a bounded body of knowledge, which an individual can master . . . the expert paradigm creates an "exterior" and an "interior"; there are some people who know things and others who don't . . . [there are] rules about how you access and process information, rules that are established through traditional disciplines . . . .and [it is] credentialized. (Jenkins 2006a: 52–54)

Where the other four categories exist within a community, decentralized authority follows. Decentralized authority cuts across and builds upon the participatory elements of authentic resistance, remix, production, and collectivity. It is also the paradigm through which the other four survive.

The internet itself is, as Tiziana Terranova describes it, the "network of networks" (Terranova 2004: 40), based on an "active implementation of a design technique able to deal with the openness of systems" (ibid., 2). In other words, Terranova argues that the internet is not a specific medium, but rather a design implementation or an "architecture" that is increasingly expandable and open-ended. It is not a static medium but its architecture is itself "geared towards expansion (ibid., 3)." Burgess and Green comment on the "hackability" of YouTube despite, or possibly because of, the site's limited architecture (Burgess and Green 2009: 64–65). The "hackability" of YouTube and other similar mediums reveal the scalability and expandability of convergence culture. Therefore, Terranova argues that the openness of the architecture's spatiality not only enables decentralized authority to emerge, but is itself open to new and divergent networks (2004: 70).

As Stephen Duncombe shows in his *Dream: Re-Imagining Progressive Politics In An Age of Fantasy,* Critical Mass is example of this kind of open, decentralized network. Critical Mass, a free-form collection of bicycle riders that take over the streets of their city, formed in San Francisco in 1992 and now happens regularly in four hundred cities around the world (Duncombe 2007: 137). Drawing on Umberto Eco's concept of the *opera aperta*, literally "open work," Duncombe argues that one way a political protest movement can operate within participatory culture is through creating an "open spectacle." An open spectacle is an open work where the movement in contrast to most modern works of art, "has no such finitude: it is left open by the artist to be completed by someone else. . . . These works are, by their very design, unfinished. Not just their meaning but the very form they take on is necessarily ambiguous" (ibid., 135–36).

Participating in the form of Critical Mass is what is essential for this kind of network. As one earlier flier about Critical Mass stated: "Critical Mass isn't BLOCKING traffic—We ARE traffic." This signals that for these riders "The experience of participating [has] the most profound effect" (ibid., 137). This is because, while there are organizers who plan where to meet, the time and day, and the basic route for the ride, the ride itself is contingent on who shows up and the direction they decide to take the ride in. "What Critical Mass looks like on any given night and the exact direction and duration the ride takes are indeterminate, contingent on who shows up (police included) and what the mass decides to do. The spectacle of Critical Mass is literally a 'work in movement'" (ibid., 138).

In a 1994 pamphlet the riders referred to their organizational structure or movement as a "Xerocracy:"

> Organizational politics, with its official leaders, demands, etc., has been eschewed in favor of a more *decentralized system*. There is no charge. Ideas are spread, routes shared, and *consensus* sought through the ubiquitous copy machines on every job or at copy shops in every neighborhood—a "Xerocracy," in which anyone is free to make copies of their ideas and pass them around. Leaflets, flyers, stickers and zines all circulate madly before, during and after the ride, rendering leaders unnecessary by ensuring that strategies and tactics are understood by as many people as possible.
>
> Xerocracy promotes freedom and undercuts hierarchy because the mission is not set by a few in charge, but rather is broadly defined by a few in charge, but rather *is broadly defined by its participants*. The ride is not narrowly seen as an attempt to lobby for more bike lanes (although that goal exists) or to protest this or that aspect of the social order (although such sentiments are often expressed). Rather, each person is free to invent his or

her own reasons for participating and is also free to share those ideas with others. (Ibid., 139)

What the pamphlet quoted here describes is a participatory system, or as Terranova calls it, an "active implementation of a design technique able to deal with the openness of systems." Egalitarianism, open-endedness, consensus, and dynamism are what Duncombe refers to as "field of relations" that gives the movement or community a structure or architecture but remains open in every other way (ibid., 140).

Therefore, participatory culture depends on a participatory way of organizing and structuring itself. Without a bottom-up structure of authority, authentic resistance would be susceptible to new forms of oppression, remix would be completely cut off from its sources, production would be seen as devious and threatening to the acting regime, and collectivity would be thwarted as a threat to established power structures. Therefore, it is not so much that participatory culture is anti-authority, chaotic or even disorganized, but rather its very design implementation is one in which authority is derived through the network and its many channels of input.

Dwight Friesen, in referring to the decentralized approach of the "network paradigm," describes the internet as a network that is made up of hubs sustained by "clusters" (Friesen 2009: 183). In this way, authority is not absent within the system but found within the system itself. For authority to have no central hub, expert systems are harder to develop and dominate (Brewin 2007: 109–13). When one link fails, other hubs are able to readjust and keep the network running. Thus, a "network paradigm" reflects a holistic epistemology rather than foundationalism (cf. Murphy 1989).

Murphy argues that W.V.O. Quine's article "Two Dogmas of Empiricism" (1951), challenged modernity's foundationalist presuppositions, and argued that instead of having epistemology constructed like a building, it should be understood as a web or net:

> The totality of our so-called knowledge or beliefs, from the most casual matters of geography and history to the profoundest laws of atomic physics or even of pure mathematics and logic, is a man-made fabric which impinges on experience only along the edges. Or, to change the figure, total science is like a field of force whose boundary conditions are experience. (Murphy 1996: 88)

Murphy describes this web-based holistic epistemology as one where

> each belief is support by its ties to its neighboring beliefs and, ultimately, to the whole. Justification consists in showing that problematic beliefs are closely tied to beliefs that we have no good reason to call into question. So the coherence of the web is crucial for justification. When inconsistencies appear—conflicts within the web or with "recalcitrant experience"—there are always a number of ways to revise in order to restore consistency. The choices that will be made here are in a sense pragmatic: how to mend the web with as little disturbance to the whole as possible. (Ibid., 94)

A participatory and decentralized authority is established by the way the community functions as that community interprets, reinterprets and remixes its "texts" within new settings. Elsewhere, Kester Brewin writes of the contrast between the top-down hierarchy of the Gnostics' secret knowledge and the more decentralized knowledge of the internet (Brewin 2007: 109). Emergent systems, as he calls them,

> Will not be marked by knowledge stored centrally. There will be no key leader who will be seen as a fount of all knowledge and wisdom on all topics. The distributed nature of knowledge will be positively celebrated, as it will prevent the collecting of power into small male-dominated pools, and thus protect people from the abuses that that power would bring. In turn, narrow preaching of Scripture will be avoided and understanding of it will become a shared project. (Ibid., 110)

Emergent systems or network paradigms are based on holistic understanding of authority, accepting that authority comes through the community of interpreters, the shared practices, and the authoritative texts of that community—or tradition (ibid., 104–5). Because there is no central hub, these networks are scalable. Because authority is derived from the community or architecture itself, knowledge and power are relational rather than top-down. It is fluid and flows across channels due to little hierarchical and structural resistance. It forms a community that is best thought of as networked friendships, utilizing dialogue and apprenticeship to hold the social identity of the group together. There are many examples of this "networked paradigm" within participatory culture that have already been mentioned: from YouTube, to the DIY of Zines—which sought to create an open space dialogue, to the remixers of hip hop, to the consensus-building of Wikipedia and the new "tactical" alliances of bloggers, these communities exhibit a model of authority that is decentralized, communal and holistic.

Networked paradigms and decentralized authority seeks to build on the assumptions behind collective intelligence, inasmuch as it downplays the expert and allows space for all people to learn and contribute (ibid., 109–13). It reflects a structure or architecture that is based on a "network of networks" paradigm. This paradigm is more fluid and web-like than authority within modernity. It is a many-voice movement, where everyone, everyone is in a sense "expert" and is able to amplify his or her voice within the fan community. In a community like this every voice counts and the interpretive community knows that experts and credentials are not enough to maintain a community based within participatory culture.

Jenkins contrasts four differences between the expert paradigm and collective intelligence that are helpful when outlining what decentralized authority looks like within participatory culture: (1) bounded knowledge that one person can master versus open-ended interdisciplinary knowledge drawing on a diversity of disciplines and experiences; (2) based on an exterior and interior position to knowledge (some have it others do not) versus the perspective that all have knowledge to contribute; (3) established by rules of access and methods of processing knowledge versus a knowledge that is "disorderly, undisciplined and unruly" which follows more of an ad hoc procedure; (4) credentialed versus trusted where a demonstration of knowledge and experience is of utmost importance (Jenkins 2006: 52–54).What holds the process of collective intelligence together is the community working together to acquire knowledge and reaffirm their ties to that particular group (ibid., 54).

Alternative Social Community

The sixth and final element is the result of the previous five: alternative social community (Jenkins 1992: 280). Fans that engage in the practices of participatory culture will find themselves a part of an alternative social community in at least three ways. First, as Stephen Duncombe writes, it is in the very process of cultural production that an alternative community is created (Duncombe 1997: 117). As society has shifted more and more towards consumerism, participatory culture emerged as a rejection and subversion of the basic tenants of consumer culture:

> We make sense of our world and construct our identities, in significant measure, out of the physical and cultural materials that surround us. Not only do we enjoy the products and entertainment that we consume; these things become an integral part of who we are. In our age of mass consumption, more and more of this stuff is produced not by us but for us, not according to the logic of community tradition or individual inspiration, but according to the pecuniary rationale of the market. The result is a historical separation between us, as individuals, and the entertainment and products we use, enjoy, and derive meaning from. (Ibid., 107)

Fans reveal one response to these divisions brought on by consumerism; in the process of their appropriating, remixing, and sharing, new communities are created. Secondly, this alternative community is a site of both possibility and resistance:

> Fandom constitutes such a space, one defined by its refusal of mundane values and practices, its celebration of deeply held emotions and passionately embraced pleasures. Fandom's very existence represents a critique of conventional forms of consumer culture. Yet fandom also provides a space within which fans may articulate their specific concerns about sexuality, gender, racism, colonialism, militarism, and forced conformity. . . . Fandom contains both negative and positive forms of empowerment. Its institutions allow the expression both of what fans are struggling against and what they are struggling for. (Jenkins 1992: 283)

Fandom creates a liberated space where an alternative community is formed. Therefore, the third element of this alternative community is that it is both nonconformist and creative; it is not simply political resistance, it is utopian, putting forward a vision of what is possible given different values and practices within a society. In identifying alternative social communities, one notices that it is neither sectarian nor tolerant but weaves together resistance and creation, refusal and empowerment, offering an alternative vision to what is available.

The Occupy Wall Street movement embodied many elements of participatory culture, not least of which is the creation of an alternative social community. Motivated by the tactics and success of the protest in Cairo, Egypt earlier in 2011—where 50,000 people were mobilized over social media to participate in a protest of *resistance*—a small group of organizers planned a major protest for Lower Manhattan in September.

Armed with signs that stated phrases like "We Are The 99%," one could infer the various grievances the group symbolized: "An ever widening gap between rich and poor; a perceived failure by President Obama to hold the financial industry accountable for the crisis of 2008; and a sense that money had taken over politics" (Chafkin 2012).[14]

Drawing inspiration from a long line of activism matched with the new capabilities of convergence culture—YouTube, Twitter, blogs and other forms of new media—the protesters created a new form of activism. Cornel West, speaking to the Occupy crowd on October 7, 2011, saw the connections to history:

> But if I'm not here my spirit is with you. Because the legacy of Martin is here. The legacy of Rabbi Abraham Joshua Heschel is here. The legacy of Dorothy Day is here. The legacy of Cesar Chavez is here. The legacy of all those who came before is here. And we refuse to move forward unless we look back and remember those who did exactly the same thing. Look, the sister got Mandela right on her shirt. South Africa had to teach the world a democratic lesson. Tunisia, Egypt, northern Africa had to teach the world some democratic lessons. And now, the USA is gonna have to teach the world some democratic lessons, even though we got those immoral drones that are being dropped. We're still in Afghanistan ten years later. Corporate interests still shaping so much of the world in its own image. (West 2011)

One organizer remembers it this way:

> What we had done up until then was very Internet-based, and this looked like it would take a more old-school kind of activism. I remember one [Anonymous member] saying, "I'm not taking part in any hippie drum circles. Stop talking about this." But then you had all these vocal people that were like, "We can get this going in the right direction. We can help steer this thing through our media." (Chafkin 2012)

This blending of old and new together worked: about two thousand people showed up on that first day in Zuccotti Park to join the protests. The protest was live-streamed all over the internet and at one point that

---

14. Cornel West voices the underlying narrative to the Occupy Protests well, "And 1% of the population has 42% of the wealth, 1% of the population had 83% of the income growth in the last 10 years, and the top 10% had 100% of the income growth. What does that mean? It means that poor people, working people, the 99% find themselves wrestling with wages that have flattened out, stagnating, with costs going up" (West, "Dr. Cornel West Brings It," 2011).

day it was reported that there were three hundred tweets per second about Occupy (Chafkin). One of the tactics Occupy used to control their narrative was to broadcast their arrests on websites like YouTube (Maslin Nir 2011). The sharing images of injured protestors through social media is another example of DIY culture at work. Instead of waiting for more traditional forms of media to shape the message of Occupy, they took it upon themselves to tell their own narrative, in their own voice.

Occupy's impact came from the fact that it has demonstrated both by its physical presence in tent-cities all around the world, as well as its presence on the web, that it is possible to build a mass movement based on alternative values and participatory practice. Occupy brought together threads of participatory culture in a way that created an alternative social community. Organizationally this is seen in their use of collective intelligence—through access to a worldwide Occupy community—and their use of decentralized leadership.[15] One way that Occupy exhibits decentralized leadership is through their "general assemblies" that use a consensus model of decision-making. A structure based on a, "group decision making process that seeks the consent, not necessarily the agreement, of participants and the resolution of objections"(Occupy 2011).

Nathan Schneider, as well as others directly involved in the movement, have noted the connection between the consensus model and Quakerism;

> The General Assembly, which would eventually morph from a planning committee into the de facto decision-making body of the occupation, was a hodgepodge of procedures and hand signals with origins as various as Quakerism, ancient Athens, the *indignados* of Spain (some of whom were present) and the spokes councils of the 1999 anti-globalization movement. Basically, it's an attempt to create a nonhierarchical, egalitarian, consensus-driven process—the purest kind of democracy. (Schneider 2011)

---

15. One of the interesting "participatory" practices that reflects *decentralized leadership* that developed out of Occupy was the "people's microphone." One New York civil-rights lawyer involved with Occupy from the beginning, Sam Cohen, says that "The people's microphone—all strangeness aside—was an incredibly effective tool to get around the amplified-sound permit because you need an amplified-sound permit to use a bullhorn or microphone. Everybody within earshot repeats what you say. Speaking in that context was a bit of a challenge: "Parsing my speech. Into sections that can be repeated. In front of large groups of people. While maintaining emphasis." That was the cadence I would use" (Chafkin, "Revolution Number 99," 2012).

Just as in other aspects of fandom, Occupy protestors—taken as a form "participatory democracy"—camping in parks around the world is not "so much an escape from reality as an alternative reality whose values may be more humane and democratic than those held by mundane society" (Jenkins 1992: 280).[16] When asked about what its main political message was, many were surprised to learn there was no key message and there was not a key leader. It's not that there was not a decipherable message from Occupy, the main point was that the group did not want to play by the rules of the very system they were trying to resist. Instead, they pointed to the actual existence of Occupy as the alternative message. As feminist and cultural theorist Judith Butler argued, Occupy sought to build an alternative system that did not reproduce the inequality of the system they challenge:

> Simply put, the appeal or demand that sought to be satisfied by the existing state, global monetary institutions, or corporations, national or transnational, would be giving more power to the very sources of inequality, and in that way aiding and abetting the reproduction of inequality itself. As a result, another set of strategies are required, and what we are now seeing in the Occupy Movement is precisely the development of a set of strategies that call attention to, and oppose, the reproduction of inequality. (Butler 2012)

The protestors of Occupy sought to represent a utopian vision of the world that offered a symbolic critique to real world issues, "the utopian dimension of popular culture . . . is linked to its ability to offer symbolic solutions to real world problems and felt needs" (Jenkins 1992: 281).

Alternative social communities within participatory culture seek to project an "image of something better" and show how utopia might look (ibid.); these are experiments, decisive answers are not the end goal. Rather than taking political activism and resistance negatively—as is often done within evangelical circles, one can understand Occupy and other examples of "politics of postmodernity" as experimental, positive and celebratory:

---

16. Cornel West has said that Occupy represents "democracy awakening" (West, "Dr. Cornel West Brings It," 2011), whereas others have referred to it as participatory democracy because of its working groups, general assemblies and "progressive stacks"—where people from marginalized groups are offered the first opportunity to speak in their meetings ("Occupy Movement," 2011).

> Opposition may be constituted by living, even momentarily, within alternative practices, structures and spaces, even though they may take no notice of their relationship to existing systems of power. In fact, when one wins some space within the social formation, it has to be filled with something, presumably [sic] something one cares for passionately. (Ibid., 283)

The point is to join in the creation of these alternative spaces, not to have them finalized or concretized. Fan cultures create an alternative social culture inasmuch as real people struggle to construct a site or space of alternative values and ethics (ibid., 282).

Thus, Occupy and other alternative social communities can be understood through the lens of *opera aperta* or "open spectacle." Duncombe describes the sentiment behind Occupy well when he argues that these open works "never [arrive] at one answer. Open to the noisy diversity of participants, observers, and settings to create the completed work, it sends (or rather, rests) in a field of possibilities" (Duncombe 2007: 142).

Like Occupy and Critical Mass, these alternative spaces may not be permanent, but the practices and the liberated spaces they create are symbolic of the kinds of values these "fans" wish to project out into the world. Thus they challenge "dominant culture and [re-create] their own relationship to it, and thus to the world" (ibid., 112). In forming a participatory culture, fandom has creative alternative social communities that often reflect the values and the "achievable utopia" they believe is possible.

CONCLUSION

In the first part of this chapter I gave a brief overview of fandom and cultural studies, arguing that fandom—as a smaller aspect of participatory culture—represents active fans who demonstrate practices of resistance to consumer culture. Henry Jenkins' work is pivotal in the area of participatory culture, fan studies, and what he now calls convergence culture. Convergence culture is a culture that is active, where new and old media collide, and where collective intelligence is at hand. Convergence culture names a newer aspect of participatory culture that now involves the influence and use of technology in everyday life.

The second part of the chapter looked at six practices of participatory culture as they have been described by both scholars in the field as well as ready examples from culture. Participatory culture is a culture that practices authentic resistance by stripping away the contrivances of the modern world through an appropriation of cultural artifacts that challenges the sanctioned meanings and interpretations. Remix names the tendency within participatory culture to create something new out of something old. By building onto original pieces of art that already have cultural reference and mixing that art with a new cultural artifact, remixers are able to create new art and meaning. Both of these previous examples show how fans within participatory culture are also cultural producers. YouTube and blogging are just two of the ways that fans are producers in today's world. Fans also create shared spaces of collective intelligence, where skills are shared and communities are built in the hopes of reaching an "achievable utopia." Decentralized authority, closely related to collective intelligence, is an architecture or structure that does not rely on an expert, but rather the participation of the whole. It is an egalitarian structure that operates out of consensus models of decision-making. Finally, communities where you find the first five elements will by their very existence create an alternative social community. These communities create liberated spaces experimenting with "image[s] of something better" (Jenkins 1992: 281).

CHAPTER 4

A Convergent Model for Participatory Renewal

A MODEL OF RENEWAL that aims to be *convergent* and *participatory* must integrate the key resources gleaned from MacIntyre, Bevans and Jenkins—pulling together their respective spheres into a synthesis represented here as tradition, mission and dialogue with today's culture. Throughout, I have argued that a faith tradition experiences renewal as it seeks to engage the *mission Dei* in the present in ways that draw upon its practices, while reinterpreting and reformulating them according to their present contexts. As a highly participatory faith tradition, Quakerism is uniquely positioned to contextual into today's culture, reformulating the movement in ways that might bring about renewal.

THEORY BEHIND THE MODEL

I will refer to the model constructed here as a convergent model, based on Bevans' model of synthesis, emphasizing the necessity of both tradition and context. This model also draws on MacIntyre's understanding of tradition as historically extended arguments that are socially embodied and is in dialogue with Jenkins who understands participatory culture to be a community of fans that resist, subvert, and challenge dominant structures by embodying alternative social practices within culture.[1] A

---

1. As mentioned in the Introduction, "convergent" within the context of today's Friends Church is a playful use of the word to mean paradoxically "conservative" to the tradition and "emergent" within today's culture. Convergent Friends are those who

synthesis of these three thinkers will provide a model for how renewal looks within participatory culture that is able to remain in dialogue with the past and the present. First, I review the key insights from MacIntyre, Bevans and Jenkins and second, integrate them into a new convergent model for renewal.

Tradition as the Only Ground for Innovation

The best hope for the revitalization of any faith tradition is to draw on the resources of its tradition. MacIntyre's view of tradition is that it is open-ended and capable of being revised. Some, following the influence of modernity, understand tradition to be "the dead faith of the living," but MacIntyre's entire philosophy is built around the conviction that a tradition can, if its apprentices become empathetic and self-aware, progress its enquiries forward through the maze of rival claims and challenges. My proposal here is for another way, based on the resourcefulness and adaptability of tradition.

Since the advent of modernity, tradition has fallen out of favor in the West. For much of the Protestant church, tradition is taken as a liability and baggage, which "in most cases means the perception of unnecessary and definitely unwanted dogmatics . . . a feeling that the traditional religions are out of touch and incapable of responding quickly enough to the massive social and cultural upheaval that many sense themselves navigating" (Taylor 2008: 13). Often within the church we see what MacIntyre identifies as two possible relationships with tradition, "unproblematic allegiance" or "large opposition:"

> A tradition of enquiry is more than a coherent movement of thought. It is such a movement in the course of which those engaging in that movement become aware of it and of its direction and in self-aware fashion attempt to engage in its debates and to carry its enquiries forward. The relationships which can hold between individuals and a tradition are very various, ranging from unproblematic allegiance through attempts to amend or

"question what it means to be faithful to their tradition (conservative) while re-imagining it within a new cultural context (emergent)," (Daniels, "Convergent Friends," 240). In other words, as Robin Mohr has stated, these are "Friends who come together 'seeking a deeper understanding of our Quaker heritage [tradition] and a more authentic life in the kingdom of God on Earth [mission], radically inclusive of all who seek to live this life [participatory]'" (ibid.).

redirect the tradition to large opposition to what have hitherto been its central contentions. But this last may indeed be as formative and important a relation to a tradition as any. (MacIntyre 1988: 326)

Juxtaposed to this, MacIntyre's thought shows that revitalization consists in apprentices becoming "aware of [their tradition] and of its direction and in a self-aware fashion attempt to engage in its debates and carry its enquiries forward" (ibid.). MacIntyre's philosophy offers at least three insights into our participatory model: the stages of progress a tradition makes, the importance of apprentices in the progress of a tradition, and the criteria for a tradition reconstituted.

According to MacIntyre, tradition is a historically extended argument that is socially embodied within a community and unified by the narrative quest of what its practitioners understand to be the good of human life. These arguments concern the interpretation of the tradition's key texts. Through ongoing debates, interpretations and argumentation, "fundamental agreements" form, helping to create a cohesive narrative. When conflicts and disagreement arise from inside, as well as outside, adherents within the tradition begin to reformulate these interpretations and their subsequent practices in ways that seek to draw on the resources of their tradition.

This happens through three stages: internalizing of the law, a breakdown of the schemata, and reformulation. Their ability to reformulate will depend, "upon what stock of reasons and of questioning and reasoning abilities they already possess but also upon their inventiveness" (ibid., 355). Their inventiveness will "determine the possible range of outcomes in the rejection, emendation, and reformulation of beliefs, the revaluation of authorities, the reinterpretation of texts, the emergence of new forms of authority, and the production of new texts" (ibid.).

Change and adaptation are essential to the life of a tradition. Traditions that are able to adapt and read their primary texts in new ways, reformulate interpretations, and even dismiss older interpretations that can no longer be justified are essential in extending the core of those traditions into new contexts. The central point is that MacIntyre demonstrates both that traditions show signs of health when they not only overcome crises but when they adapt through reinterpretation and "invention" over time (ibid., 354–55). Moving through the stages is a sign of health; being unable to interpret and progress is a sign of degeneracy (MacIntyre 1984: 146).

The ability to adapt and change is related to adherents having first become apprentices of their tradition, taking it as a craft through which they are formed by the virtues and practices of that tradition. An apprentice of a tradition is someone who shares in the "contingencies of its history, understanding its story as one's own, and finding a place for oneself as a character in the enacted dramatic narrative which is that story so far" (MacIntyre 1990: 65). Once an apprentice is so shaped by the virtues and practices of that tradition that he or she has mastered their craft, then she can extend her practices in new ways:

> Using what can be learned from the tradition afforded by the past to move towards the *telos* of fully perfected work. It is thus knowing how to link past and future that those with authority are able to draw upon tradition, to interpret and reinterpret it, so that its directedness towards the *telos* of that particular craft becomes apparent in new and characteristically unexpected ways. (Ibid., 66)

It is critical to recognize that renewal of a tradition does not come at the whim of any person whether inside or outside the tradition, but by the very practitioners who have devoted themselves as apprentices to its texts, virtues and practices. It comes by way of adherents, or "fans" of that tradition paying homage to it by not allowing it to die a forgotten death, nor by protecting it from revision. They do not accept the maintenance of the status quo, they take seriously the challenges it faces and seek to help their tradition move forward in light of them. These are the people who enter the practices in such a way that they have become subordinate not only to the community that now constitutes those practices, but to the historical community of practitioners—those who precede the community now and whose acheivements have made possible the existence of that present community; in this way they accept the authority of tradition and have the best possibility of extending it into the future (MacIntyre 1984: 194).

Finally, MacIntyre offers three criteria for reconstitution of a tradition in the aftermath of an epistemological crisis. Through a process of both same-saying and concept-borrowing, a tradition in crisis is able to catalogue the contentions of a rival tradition into its own schema and borrow new resources that may help the floundering tradition be reconstructed. The criteria for newly reconstructed tradition demonstrate how the problems that led to the crisis can be resolved, explain why the crisis happened and show some continuity of shared beliefs and practices within the tradition (1988: 362).

A tradition that is able to write a newly revised history, taking into account these criteria, will have passed through the stages successfully; however, even this history must remain open-ended and provisional.

A tradition revitalized is a new masterpiece, a new work of art that resembles the original but has truly original and contextual additions integrated within it. There must be the possibility of a new historical narrative written about the changes, and some clear resemblance with the past. Success is not guaranteed. The possibility for misinterpretation and unsatisfactory developments are always at hand. Yet, a faithful reinterpretation of one's past is not only possible, but is the only way forward.

We learn from MacIntyre that tradition is the only grounds for innovation. In the Quaker case, for the possibility of a new synthesis, the Quaker tradition must be seen as offering many of the resources for its own renewal. MacIntyre gives us an approach to history that takes seriously a tradition's ongoing struggle to progress as a socially embodied community by pointing to that tradition's resources for reinterpretation and renewal in today's context.

Mission Embedded within Context and Tradition

If for MacIntyre tradition is the grounds for reinterpretation and innovation, then for Bevans context is the catalyst to innovate. The church and its understanding of mission in the Enlightenment is one such example. For an innovation to be successful it must make sense of its present context, be up-to-date, and form a culturally appropriate expression of faith (ibid., 5). All contextual theology must connect today with yesterday, and yesterday with today. Mission is essential for the existence of the church. The church is a tradition in mission, the goal of which is to pursue God's Spirit in the world, discerning how to participate in that work, while giving witness to Jesus Christ. The point of the church is not to be faithful to its tradition at all cost, as Cattell warned, but to be faithful to the eternal within the tradition, which is also at work in the world. Therefore, while tradition is essential, it is not enough for the church who are the people of God responding to the work of Jesus in the world.

Inasmuch as the Enlightenment affected the West's relationship to tradition, it has also had a profound impact on mission. Until contextual theology, mission was understood in terms of universality and objectivity. What was perceived as God's work in one place was taken as true for every culture. The universality and objectivity of modernity combined with mission led to colonialism. With the advent of contextual theology, there was a move to respect local cultures and find the places where God was at work within a given context (Shenk 1999: 56). Bosch has said, "the gospel always comes to people in cultural robes. There is no such thing as a 'pure' Gospel, isolated from culture" (2005: 297). While Bevans remarks, "there is no such thing as 'theology'; there is only contextual theology." Therefore contextual theology points to the reality that the church is inescapably embedded within both tradition and context; any attempt to break free from one or the other returns us back to the problems inherent in both Christendom and modernity; any attempt to renew the church must involve both.

Bevans offers a model of contextual theology that demonstrates how the church can be faithful to both its history and its present because it takes into account the past as it has been passed down, while taking seriously the present experience of context (Bevans 2002: 5). The synthetic model draws together tradition and context in a dialogical approach that "makes creative use of whatever is at hand" (ibid., 88). It does in three ways: by seeking to preserve the gospel and tradition; borrowing resources and learning from the context to aid in new reformulations of faith as it emphasizes its complementarity and uniqueness; and finally, by creating a new contextual theology by bringing together these various threads in a dialogical and imaginative way. Synthesis shows us that theology is always on the go, draws upon resources both traditional and contextual, and is constructed by those within the culture—that is those who, like apprentices, have the skills necessary to create meaning out within their setting.

The convergent model takes into account the essential nature of the present context as it seeks to understand and reinterpret a tradition into a new synthesis. A contextual theology that draws upon the synthetic model looks back to its tradition in order to make sense of its own present context, while actively participating in its context and using that to understand tradition. Revitalization for the church consists of creating a synthesis that contains a back and forth dialogue between past and present, apprentice and cultural context.

Everett Cattell understood that the tradition of Quakerism was in its very formation missionary, and believed that by abandoning everything to grasp onto God's work in the world they would retraverse the original Quaker vision. As Ron Stansell writes, Cattell believed "that obedient mission itself produces renewal and fresh breezes from the Spirit. We discover God's blessings only when we give ourselves away to Jesus and to the world" (Stansell 2009: 131). What Cattell left unsaid was in what ways the tradition was missionary, what interpretations and practices might be brought forward in today's context, and in what ways today's context sheds new light on the Quaker tradition. What MacIntyre and Bevans add to our convergent model is that any contextual theology will rely on the texts, interpretations and practices of one's tradition while learning from and adapting to one's own context, anything less is too short-sighted.

Participation and Today's Context

If Quakers are to find renewal by constructing a convergent model that builds on both MacIntyre and Bevans, within the present context then participatory culture is a fitting dialogue partner. Not only does participatory culture name a dominant cultural thread within the today's context, but it also shares many of the same qualities found within MacIntyre and Bevans—reinterpreting texts, apprentices, subjectivity, a rejection of the dualism of modernity and the creation of new syntheses of cultural texts are a only few. When participatory culture put in dialogue with early Quakerism, as I demonstrate in the following chapter, many of the practices that formed a unique approach to mission is brought to light.

Through his research and writing, Henry Jenkins has challenged popular understandings of fandom by insisting that there are legitimate ways of working within a cultural system of domination in ways that resist what that system values. In doing this, these "fans" form a socially embodied community that presents a different vision, an achievable utopia, in the world. Those within participatory culture are active, reject the dualism between producer and consumer, and use whatever is at their disposal to produce new cultural artifacts. As Jenkins has argued, "fan cultures . . . [are] a revitalization of folk cultures in response to the content of mass culture" (Jenkins 2006: 12). In their production of new cultural artifacts fans create an alternative social community within mass culture.

Participatory culture is a landscape through which a missionary today must listen and learn where God is moving. If God is moving in participatory culture, then discerning the practices of that culture will help understand how the church might engage with it appropriately. In the previous chapter, I described six practices that can be extrapolated from participatory culture: authentic resistance, remix, producing culture, collective intelligence, decentralized authority and the creation of an alternative social community. Each of these practices describes ways in which fans foster new forms of community within preexisting culture, create new cultural texts by drawing on existing material, lead by consensus and challenge the dominant systems and practices of consumer culture. In the following chapter, it will be argued that these are practices similar to those within the Quaker tradition.

One of the central practices within participatory culture that connects back to MacIntyre and Bevans is remix. Fans take cultural texts and poach them, remixing them in ways that bring about new and sometimes subversive meanings. This type of cultural poaching describes a practice that takes seriously texts and cultural objects insofar as it seeks to internalize them and then rewrite them within their own personal contexts. This appropriation of texts blurs lines between producer and consumer, and challenges sanctioned interpretations. This is a practice that represents a synthesis of "original texts" and "cultural context" within today's culture. Poaching, or remix, is itself a synthesis, a contextual theology of sorts. Remixers can be thought of as apprentices within their particular fields of knowledge—whether media, literature, art, hip hop, and so on—who in a MacIntyrean way internalize their texts, deconstruct their schemata and find new ways of interpreting them. Remixers are an example of practitioners within participatory culture that extend their tradition in innovative ways.

A CONVERGENT MODEL OF RENEWAL

These three threads are brought together to create a convergent model of participatory renewal for faith traditions. Below I will develop the elements of this model and explain how to use it. This convergent model is for faith traditions that hope to bring about social and spiritual change in a way that is faithful to its tradition and engaged within its context –while fostering deeper participation within the movement. It is a model that draws directly from the key insights of MacIntyre, Bevans and Jenkins, and is constructed in a way that mirrors the four components of Bevans' synthesis model: tradition, context, dialogue and praxis.

The process begins when participants within a tradition experience a crisis that causes them to rethink their tradition in light of their context. By putting their tradition in dialogue with their context, examining each from the other's perspective, as only people who are able to speak the language of both can do, they are able to find places of continuity and discontinuity in both. Dialogue between the tradition and context involves same-saying, concept borrowing, and in some cases, as Bevans puts it, "exorcism" of aspects of that culture. There are many ways in which tradition and context can be put in dialogue with one another, but if this community wishes to bring about a participatory community then there are three core qualities—based on the original six elements of participatory culture—the community will exhibit: (a) *remixes* of the original texts of the tradition in new ways and with new texts maintaining their uniqueness and complementarity; (b) as it *resists* a passive culture of consumerism in order to foster an authentic subjective experience by producing something new; (c) while it draws on many voices, forming an *open work* of shared power and knowledge; (d) and by doing so they will have created practices of a *participatory community* that gives a renewed witness in the world.

The six elements of participatory culture are condensed down to four essential elements: remix, authentic resistance, open work and renewed participatory community. Authentic resistance is combined with cultural producers because both are concerned with the authentic production of something new in the midst of something old. Authentic resistance is more about dismantling, while cultural production is about the construction of something new. Open work is the combination of collective intelligence and decentralized authority. It names both a holistic epistemology as well as the very structure of authority within a participatory community. Bevans synthesis model is made up of four interacting parts: dialogue of the community, context, tradition and praxis. The convergent model has these same four working parts: the apprentices put into dialogue their context and tradition in ways that bring about new praxis: remix, resistance, open work and renewed participatory community.

Finally, MacIntyre's three stages of a tradition in renewal are also present. Stage one is the internalizing of the law and an unquestioning context; this is the tradition prior to crisis. The second stage is the conflict that brings about the need for change. This is the stage in which the apprentices of the tradition realize that something must be done if their tradition is to continue into the future, and where they begin to put tradition and context in dialogue. The third stage is the reformulation of the tradition which is the working out of remix, resistance, open work and building up a participatory community. Below I offer more detail into how each of the elements are informed by and interact with MacIntyre, Bevans, and Jenkins.

Remix

The concept of remix, as I developed in chapter 5, offers a poignant metaphor from participatory culture for how a tradition, or original text, is respected as the source of creativity, while allowing new cultural material to be the catalyst for a new rendition or reading of that original piece of art. Remix is the blending together of various threads both traditional and contextual and making something out of it. Bevans' understanding of synthesis is closely related to how I use the term "remix." Bevans writes:

> A fundamental presupposition of the synthetic model is the composite nature of the human context as the situation in which men and women live. Practitioners of the synthetic model would hold that every context has both elements that are unique to it and elements that are held in common with others. What is for the synthetic model is to emphasize *both* uniqueness and complementarity, since one's identity emerges in a dialogue that includes both (Bevans 2002: 90).

In this way remix names the possibility of drawing two things together that may at first seem unlikely components, but may in fact form something appropriately new. It also names the fact that for a faith tradition there is always something to be learned and borrowed from culture while still maintaining its uniqueness (ibid.).

Lawrence Lessig describes remix culture as a blending between old and new, similar to Jenkins idea of convergence, where the meaning of one builds on the reference of the other. According to Lessig, even if at first the pairing is counter-intuitive, remix, done well can produce something entirely new: "Whether text or beyond text, remix is collage; it comes from combining elements of [Read-Only] culture; it succeeds *by leveraging the meaning created by the reference* to building something new" (Lessig 2008: 76; italics added). Rather than seeking to create something original out of nothing, remix draws on the already-existing power of the many layers embedded within the symbols that it combines (ibid., 69). Remix takes preexisting Read-Only culture and transforms it—often in ways that challenge the sanctioned interpretations—in a personal and creative way that borrows and builds on established symbols.

In the context of a remix within a faith tradition, it is essential to consider what a successful remix consists of. Not all remixes are equal. Within remix culture, a successful remix is one in which a reference to the old track or original artwork is still recognizable, and the new work derives or leverages reference to the original in a new way. While MacIntyre does not refer to the concept of remix specifically he covers similar ground when he talks about the reformulation of a tradition:

> What responses the inhabitants of a particular community make in the face of such stimuli toward the reformulation of their beliefs or the remaking of their practices or both will depend not only upon what stock of reasons and of questioning and reasoning abilities they already possess but also upon their inventiveness. And these in turn will determine the possible range of outcomes in the rejection, emendation, and reformulation of beliefs, the revaluation of authorities, the reinterpretations of texts, the emergence of new forms of authority, and the production of new texts. (MacIntyre 1988: 355)

MacIntyre's understanding of the formation of a tradition sheds light on the process of how a text could be remixed:

> We are now in a position to contrast three stages in the initial development of a tradition: A first in which the relevant beliefs, texts, and authorities have not yet been put in question; a second in which inadequacies of various types have been identified, but not yet remedied; and a third in which response to those inadequacies has resulted in a set of reformulations, reevaluations, and new formulations and evaluations, designed to remedy inadequacies and overcome limitations. (Ibid.)

Salient for a discussion on a successful remix is MacIntyre's point that the development of a tradition is different than the transformation of beliefs, however gradual or systematic: "A rational tradition's modes of continuity differ from those of the former [transformation of beliefs], its ruptures from those of the latter [a sudden conversion]. Some core of shared belief, constitutive of allegiance to the tradition, has to survive every rupture" (ibid., 356). Reformulations require both intellectual insight and "a rare gift of empathy" on the part of the protagonists in a tradition (ibid., 167). Finally, Bevans development of criteria for orthodoxy within the context of faith communities constructing new contextual theologies reinforce MacIntyre's criteria.

Bevans argues the three criteria the new synthesis should exhibit are: (1) the basic intentions of the tradition should be left intact; (2) it should be rooted in Christian orthopraxis; and (3) it should be formulated and accepted through a consensual process. A community that knows what constitutes a good remix from a bad one will be better able to know what parts of the context that should be kept and which parts should be exorcised (Bevans 2002: 91).

MacIntyre's criteria differ in their focus but supplement rather than detract from Bevans. Above I summed up MacIntyre's criteria saying that a newly reconstructed tradition needs to (A) find a resolution of the previous problems that initiated the change or conflict, (B) explain of what went wrong and why, (C) demonstrate a continuity of some shared beliefs and practices with the tradition of enquiry, and finally (D) accept that it is provisional and open to further revisions: it only offers a "best account so far."

Bevans' #1 and #2 fit into MacIntyre's C—the shared beliefs and practices from the tradition should share the same intentions and match orthopraxis. Whereas Bevans' #3 is connected to MacIntyre's A, B and D in that they name the process through which this work is done. This names the content that arises from change. Finding resolutions and acceptable explanations needs to be done within the community undergoing change—one isolated individual or argument is not enough to bring about the kind of social change the convergent model aims for. Accepting the provisional and open-ended nature of new formulations also needs to be arrived at by consensus if the tradition is to allow itself to return through this process again in the future, otherwise a new reformulated tradition can easily become entrenched in old ways when new conflicts arise.

The underpinning criteria of the convergent model can be summarized as follows: when facing conflict and challenge the apprentices of a tradition must be able to find resolutions to the problems and explain why the problems existed and accept the provisional nature of their newly formulated community through a provisional process that can once again start over again if new conflicts arise. The renewed community will demonstrate its shared belief and practice with its predecessors in ways that have both the right intention and the right practice.

Authentic Resistance

The second way a participatory model of renewal puts tradition and context in dialogue is through the community's authentic resistance. This combines the two complimentary characteristics authentic resistance and cultural producers. What is essential to this productive and authentic resistance is that it strips away all that encumbers, all the social contrivances that become obstacles to a deeply authentic experience. Productive resistance is about emotional investment; it is rooted in the subjective experience.

This model argues that it is necessary for those working for change or renewal of a tradition to be participants, fans, or apprentices of that particular community. Bevans argues that modern, Enlightenment-oriented theology was considered objective, discursive and academic. This is a form of "trickle down" theology that is left to the "highly trained specialist" (Bevans 2002: 18). The subjective-shift of contextual theology, under the influence of postmodernity, recognizes instead that today theology is "conceived in terms of expressing's one's present experience in terms of one's faith," therefore ordinary people are inadmissible to the project. "If theology is truly to take culture and cultural change seriously, it must be understood as being done most fully by the subjects and agents of culture and cultural change" (ibid.). For authentic theology and practice to form within that tradition and context there needs to be a shared experience rooted in that culture.

It is important to note that Bevans argues a "non-participant," or outsider, can do limited theology. The trained theologian acts as a midwife for the subjects of a given culture "as they give birth to a theology that is truly rooted in a culture and moment of history" (ibid.). Theologians or those who are outsiders can act as "brokers" to the ongoing task of writing and reformulating contextual theology, but this must be done carefully and always within the

> constant practice of dialogue between the people—who are the subjects of culture and cultural change and so have a preeminent place in the enterprise of seeking to understand Christian faith in a particular context—and the professional theologian which

articulates, deepens, and broadens the people's faith expression with his or her wider knowledge of the Christian tradition and, perhaps, the articulation of faith in other contexts. (Ibid.)

We have seen this emotional investment and subjective experience in the zine culture of the 1970s and 1980s, as well as the example of Harry Potter fandom, and the rise of bloggers in the twentieth century; people write about what they love and care about most, creating pockets of resistance where they can produce the kind of culture they wish to see in the world. Another way this can be put is that change and renewal comes by way of those who are apprentices of a tradition and context. Apprentices are those who accept the importance of their tradition and under the tutelage of authority allow themselves to be shaped by the virtues and *telos* of their tradition (MacIntyre 1990: 64). Under the teaching of masters, these apprentices will learn how to take their tradition further (ibid., 65).

Finally, this authentic and productive resistance leads a community to be cultural producers. Not satisfied with the maintenance of the status quo, they look for new ways to create new culture where authenticity is central. There is no one "product" these communities create, rather, it ranges from new forms of media, social criticism, satire, to new communal identities, all of which form what could be called "liberated spaces." In these spaces, subjects are able to express freedom to speak, learn, write, and gather in ways they may not be permitted to by the dominant culture. For instance, the Do It Yourself (DIY) movement within youth culture:

> [W]anted to reject the continual cycle of consumption by creating self-sufficient alternative spaces" so they created liberated spaces for it to happen. Spaces created by DIYers often combine "social criticism" with "cultural creativity in what's both a utopian gesture and a practical display of resistance. (Quart 2003: 209–11)

American culture today could be described as a "society of spectacle," where desires are manufactured and emotions manipulated. Ours is a society driven by consumption and branding, forcing inauthentic and manufactured choices for happiness on people. On the one hand, inauthenticity is passivity. A consumer is one who is an outsider to authentic experience and emotional investment. On the other hand, a producer is an active subject who breaks down the divisions between consumption and production, circumventing restrictions around authority, skill, and professionalization (Duncombe 1997: 124). Those who challenge the ritualization of consumption foster our second element of renewal.

Open Work

The Third Key element is the open work, which builds on the synthesis of collective intelligence and decentralized networks found within participatory culture. It is about the redistribution of knowledge across networks both human and technological. It represents a shared and inclusive approach to power that remains organized while non-hierarchical, congruent while not restrictive, and is flat or mutual inasmuch as the architecture of the network is "many voiced" and based on consensus models of authority.

Collective Intelligence concerns itself with forming social relations where knowledge and power are shared, and where "knowledge culture" enables the community to move towards an "achievable utopia." As Jenkins calls it, "Dress rehearsal for the way culture might operate in the future" (Jenkins 2006b: 134). This is done in the context of communities bonded together through "collective intelligence," where a mutuality of learning and teaching is exhibited in the group: "Each activity, each act of communication, each human relation implies an apprenticeship" (Lévy 1997: 11–12). Collective intelligence forms communities of new knowledge and new skills, raising the capacity for productivity, even within smaller groups, because everyone is able to collaborate and contribute. A collective approach to knowledge allows for a diversity of ideas and skills within the community, without necessitating uniformity. Collective intelligence within our model is not limited to the intelligence within the present community, but includes all of the intelligence present within that community's ongoing tradition. Thus, as in Bevans' synthesis, dialogue with tradition and context are essential components of collective intelligence.

A decentralized network, the structural side of collective intelligence, is the architecture or organization implementation that allows for decentralization to occur. This aspect of the model looks for ways in which the community organizes itself, how it determines what is an authority, and whose voice gets heard. In a decentralized system, organization is based on consensus models of decision-making, every voice is sought after and heard. As with Bevan's synthesis model, it is dialogical in nature, conversational in tone, relational in its make-up. Just like Critical Mass, the make-up of the group and its identity "is broadly defined by its participants." Because it is consensus based and relies on the voices of participants within a tradition or community, a decentralized network is itself an open work. This network is dynamic, open and provisional—it lends itself to a "hackability" and expansion.

Finally, taken alongside MacIntyre, this element is understood to be holistic in its understanding of authority and knowledge, just as within collective intelligence there is no one text, person, or interpretation that is indubitable. This holistic approach is strengthened greatly by the formation of apprenticing communities, where the virtues and practices of the present and historic community is passed on. This happens because of how the community functions; its existence is predicated on the participation and knowledge of that whole community. Unlike in some movements where an expert or text is the foundation, a decentralized community will identify multiple sources for tradition and create space for multiple voices and interpretations.

Alternative Participatory Community

The final element within the convergent model is that this renewed community or movement embodies an achievable utopia, or what I have referred to as a "free space," that fosters an "alternative participatory community." This community is alternative on the basis that it is a space of resistance to the cultural norms of consumption, violence, hierarchical control, authorized meaning.[2] In other words, it is a participatory community that creates a space where the values it wishes to see within the world are embodied within its social movement. This alternative participatory community is at the same time a new or "fresh expression" of a particular community and one rooted within a tradition. It is MacIntyre's concept of tradition being reformulated by the work of that tradition's apprentices, and finally embodied by a new vision of their world where the prevailing ideology of the time is resisted by alternative practices.

An alternative participatory community is the space where synthesis comes together into both contextual theology and contextual practice.

---

2. Gay Pilgrim draws on Foucault's idea of heteroptia to discuss how early Friends "set up alternative discourses/spaces that led to dissonance between themselves and the world they inhabited" (Dandelion, *The Liturgies of Quakerism*, 36).

This is a "socially embodied community" in the MacIntyrean sense; it is a community whose practices are rooted in the ongoing interpretation of texts and the weaving together of contextual elements. They are themselves liberated spaces that create resistance and possibility. They are a new embodied witness to the possibility of a faith tradition always in revision within the present moment; under the guidance of God's Spirit, always in dialogue with the apprentices of that tradition and context. The community is one in which the *eternal* of one's tradition lives on unencumbered by either the dominance of one's culture or the ritualization of one's tradition. It is at once a retraversal of the past in the present, a repetition of something profoundly old and yet always new. It is, in the words of early Friends, "primitive Christianity revived;" or, as we might say today, primitive Christianity remixed.

This final feature builds upon the previous three elements of the model, while also including this embodied sense of a new vision for the world. The questions this final aspect of the model asks are: How does this community practice remix? In what ways does the community exhibit resistance? What structures are in place for fostering collective intelligence, consensus, and the amplification of many voices? How does this community embody within itself what it wants to see from the rest of the world?

SUMMARY: A PARTICIPATORY MODEL OF RENEWAL

A convergent model for participatory renewal is based on the insights of MacIntyre, Bevans and Jenkins. The process is initiated when apprentices seek to overcome the confrontations, incoherences and break down of schemata that arise within their tradition.[3] In order to bring about convergent renewal they must put in dialogue the original texts and interpretations of their tradition and current cultural artifacts and practices, putting them together (through same-saying and concept borrowing) in a way that (a) remixes the original texts of the tradition with new texts while maintaining their continuity—their uniqueness and

---

3. It is important that those initiating renewal are insiders of the tradition and context, not simply a "missionary," but one who has fully apprenticed within. This is a group of people who exhibit, "the virtue of having an adequate sense of the traditions to which one belongs" (MacIntyre, *After Virtue*, 258) people who love both tradition and their context and learn one as their primary language and the second as their second-first language.

complementarity; (b) as it resists a passive culture of consumerism in order to foster an authentic subjective experience; (c) and drawing on many voices forming an open work of shared power and knowledge; (d) and by doing so they will have created practices of an alternative participatory community that gives witness in the world.

CHAPTER 5

The Convergent Model and Early Quakerism

IN THIS CHAPTER, I put the convergent model of renewal to work on our first case study: seventeenth-century Quakerism. When putting this model in dialogue with the early Quaker tradition, one finds that Quakerism was indeed a participatory renewal movement. As they placed the original texts of Christianity in dialogue with their seventeenth-century English context, early Friends exhibited high levels of participation in the way they remixed biblical texts, built a decentralized network of leadership and fostered authentic resistance, leading to a new set of practices that were socially embodied in an participatory Christian community. I argue that early Quakers were radical Christians who sought renewal by putting their tradition in dialogue with their context in ways that demonstrate all three of the core features of my model, thus forming an alternative social community.

TRADITION AND CONTEXT: SEVENTEENTH CENTURY DISRUPTED

Early Quakerism was born into a context that saw emergence of dissenting movements, capitalism and the continued reign of Christendom. In this section, I offer a very basic summary of the tradition and context that set the stage for the next two sections which look at the Quaker response, the practices that helped form Friends as an alternative social community.

Religion and Politics: Seedbed for Dissent

The religious and political climate of seventeeth-century England was marked by social unrest, civil war and various Christian groups vying for control over Christendom. This is the cultural context that would become the seedbed for many dissenting groups, not least of which is the Quaker movement. The unrest at this time not only threatened to tear the fabric of society apart, but Christianity was in crisis as well. However, crisis also creates the opportunity for new possibilities.

In the early 1600s England enjoyed prosperity under the reign of James I (1603–1623). The movement from feudalism towards capitalism was rapid; agriculture expanded immensely during this period as workers cleared forests, introduced by new modes of production and better distribution (Gwyn 2006: 74). Agriculture during this period was still the foundation of English economy, but industry began to flourish. As Quaker historian Douglas Gwyn points out, "New industrial processes required more capital investment. London was the leader in new industry and commerce, producing new wealth favorable to the politics and life of Puritanism" (ibid., 74–75). Men from the ruling class endowed with significant property were the only people permitted to vote in the elections of parliament (ibid., 75). Politics in this period was no place for women's rights or equality of any kind; except for men of the ruling class, all were excluded. Gwyn remarks, "80–90% of the populace therefore had no voice in English politics." Here the ruling classes saw the mass population as potentially dangerous, on the verge of anarchy and chaos, a "many headed monster" just waiting to be ruled over (ibid.).[1]

However, this all began to change drastically by 1639. In Scotland, an uprising by a nationalist party forced Charles to seek new funds from Parliament to establish a military to squelch the rebellion. During the elections, great political turmoil unfolded in England, with streets filled with rioters during the sessions (ibid., 82). What took place next led to civil war. Charles, wanting to create a military force, needed Parliament's consent, but Parliament was concerned that Charles would create

---

1. This was the common view of the "working classes" or what F. R. Levis would later refer to as the "common culture" (Barker, *Cultural Studies,* 41). Another cultural theorist, Matthew Arnold of the nineteenth century, would argue "The best that has been thought and said in the world. Here 'reading, observing and thinking' were said to be the means toward moral perfection and social good. Culture as the form of human 'civilization; is to be counterpoised to the 'anarchy' of the 'raw and uncultivated masses'" (ibid., 58).

a military and retaliate locally on his opposition. When they would not consent, Charles assembled those in the military who were loyal to him. In response, Parliament formed its own military. Afraid of being outnumbered and losing the cause, Parliament joined with the Scots promising that if they were victorious the Scots could resettle "according to the Word of God, and the Example of the best Reformed Churches" which Scots took to mean that England would be "under Presbyterian rule" (ibid., 83). However, Parliament kept the language vague enough to incorporate Scottish factions opposed to this outcome. While Parliament, with the help of the Solemn League and Covenant of Scotland, won the battle, the war, so to speak, was lost. The newly ordered religious hierarchy brought division among the Puritans of Britain.

This division created an unsettling situation in the 1640s where new religious dissenters and political ideas were able to surface (ibid.). New radical ideas broke into public discourse thanks to the printing press and a breakdown of political censorship. This gave rise to voices not typically represented within the larger religious and political discourse of the day. Gwyn writes, "The new trends particularly enlivened the lower-middle classes, raising the specter of a chaotic and rebellious "rabble," the threat the ruling classes feared most" (ibid.). Here the "many headed monster" loomed, waiting for the very moment when it would break free from its oppressive chains. In their inability to secure power in England, the Puritans lost more than just a chance at political power; the ruling class ideology with which they sought to control the masses was now being called into question by the masses—whatever stability James and Charles had secured was now lost. In the religious sphere of society, dissenters managed to challenge deeply held convictions about what it meant to be the church in the seventeenth century:

> A full-scale sectarianism now flourished, often informed by Anabaptist ideas: separation of Church from state; reliance upon the Spirit in Worship and decision-making; re-ordering of Christian life according to the Sermon on the Mount, with its strong critiques of power and wealth; and expectations of Christ's imminent return, bringing God's reign on earth. (Ibid., 84)

Within this backdrop of political and religious anxiety, a number of alternative religious and political movements emerged, such as the True Levellers, Ranters, Diggers and Seekers.

Each dissenting group offered rival claims to the interpretations and practices of the time and called into question the entire system of which they were a part. For example, the Levellers wanted "elections for sheriffs and justices of the peace, legal reforms, greater security for tenant farmers, a ban on military conscription, the abolition of tithes, and the end of the state Church" (ibid., 85). While the Diggers, led by Gerrard Winstanley, were more radical still. They rejected private land ownership, saying that it was a result of the Fall (ibid., 86). They also believed that "The kingdom of God would surely include the abolition of wage-labor and a communality in both material and spiritual affairs" (ibid.). In the earlier parts of the movement, they also created "a small network of agricultural communes on common lands," but these lands were lost through legal battles and violent mobs (ibid.). As is true in moments of great crisis, everything was up for grabs. The English ruling classes faced the terrifying reality that they could lose control of the masses. Gwyn writes, "All concepts of traditional authority were under attack, with far-ranging, often vague alternatives proliferating everywhere" (ibid.).

There are traces of each of these dissenting groups within early Quakerism but two key groups were the Seekers and the Baptists. The Seekers attacked the religious system of their time by "eschew[ing] outward forms as part of worship, convinced they were trappings of apostasy" (Dandelion 2007: 14). Therefore, Seekers met in silence, and waited until a minister stood to offer spoken ministry. Seekers, or "waiters," were people who gave up on the established church because of the consistent religious and political conflict in their day; they were seeking—by waiting—for a new movement of the Spirit to begin. Their seeking took on the dialectical quality of seeking by standing still (Gwyn 2000: 8).[2] They did not believe they had yet found the answers to society's dilemmas (Gwyn 2006: 89). Significantly:

> Their teachings tended to confirm the millenarian hopes and spiritualist pieties of most radical groups, but with a new, chastened mood. They met in silence, without use of formal sacraments, without any official clerical leadership, speaking only if

---

2. Gwyn writes that the moment of seeking by *standing still* is signaled by three things: "This moment may arrive with the attainment of some aim of seeking and be a time to consolidate newfound wisdom. Or standing still may embody a resistance to the forces of change ... finally, standing still may arrive as a moment of cumulative fatigue and frustration with wandering among many different truths (Gwyn, *Seekers Found*, 8).

moved by the Spirit. Sometimes called *waiters,* they awaited a new revelation from God. (Ibid.)

The Seekers were not the only group to offer a number of key ideas to early Quakerism. The Particular and General Baptists also were sources of inspiration. The Particular Baptists were a group of radicalized Puritans who challenged the "clerical monopoly" by denouncing infant baptism—"a cornerstone of state-sponsored Christianity," led by untrained, spirit-led, "mechanic preachers" who were tradesmen, but included a few women (ibid., 84). The Anabaptist-influenced General Baptists were even more radical and espoused ideas of separation of church and state, the centrality of Jesus' teachings from the Sermon on the Mount and his imminent return, the importance of spirit-led decisions and worship, the wickedness of power and wealth as it had been abused within their society (ibid.). As young George Fox began his spiritual wanderings through the Northern parts of England he not only found his early success among these groups, but some of his most lasting ideas.

Covenant of Grace and the Rise of Capitalism

While dissenting groups found their momentum and voice in the rising cacophony of cultural unrest, others tried to maintain or secure their own monopoly at the top. Of those groups, Puritans are central to the struggle at hand and provide a ready example of how capitalism in this period began to influence Christian theology and practice. Puritans, under the influence of reformed theology, used the language of "covenant" to reflect a sense of God's new order unfolding in sixteenth and seventeenth-century England. They too saw imminent change at work in the world. As Gwyn notes, this "covenant theology expressed the dramatic transformations in economic, political, and religious interaction culminating in the Civil War of the 1640s" (ibid., 65).

Puritans, largely from the mercantile class, wanted to bring reform to society with a number of changes that included a shift of authority over the church from the Crown to Parliament (ibid., 71). The Puritan "covenant of grace" was the way they began to change the "social contract" (ibid., 75). It provided a biblical paradigm that could enable a redefinition of the social order that had been rooted in medieval understanding of natural law and the divinely ordered chain of authority (ibid., 72).

The reformers asserted that natural law was evident to Adam before the Fall, through the natural light of reason. Adam was placed in creation under a covenant of works, to live in harmony with natural law. But Adam's failure resulted in an impaired human capacity to perceive natural law. God chose to redeem the descendants of Adam through a second covenant, a covenant of grace, first established with Abraham through God's binding promise and Abraham's faithful response. The covenant reached its full, universal implications in Jesus Christ. The covenant of works remains operative, leaving humanity with some residual awareness of sin in the conscience, and thus fully accountable before God. Nevertheless, since in Adam human strive and fail, the covenant of grace offers salvation as an undeserved gift, through faith in Christ, communicated by the gospel message contained in Scripture. Christ's sacrifice atones for continued sin and will present believers acceptably before God at the Last Judgment. (Ibid., 72–73)

For Puritans, the natural law was not a secure place from which to build because of human sinfulness, thus the state apparatus needed instead to derive its authority from a position of grace. The covenant of grace became a sweeping theological critique of the crown, but it was not broad enough in its scope. According to Gwyn, Puritanism and its "covenant of grace" operated on at least three levels, stimulating change in seventeenth-century England:

> An overview of the Puritan covenant of grace suggests that it existed (at least in its intention) on three levels: the personal level of the soul's commerce with God; the ecclesial level of the clerical class; and the political level of a Christian commonwealth united by a constitutional monarchy, serving God in all aspects of creation. (Ibid., 82)

Politically speaking, while the Church of England held the position of state-sponsored power, the Puritans sought to seize the reigns of power.[3] During the reigns of James and Charles, 1623–1642, there was a struggle over resettling church and state (ibid., 78). When James, who was raised a Presbyterian in Scotland, came into power there was political hope that he would overturn the Episcopal hierarchy with a Presbyterian

---

3. Gwyn suggests that Luther, Calvin, and Zwingli were known as "magisterial reformers" or those who "tended to ally with and sanction the existing political powers–especially since those powers protected them against Roman reprisals (Gwyn, *Covenant Crucified*, 73).

one; instead James buttressed the divine right of the king (Gwyn 1986: 9). He favored the saying "No Bishop, No King" to show that ideology and political power needed to stick together (Gwyn 2006: 78). He was not in favor of becoming subject to a church-run Parliament and worked to oust Puritan influence from within the church through the passing of new canons (ibid.).

Theologically, Puritans were centered on devotion to the sacred texts of Christian Scripture. Their movement was motivated by the preaching and teaching of a new influx of ministers during the last quarter of the sixteenth century from Oxford was Calvinist in theology and centered on biblical preaching—counter to Elizabeth's directives which forced clergy to preach from *The Book of Homilies* rather than the Bible (Gwyn 1986: 8). Building on the covenant of grace, Puritans believed that the church was the marketplace of the soul:

> Here the offer of salvation was made public through gospel preaching. Here the sacraments of baptism and communion served as manifest seals of one's covenantal participation. Yet one stepped forward for communion at great risk: if one was not truly among the elect and redeemed of God, to drink from the cup was to drink one's own condemnation (1 Cor. 11:35). Spiritual fraud in the Church was considered just as dangerous to society as was commercial fraud in the marketplace. (Gwyn 2006: 80)

Gwyn notes that Puritanism propagated a restricted participation. On the one hand, this was in part because of the theology of double predestination, which created a division between those elected and those damned within the church.[4] On the other hand, the clerical class "dispensing and controlling the two instruments of the covenant—preaching and sacraments—maintained a two-class religious society within the church" (ibid.). This was essentially the same view as those within the ruling class of England who believed that in order to maintain control within society there needed to be two social classes (ibid., 73). Therefore, rather than usurp the old system, Puritanism sought essentially to

---

4. Gwyn writes, "Calvin and his followers stressed the unconditional, promissory aspect of God's sworn obligation to aid lost humanity. But Calvin qualified this unconditional, universal sense of covenant with his doctrine of double predestination. God retrains sovereignty by choosing before the beginning of time which souls will be saved. The rest are predestined to remain lost and suffer final condemnation" (Gwyn, *Covenant Crucified*, 73).

maintain the social structure while replacing the Church of England as the official state church.

Underlying this, as Gwyn argues, Puritanism developed alongside the expansion of capitalism: "Just as capitalism fostered a possessive individualism through mechanisms of the market, so Puritan covenantal language articulated a sense of the soul's striving to acquire Christ, to procure personal salvation" (ibid., 79). In the same way that goods or capital are accumulated within capitalism, Puritans would work their whole lives to accumulate grace. This is illustrated by the fact that at least some Puritans maintained ledger books accounting for their moral debits and credits (ibid., 80). One's standing with God was like that of a balance sheet always in need of reckoning.

This was the birth of spiritual consumerism. This way of being the church did not foster a participation out of freedom but rather a faith that was calculated and commodified. Finally, as mentioned above, the capitalist ideology was also expressed in seventeenth-century Puritanism by its inherent class structure. Based on a specialized, expert model of ecclesiology, Puritan clergy exercised control over interpretation of Scripture and sacrament, "maintain[ing] a monopoly of revelation" which created levels of class within their ranks: hierarchy, parish clergy, and laity (ibid., 81).

Christendom Challenged

While the dissenters began to find their voices and momentum and capitalism began influencing not only Western economy but also religion as well. Hierarchy and control were central tenants of Christendom in this period. However, the stalemate of the 1640s between the church and state provided enough crack in the dam that the waters finally broke loose. New voices and movements were able to challenge those in power in a way that finally brought about the necessary change.

The ruling ideology of the day was based on interpretations of Scripture that gave rise to and underwrote a class-based society, the interconnectedness of the state and church, and a religious community that controlled who could hear, let alone read, interpret or speak from those primary texts. Since the time of Constantine, church and state were politically intertwined. As dissenting voices emerged, they leveled challenges against the religious underpinnings in these interpretations and practices in the society. Quakers, along with Baptists and others, challenged the hierarchical control and the called for the separation of church and state. Their voices demanded more involvement in the political process, and more participation by the people within the church itself. They rejected the compulsory tithes, state-sanctioned sacraments, and the violence the state-church perpetuated.

Tithes were an especially vulnerable target of protestors in this time period. To challenge the tithing system was to challenge the financial storehouses of the dominant system. As Gwyn notes, "Tithes upheld and empowered a large, entrenched ecclesial structure that inevitably aimed to repress all alternative groups. And that structure in turn upheld the class divisions of the wider social order" (ibid., 84). Everything in this period of religio-political history was about upholding the hierarchy at all costs.

From the earliest stages Quakers challenged this hierarchy, not just in their rejection of compulsory tithes, sacraments, lineage of the priesthood, etc. but also in their own theology about Jesus Christ. George Fox's almost liturgy-like chant, "The Lord has come to teach them himself, and of the seed Christ in them" was guided by the conviction that there was literally no authority but the risen Christ (Fox et al. 1985: 48).[5] This phrase "teach them himself," which is often used to support the interpretation that early Quakerism, was based on a realized eschatology, but is, in my view, better understood as a challenge to the religious and political authorities of Fox's day. His preaching and declaration that "the Lord has come to teach them himself," was to those in power, those who believed they spoke on behalf of God. Fox's is an anti-Christendom, anti-authoritarian statement. It was this conviction that led Quakers to denounce clergy of any kind, refuse to pay compulsory tithes, and reject the sacraments, enabling them to become a participatory movement in the seventeenth century.

Conclusion

The history of Quaker origins is the story of a radical Christian movement that emerged during a tumultuous time in England. This Christian

---

5. The context of this statement being in a steeple-house on a Sunday morning during worship seems equally important: "And when the priest had done I spoke to him and the people the truth and the light . . . and of their teacher within them" (Fox et al., *The Journal of George Fox*, 48).

movement was a radically egalitarian, grassroots, and counter-cultural response to the state and established church of the time. As demonstrated below, against the control, hierarchy and inequality of the political and religious culture of seveneeth-century England, Quakerism was a convergent and fully participative renewal movement within the seventeenth century. It was a movement that was inclusive, prophetic and participatory, calling the established church back to its Christian roots in new ways.

RESPONSE: ELEMENTS OF PARTICIPATION

In this section, I demonstrate how early Quakers responded to their time by putting their Christian tradition in dialogue with their context in ways that exhibit remix, resistance and decentralization.

Remix: Dissenters, Empathy and Reenactment

Quakers exhibited remix in a number of ways; I refer to three here: First, by the way they drew together dissenting ideas and people in a new and more organized—albeit, decentralized way; second, by the way they read the Bible empathetically, entering into the biblical narrative as though it were their own; and third, in their reenactments of the Biblical narrative within their context.

Organizing Dissenters

Quakers drew on the dissenters of their time and incorporated their theology and practice into their readings of the Bible. It was a movement that was not only able to incorporate the ideas of dissenting groups, but the dissenters themselves greatly populated the early movement. Friends were able to remix dissenting ideas into a new contextual theology. Central Quaker leaders including James Nayler, Richard Farnworth, William Dewsbury, Edward Burrough, Francis Howgill, and Richard Hubberthorne, were all Seekers when George Fox met them in 1652 while he was gathering people into the Quaker movement (Dandelion 2007: 15). It's also important to note that there were two kinds of seekers,

> Seeker A types wished to restore primitive Christianity, awaiting a prophet to help achieve this. Seeker B types believed God would not take humanity backwards, especially to a faith which

had been so easily corrupted before, but that they were living in a new and distinct age. (Ibid., 14)

Dandelion argues that James Nayler was a Quaker who was heavily influenced by the latter, while George Fox tried to incorporate both threads. Practices such as waiting in silence until one was led to speak by God's Spirit quickly became orthopraxis within the movement.

The nineteenth-century Quaker historian, William Tallack, similarly suggests the new remix Quakers created. In *George Fox, the Friends, and the Early Baptists* (1868), Tallack argued that Fox appropriated many of the General Baptist viewpoints and turned them into distinctly Quaker practice. Some of these Baptist-influenced practices included, "The peculiarities of language and dating; the system of ecclesiastical discipline; continuing revelation; the use of queries; opposition to music and signing; and commitment to plainness and pacifism" (Hamm 2004: 12). Tallack summarized the six essential features "promulgated by Fox and his followers" that—as he put it—"were, and are the essentials of Quakerism:"

> The necessity for a practical individual experience of God as manifesting a *living*, energizing, and *perceptible*, presence of the Spirit in the souls of men...

> The uselessness of only studying the Bible as a record of past events, dead men and ancient experiences, instead of searching it for practical applications to the every-day-life and present wants of the reader.

> The duty of "honouring all men," therefore avoiding undue partiality, flattering titles, or cringing to the few whilst neglecting the many who were all alike to be recognised as being God's children.... Hence Christians should seek to elevate and bless all men, even the repulsive and debased; for these latter should be loved as possessing dormant *capacities* of boundless future development for God.

> The call and right of *every* Christian to some recognised sphere of usefulness in "The Lord's Body,"—the Church universal, which consists of "many members," and has need of the faithful performance of the respective function of each and every one of them...

> The primary importance of aiming at "the essence and marrow" of all religious matters, rather than resting in verbal creeds, visible ceremonies, or mere professions. . . .
>
> That the ministry of the Gospel, or other spiritual service, is only to be entered upon under an honest sense of duty, and to be performed throughout in continual, humble, prayerful dependence upon the one "Giver of every good and perfect gift." (Tallack 1868: 66–67)

Tallack's reading of history suggested that Fox did not innovate these features but rather drew almost exclusively from the Radical Reformers:

> But these and other principles had, with little exception, been previously the characteristics of the Baptist theology also, and more particularly of the "General," as distinguished from the "Particular," Baptists. Both divisions of the Baptist had anticipated most of the doctrines, and also the system of discipline, adopted by George Fox and the Friends. But it was the General Baptists, (who were a distinct body as early as 1608,) that had most fully arrived at the views and usages which have been subsequently attributed to Quaker origin. (Ibid., 67)

According to Tallack, the Civil Wars created major divisions among the Baptists and "resulted in many thousands joining the ranks of Fox and the Friends" (ibid.). Thus, Fox's gift lay not in his ability as a religious innovator but as an organizer (ibid.). He was not the founder of Quakerism but rather a great organizer and remixer, who was able to bring together various threads of theology, practice, and dissenting groups who joined the Quaker movement.

Reading the Bible with Empathy

If early Friends remixed theology, borrow from preexisting ideas within the religious landscape and organizing them in a way that created something new within Christianity, then their practice of reading of the Bible empathetically was a direct challenge to the sanctioned interpretations and clerical monopoly over Scripture itself. For early Friends, the Bible was immensely influential and important to their development as a movement and their critique of the powers they challenged. However, the way they read and interpreted the Bible was an affront to those in power (Palmer 2013). By remixing the Bible, Quakers sought to further break the control that experts held over Scripture just as Anabaptists did on the Continent:

> In the Reformation groundswell of vernacular Bible reading, the rule of the expertise maintained a certain control over Scripture, which any literate person might read and interpret. Hence, university-trained ministers, the first modern professionals, controlled interpretation by standardizing their expertise and maintaining a monopoly over revelation. The challenge to that rule of expertise had been one of the primary scandals of Anabaptism on the Continent. (Gwyn 2006: 81)

Over the need to have an ordained clergy or expert interpret the Bible, Quakers took the Reformation to its extreme conclusion and suggested that it is the Holy Spirit who is the ultimate interpreter of the Bible because it is the source of everything written there. Robert Barclay, eschewing the role of the expert in his seminal work *An Apology* (Barclay 2002), argues that even the authority of Scripture is ultimately subject to God's Spirit:

> Nevertheless, because they [Scriptures] are only a declaration of the fountain, and not the fountain itself, therefore they are not to be esteemed the principal ground of all truth and knowledge, not yet the adequate primary rule of faith and manners. Yet because they give a true and faithful testimony of the first foundation, they are and may be esteemed a secondary rule, subordinate to the spirit, from which they have all excellency and certainty. (Ibid., 62)

Friends believed that the same Spirit who authored the Bible was alive and active in their movement and within each other, enabling them to not only understand and interpret Scripture, but to be able to *read it* and *write about it* in a way that mirrors remix culture.

In *Early Friends and the Bible: Some Observations* (1993), Quaker theologian T. Vail Palmer Jr. argues that early Quakers read the Bible empathetically. Palmer's understanding of reading the Bible with empathy mirrors the concept of remix within a faith tradition. Borrowing from the biblical theology movement, Palmer argues that reading the Bible empathetically is as Bernhard Anderson once said, an "attempt to stand within the Bible and to look out at the world through the window of biblical faith" (Palmer, *Forthcoming*, chapter 1), or in the words of G. Ernest Wright, "Biblical theology is first and foremost a theology of recital. The worshipper listens to the recital and by means of historical memory and identification he participates, so to speak, in the original events" (ibid.). Palmer argues this Quakers entered fully into the biblical story as though they were there when it was written: "For Fox and Fell, the biblical history was indeed the history of their own time; every player in the drama of 17th century England had a counterpart in the biblical drama of the people of God and its enemies" (Palmer 1993: 44). Just as in remix, they integrated themselves into the biblical narrative in a way that drew upon the symbols and leveraged its references in new ways.

There are two ways they remixed the biblical narrative. The first was by the way they incorporated the words of Scripture into their own voices without citation or quotation like a tapestry woven together.[6] They did this by reassembling phrases and images in a way that formulated a new argument or statement that was at the same time personal and yet rich with biblical metaphor (ibid., 48). This was not simply Bible memorization, this was re-writing biblical text as a part of their own speech. For example, in Fox's one-page Epistle II Palmer counted twenty-five quotations, while in Edward Burrough's one-and-a-half paged "An Epistle to all the Saints Whom God hath Called" (1657), he counted fifty different biblical references without quotation or citation (ibid., 42–43). Consider this example from George Fox's Epistle 227 (1663) written during a time of severe persecution:

> Sing and rejoice, you children of the day and of the light; for the Lord is at work in this thick night of darkness that may be felt. And truth does flourish as the rose, and the lilies do grow among the thorns, and the plants atop of the hills. And upon them the lambs do skip and play. And never heed the tempests nor the storms, floods nor rains, for the seed Christ is over all, and doth reign. And so be of good faith and valiant for the truth; for the truth can live in the jails. And fear not the loss of fleece, for it will grow again; and follow the lamb, if it be under the beast's horns, or under the beast's heels; for the lamb shall have the victory over them all. And so all live in the seed Christ, your way that never fell. In him you do see over all the ways of Adam's and Eve's and daughters in the fall.

---

6. Palmer suggests that a citation is a "paraphrase of a Bible passage, close enough to the actual wording that [a Friend] must certainly have had that passage in mind" (Palmer, *Friends, God and the Bible*, chapter 2).

Within just the first three lines we can identify these seven references: Sing and rejoice (Zachariah 2:10); you children of the day and of the light (1 Thessalonians 5:5); for the Lord is at work in this thick night of darkness that may be felt (Exodus 10:21); flourish as the rose (Isaiah 35:1); lilies do grow among the thorns (Song of Songs 2:1); plants atop of the hills (Jeremiah 31:3–5); lambs do skip (Song of Songs 2:8). There are doubtless other metaphors and wordplays within this text—drawing from other biblical books such as book of Revelation, Genesis, Jeremiah, Judges, and others, but what it demonstrates is that early Quakers were remixing the Bible, treating it as fan fiction, re-writing the texts within their own words and bringing about new meanings that leveraged well-known biblical symbols and phrases.

As Palmer puts it, "Clearly, Fox and Burrough did not seem to be appealing to these quotations and citations as external sources or as authorities to which they were asking Friends to conform themselves" (ibid., 43). Whereas the Bible is—at least for a majority of Christendom—a Read-Only text, early Quakers used it in Read-Write ways. By incorporating the language and phraseology of Scripture into their own arguments, they challenged the sanctioned readings and interpretations by building creatively on the power of biblical reference.

A second way they remixed the biblical narratives is seen in how they opened up new possibilities for reading and interpreting biblical teaching and Christian doctrine, which subsequently made way for alternative Christian practices. One of the most important remixes of early Friends is found in Margaret Fell's *Women's Speaking Justified* (1666), which addressed the issue of women preaching in public worship. This is one area where Quaker theology sharply contrasted with a majority of Christian theology in that time. From the beginning, Quakers identified and encouraged the work of women ministers. Elizabeth Hooten was the first female preacher among Friends (1647), and she was certainly not the last (Palmer 2010: 5).

Women were among the early Quaker missionaries to travel across the British Isles, to America, Turkey, and beyond (ibid.). There were a number of Friends who wrote in support of female preachers, but Margaret Fell, the "Mother Superior" of Quakerism (Garman 1996: 6), authored the most profound and popular tract on the equality of women.[7] Fell's tract looks at every passage in the Bible that can be taken in support

---

7. Some women have cited Fell's tract as the first key text of the feminist movement (see Thickstun, "Writing the Spirit,").

of women speaking, and looks at passages that have been used against women, weaving together biblical text in a convincing personal, rather than legalistic manner (Palmer 2013: chapter 2). The thrust of her argument is that God's Spirit makes no difference between male and female and speaks through whomever is a willing vessel. She writes:

> And so let this serve to stop that opposing Spirit that would limit the Power and Spirit of the Lord Jesus, whose Spirit is poured upon all flesh, both Sons and Daughters, now in his Resurrection; and since that the Lord God in the Creation, when he made man in his own Image, he made them *Male and Female*; and since that Christ Jesus, as the Apostle saith, was made of a Woman, and the power of the Highest overshadowed her, and the holy Ghost came upon her, and the holy thing that was born of her, was called *the Son of God,* and when he was upon the Earth, he manifested his *love,* and his *will,* and his *mind,* both to the Woman of *Samaria,* and *Martha,* and *Mary* her sister, and several others, as hath been shewed. . .And thus the Lord Jesus hath manifested himself and his Power, without respect of Persons; and so let all mouths be stopt that would limit him, whose Power and Spirit is infinite, that is pouring upon all flesh. (Fell 1980: 11)

Palmer points out that Fell's tract responds in depth to two key passages used against women speaking: 1 Cor 14:34–35 and 1 Tim 2:11–12 (Palmer, *Forthcoming*, chapter 2). Fell's closing line plays off the oft-quoted Pauline passage from 1 Timothy 2:11–12 "Let the woman learn in silence with all subjection. But I suffer not a woman to teach, nor to usurp authority over the man, but to be in silence" (KJV) by turning it back around on her opponents who she suggests should "remain silent" when she says, "so let all mouths be stopt that would limit him, whose Power and Spirit is infinite, that is pouring upon all flesh."

Fell's reinterpretation of the biblical text within her culture shows how it is possible to draw on original sources in new ways. By leveraging metaphors from Old Testament and New and appealing to the Spirit of God at work, she was able to put something new forward within Christianity. For Fell, "the biblical history was indeed the history of their own time; every player in the drama of 17th century England had a counterpart in the biblical drama of the people of God and its enemies" (Palmer 1993: 44).

Similarly, George Fox wrote on the subject of women speaking. In his tract "The Woman Learning in Silence, or the Mystery of the Woman's Subjection to her Husband," Fox begins with the popular anti-egalitarian text of I Timothy and responds to it by appealing to the work of the Spirit as it is described in Acts 2 by the apostle Peter. "I will pour out my Spirit upon all flesh, and your sons and your daughters shall prophesy" (Acts 2:17 NRSV). For the remainder of the tract, Fox works through a plethora of counter-examples, showing the "women who preached the gospel, taught, and exercised leadership in the early church" (Palmer 2010: 5). He then concludes:

> Who is it that dare stop Christ's mouth? That now is come to reign in his sons and daughters, Christ in the male, and Christ in the female? And you that will not have him to reign in the female as well as in the male, you are against Scripture, and will not have him to reign over you. (Ibid.)

Here the claim is that if someone has an authentic connection to Christ—participating in his work, empathizing with the biblical narrative—any who stand in the way reject Christ's kingship. Early Friends practiced participation and co-laboring with God in the very way they read the Bible, seeing themselves as a central part of the unfolding biblical drama:

> It resembled the community of the first disciples precisely because the early Quakers had internalized the life of the early church with such deep empathy, because the history of the first apostles had become their own. They "were there when they crucified my Lord." (Palmer 1993: 46)

Reenactment

One last way that early Quakers remixed the Bible is through their re-enactment of biblical drama in theatrical ways. This was because, as Fox wrote, they believed they were to "come . . . into the same power and Spirit that the prophets and apostles were in." This kind of self-identification with the biblical text led many Quakers to take up various signs or public "street theater;" they were known for "repeat[ing] precisely the actions of some of the biblical characters" (Palmer 1993: 45). Robert Barclay was known to have acted on a call from God to walk naked as a sign (ibid.). Fox quoted Ezekiel 24: 6, 9 and Nahum 3:1 which says "Woe to the bloody city!" When Fox entered Lichfield he said, "The word of the Lord came unto me again to cry, 'Woe unto the bloody city of Lichfield!'" (Palmer 2013: chapter 2). This witness through reenactment was part and parcel of their entire way of carrying out what they understood their message to be. They were both the carriers of a message and the message; they were co-heirs with the apostles and prophets helping the biblical drama unfold.

James Nayler, an early Quaker leader, provides the most prominent illustration of empathy and biblical reenactment in early Quakerism. On the afternoon of October 24, 1656 Nayler and a group of his Quaker followers decided to reenact Jesus' triumphal entry into Jerusalem. They marched into the city center of Bristol with Nayler riding on the back of a donkey, those around him saying "Holy, Holy, Holy, Hosanna." Nayler was arrested and convicted of blasphemy charged with the crime of believing that he was Jesus. This was not the first time Nayler and his followers had done something like this, but Bristol was the tipping point:

> This group had enacted the same sign in Glastonbury and Wells but Bristol was a powder-keg and the city was eager to use the sign as an excuse to react against the Quaker successes there. Martial law the previous year had placed Major General Desborough in control of the city and he had been overly lenient towards the Quakers in the minds of many. The Quakers were rude and arrogant in their theological claims of perfectability and the unfolding second coming, and disturbing in their vision of spiritual egalitarianism and social revolution. (Dandelion 2006: 6)

Generally speaking, this kind of action was nothing new for Quakers. Plenty of early Friends participated in public theater of this sort as denouncement of the spiritual inauthenticity of their times (ibid.). Yet, it was the location they chose and the circumstances that surrounded the event that made this a powerful, if volatile demonstration.

Nayler's action was considered to be a direct challenge to George Fox's leadership because he did it "at just the time that Fox was working with key Bristol Quakers and sympathisers to gain greater religious toleration from parliament" (ibid.). Nayler's public theater undermined Fox's leadership and was an affront to the toleration Fox felt was necessary for the survival of the movement. Just as Fox was beginning work to stabilize the movement, Nayler was pushing for greater challenge of the structures they opposed. Doug Gywn writes,

> James Nayler's entry into Bristol offered a similar critique of traditional, hierarchical kingship. We will recall that the sign was enacted at the very time Parliament was considering whether to make Cromwell's position as Protector hereditary. This "monarchical" scheme clearly represented a decisive step backwards from the more democratic initiatives of the Army and the radicals; it symbolized a reversion to archaic relations of feudalism. These developments in parliament were public knowledge and the focus of intense criticism by Friends, who bid Cromwell to "lay they crown at Jesus' feet." (Gwyn 2006: 177)

In the eyes of Nayler and his sympathizers, Fox's strategy was simply a compromise. Nayler was in a position to challenge Fox's posturing; for some, he was even seen as the leading Quaker authority (Dandelion 2007a: 40). Doug Gwyn argues that, "Nayler himself may have been struggling at this point to produce a sign that would make clear the Quaker claim in general—and his own in particular" (Gwyn 2006: 165).

The action ended badly for Nayler. He avoided the death sentence but received "310 lashes, his tongue was bored and he was branded on the forehead with 'B' for blasphemer." He received his punishment in two halves because it was so severe authorities were afraid it would kill him. They then forced further humiliation upon Nayler by having him ride backwards through the city of Bristol as though to reverse the effects of what he had done (Dandelion 2006: 14). A year after release from prison in 1659, he died after being mugged.

While Nayler's example ended poorly—Fox and Nayler never found reconciliation before Nayler's death—what this example illustrates is that remix challenges the sanctioned interpretations of a text. By reenacting the biblical story, Nayler took the original intent of Jesus' riding into Jerusalem and remixed it in his contemporary setting. This action got Nayler literally branded a blasphemer because it was interpreted through a Read-Only understanding of the Bible, which was fundamentally opposed to the Quaker understanding of Scripture. What made the sign work is that it leveraged meaning from the past and brought it to bear on present issues; in seventeenth-century Read-Only society that kind of action cost Nayler his life. A remix reading of Nayler's action demonstrates how early Friends participated in the biblical drama in their own time, drew upon biblical texts and leveraged there meaning in new and creative ways.[8]

Criteria

While the interpretations challenged the dominant powers of the day, Quakers understood what they were doing to be in line with Christianity. They believed that what they were doing was in the same direction, rooted in "orthopraxy" and while not acceptable to Christians in power, was representative of many of the marginalized people of faith within their context. Quakers went to lengths to prove how their teachings and practices were harmless to the King and should be acceptable to all who truly know the Spirit behind the Bible. For instance, Robert Barclay writes in his *Apology* (1678) in defense of Friends who were "evilly entreated," beat, imprisoned, persecuted even though they were people for whom God:

> Had made to 'beat their swords into plowshares and their spears into pruning-hooks,' and to learn carnal war any more: but he raised them up and armed them with spiritual weapons, even with his own Spirit and power, whereby they testified in the streets and highways and public market places and synagogues

---

8. Scholars have debated the intentions and interpretations of Nayler's actions for years. In the interpretation above, I am demonstrating how the concept of remix not only identifies a style of biblical interpretation, but brings about the possibility of an alternative account of historical events. Three works dedicated to the life and times of James Nayler are *The Sorrows of the Quaker Jesus: James Nayler and the Puritan Crackdown on the Free Spirit* by Leo Damrosch (1996); *James Nayler: Revolutionary To Prophet* by David Neelon (2009) and *James Nayler, 1618–1660: The Quaker Indicted by Parliament* by William G. Bittle (1987). Some of the interpretations that deal with Nayler see him as a victim of the pride that comes with having the kind of power he had, Walter Williams, *Rich Heritage of Quakerism*, 94–95; or as an outworking of the early Quaker understanding of the inward Light of Christ at work within his followers (Rosemary Moore, *The Light in Their Consciences: Faith, Practices, and Personalities in Early British Quakerism* [39–40]), or as Doug Gwyn suggests, it may be understood as a form of political drama (Gwyn, *Covenant Crucified*, 167) rooted in a claim of apostolic authority that many early Friends believed they had (ibid., 165). Finally, Carole Spencer sees Nayler's action should be seen as a union with Christ, comparable to St. Francis' stigmata, which could be understood as a literal reenactment of the triumphal entry (Spencer, "James Nayler," 2001). Gwyn and Spencer's points comes closest to the understanding of empathy/remix being proposed here. Of the Nayler event Rosemary Moore astutely observes, "Nobody can be sure what was going on in the minds of the participants in these events" (*The Light in Their Consciences*, 39).

against the pride, vanity lusts, and hypocrisy of that generation who were righteous in their own eyes. (Barclay 2002: 2)

And even when they were so gravely mistreated, Barclay points to the fact that Quakers kept their integrity:

> They have boldly stood to their testimony for God without creeping into holes or corners or once hiding themselves, as all other dissenters have done; but daily met, according to their custom, in the public places .. [not] catched ... lurking in their secret chambers. (Ibid., 3)

Instead, they were out in the open, publically speaking Truth and testifying to God (ibid.). Barclay suggests that the fruits of Quakerism should be enough to suggest that they were oriented in the same direction as early Christianity, "Those that have an eye to see may observe their Christian patience and courage, constancy and suffering, joined in one, more than in any other people that differ from them or oppose them" (ibid.). Despite their uniqueness, Quakers sought to prove their complementarity with the rest of Christianity.

The *Apology*, and many other writings—such as George Fox's *Letter of George Fox and other Friends to the Governor of Barbadoes* (1671)—were motivated by the challenge early Friends posed by their use of remix within a Read-Only culture. Sometimes Friends even went so far to convince people they were Christians that they downplayed their differences as William Bacon Evans writes in his forward to Fox's *Letter to the Governor of Barbadoes*,

> In order to clear both the Truth and themselves from these slanders [false reports about their faith], it was judged needful to issue a statement, which they addressed to the Governor of the island. Since the charges consisted largely in accusations that the Quakers were no Christians, that they denied a belief in the Christ of history and in his saving work, their letter concerned itself chiefly with positive affirmations of these basic truths. Because of this, and because only passing reference was made to the inward work of Christ, some critics (including some Quakers) have felt that the Letter was one-sided, and that it failed to represent the original Quaker message as preached by Fox and his immediate followers during the twenty years preceding this visit. (Fox 1959: 1)

While they considered themselves Publishers of Truth, their opponents constantly saw them as heretics, or as one might say, publishers of "untruth." This challenge persists for any group that wishes to offer an alternative reading or reinterpretation whether it is a biblical text, a highly respected musical number, or world-renowned work of art. Remix challenges because it takes tradition seriously enough to allow it to change and become something new.

The religious and political upheaval of seventeeth-century England was marked by reinterpretations of Christianity and the clamor of dissenting voices struggling to be heard, pointing in disparate directions. Quakers responded to this by challenging their context in the way that they drew upon dissenting ideas and incorporated them into a new Christian movement. Besides remixing dissenting ideas and practices, they remixed the Bible by reading it empathetically. Drawing on the language and the symbols of Scripture, they leveraged its meaning in new ways. These new ways manifested themselves both in reenactment of biblical passages, as well as new teachings and practices rooted in Scripture but radically different from the dominant interpretations of the day, but were clearly Quakers extending the texts of their tradition out in new and innovative ways.

Authentic Resistance: Convincement and Challenge

Building on Fox's convincement narrative, I argue that the Quaker tradition demonstrates the authentic resistance of consumerism in at least three ways: first, Fox's despairing spiritual pilgrimage shows the depth to which Fox—and other early Friends—was disillusioned by the inauthenticity of those professing to be Christians within the state church and even many dissenters. Second, Fox's convincement sealed a conviction of resistance to all outward symbols and authorities because neither could bring about an authentic experience; only communion with the inward Light of Christ could bring about true transformation and new life in a person. Finally, this authentic resistance led them to reject the "trickle down" theology of Christendom; as "Publishers of Truth," early Quakers challenged the ritualization of religious consumption by becoming active producers in their own time.

Convincement and Fox's Dark Ocean of Despair

While George Fox would become a well-known Christian leader, his initial spiritual wanderings through the northern parts of England were marked by despair. Fox, born in 1624 in Fenny Drayton in Leicestershire, set out at the age of nineteen (1643) to find answers to his penetrating spiritual questions: "He sought answers to these questions through extensive study of the Bible and conversations with Puritan ministers and 'professors.'" But none of his mentors could supply answers commensurate with the depth of his questions" (Gwyn 1986: 22). He visited groups of dissenters, learning from them, debating them, arguing theology with Puritan pastors, and wrestling with the state of his own despair and constant temptation (Barbour and Frost 1988: 26). He rejected many of these Christians who he claimed were professors but not possessors (Fox et al. 1985: 37).

Fox was deeply unsatisfied with the answers he received and grew weary of learned people, feeling that their commitment to "outward religion," as he called it, betrayed an allegiance to a broken system.[9] More deviously, it was a system that promoted hypocrisy and a false encounter with Christ. While his wanderings and spiritual questions were a sign of his own inward struggle—given the tumultuous religious and political context of Fox's early life—they also mirrored the "external" crisis within society as a whole. The urbane responses of priests and "professors" may have sounded to him like coping mechanisms, reinforcing the despair he felt.[10] He wrote:

---

9. As Dandelion writes: "Fox had already become clear that the university-trained priests were not of any particular or necessary help to him in [his] spiritual quest. Consequently he had spent time with the dissenters, a year with his uncle, William Pickerling, a Baptist, in London, and time moving around the army camps which were where the most radical religious ideas of the day were circulating. However, no one he had met had been able to respond adequately to his soul's search," (Dandelion, *An Introduction to Quakerism*, 20).

10. Another word for this is "instrumentalism," which is the word MacIntyre uses to describe when a tradition's stance becomes self-defensive towards rival accounts. Instrumentalism happens when theories become coping mechanisms against competing epistemological challenges. In this phase, traditions are unable to incorporate new meaning into their schemata's of meaning and thus it is unable to extend its arguments out into the future. Instrumentalism is a deadening of the senses within a tradition, a climate of antipathy to change and creativity; it can often be a blinder, protecting the status quo of that particular narrative. Instrumentalism is itself a sign of a tradition in crisis (MacIntyre, "Epistemological Crises," 161).

> Now after I had received that opening from the Lord that to bed at Oxford or Cambridge was not sufficient to fit a man to be a minister of Christ, I regarded the priests less, and looked more after the dissenting people. And among them I saw there was some tenderness, and many of them came afterwards to be convinced, for they had some openings. (Ibid., 11)

But even the dissenters ultimately left him unsatisfied. As he wrote in his journal, "for I saw there was none among them all that could speak to my condition" (ibid., 11). One might interpret this experience of despair as discovering the deep brokenness of what was being offered, yet with a persistence to continue the search. And that hope he found, as he wrote later in his journal: "I saw also that there was an ocean of darkness and death, but an infinite ocean of light and love, which flowed over the ocean of darkness" (ibid., 19).

Whereas the Puritans wanted to simply maintain the basic container of Christendom, replacing Anglican contents with their own, Fox felt the entire container needed to be stripped away, that it had become an obstacle to people knowing God authentically. The problem with the Reformation is that it was not radical enough. Maurice Creasey explains that:

> [The Reformers] had lopped off the branches of false doctrine and practice but had not grubbed out the roots. But it is important to notice that they did not ground their criticism in a claim that some new revelation had been given in their own century, which should supersede the Christian one. Rather, they condemned their contemporaries for their failure to see and to be faithful to the truth as it was embodied in Jesus and as it was experienced and proclaimed in the "days of the apostles." (Creasey and Johns 2011: 7–8)

Part of the concern was that society, especially as it pertained to the religious culture of the time, had become inundated with "notions" about, rather than "acquaintance with" God's Spirit (ibid.). In utter despair Fox abdicated his search:

> But as I had forsaken the priests, so I left the separate preachers also, and those called the most experienced people; for I saw there was none among them all that could speak to my condition. And when all my hopes in them and in all men were gone, so that I had nothing outwardly to help me, nor could I tell what to do. (Fox et al. 1985: 11)

It was in the context of this seeking and despair that Fox had a decisive experience that altered the course of history:

> Then, oh! Then I heard a voice which said, *"There is one, even Christ Jesus, that can speak to thy condition"*: and when I heard it, my heart did leap for joy... and this I knew experimentally. My desires after the Lord grew stronger and zeal in the pure knowledge of God, and of Christ alone, without the help of any man, book, or writing. For though I read the Scriptures that spake of Christ and of God, yet I knew Him not, but by revelation, as He who hath the key did open, and as the Father of Life drew me to His Son by His Spirit. (Fox et al. 1985: 11; italics added)

This "convincement" as Friends call it marks the turning point in Fox's life. It reveals a loss of hope in "outward contrivances" and desire to have complete emotional investment in his spiritual experience. It suggests a move towards a high level of ownership in his understanding and practice of Christian faith. Fox's experience would become paradigmatic for early Quakers.[11] His convincement marked a turn inward, away from ritual, sacramental, and other earthly structures; it placed the authority of experience squarely on the resurrected Christ Jesus present and speaking to his condition.[12] Those who followed Fox started calling themselves Friends of Truth or Children of Light.[13]

As I mentioned above, a common criticism from Quakers was that their Christian contemporaries were inauthentic; they were "professors" but not "possessors" of the Truth. This was a defining critique that demonstrates the Quaker challenge of inauthenticity. Francis Howgill, a

---

11. Dandelion argues that there are six stages of convincement—building on Nikki Coffey Tousley's work—"Technically, convincement meant literally conviction, the experience of the day of visitation. However, I am using the convincement here to refer to all of these processes. Convincement then, in the sense I am using it, was about (a) a powerful in-breaking of God, (b) a sense of conviction of sin, (c) a choice, repentance, and (d) being born again into perfection, or a measure of perfection.... Ultimately, this experience would lead to (e) the convinced gathering together... (f) calling 'the world' towards a new mode of religious experience (Dandelion, *An Introduction to Quakerism*, 23–24).

12. Typically convincement underwent six stages "an in-breaking of God's power; a realization of how sinful the believer's life had been, how far it had fallen short; the chance to repent and accept the new life; the experience of regeneration; an impulse to gather with others who had had this experience; mission to those who had not yet had this experience" (Dandelion, *The Quakers*, 6).

13. The early Quakers called themselves "Friends of Truth" or "Children of the Light;" the nickname "Quaker" was one given to them in derision by their opponents.

Seeker turned Quaker minister, wrote of the spiritual preachers of his day:

> Then some preached Christ within, but they themselves were without, had but words, and they said all must be within (unto which my heart did cleave), and they spoke of . . . God appearing in man, and overcoming the power of the devil. And. . .a true love I had to all that walked honestly in what profession soever, and I hated reviling one another, and that they should smite one another, and persecute one another, and with the sufferer I always took part . . . But still I saw, though they spoke of all things within, that they enjoyed not what they spoke . . . till at last I saw none walked as the ministers of Christ. (Gwyn 2000: 231)

Howgill was looking for that authentic, emotionally invested spirituality that came from an *internalizing of the law*, a *possession* of truth that so many could only *profess*. Margaret Fell recalls this same tension when she first heard George Fox preach:

> And when they were singing, he stood up upon a Seat or Form, and desired, that he might have liberty to speak: And he that was in the Pulpit, said he might. And the first words that he spoke were as followeth: He is Not a Jew that is one outward, neither is that Circumcision which is outward: But he is a Jew that is one inward, and that is Circumcision which is of the heart. And so he went on and said How that Christ was the Light of the World, and lighteth every Man that cometh into the World; and that by this Light they might be gathered to God, andc. And I stood up in my Pew, and wondered at his Doctrine; for I had never heard such before. And then he went on, and opened the Scriptures and said, The Scriptures were the Prophets' words, and Christ's and the Apostles' words, and what, as they spoke, they enjoyed and possessed, and had it from the Lord: And said, Then what had any to do with the Scriptures, but as they came to the Spirit that gave them forth. You will say, Christ saith this, and the Apostles say this; but what canst thou say? Art thou a Child of Light, and hast walked in the Light, and what thou speaks, is it inwardly from God? andc. This opened me so, that it cut me to the Heart; and then I saw clearly we were all wrong. So I sat down in my Pew again, and cried bitterly: And I cried in my Spirit to the Lord, We are all Thieves, we are all Thieves; we have taken the Scriptures in Word, and know nothing of them in our selves. (Fell 1690: 235)

The early Quaker impulse was to reject anything that lead to an inauthentic faith, to call attention to the "thievery" inherent within Christianity in their time, and return to the simple inward possession of God's Spirit. This striving for authentic Christianity led Quakers to strip away much of what institutional Christianity considered essential at that time. Fox's experience that Christ could speak and lead him directly outside the ritual and hierarchies of the church was radical and revolutionary (Dandelion 2007: 21) and led to the creation of a movement that would become a fully participatory church.

Resistance: Ministry and Manner Critique

Quakers did not just want a highly invested and authentic spiritual experience of the Inward Christ, they wanted their practice of Christianity to reflect that conviction even when it meant going against the sanctioned interpretations of "Orthodox" Christianity. Their desire, like those within participatory culture, was to be "unshackled by the contrivances of society" (Duncombe 1997: 32). Two of the most radical places early Quakers challenged Christianity were in their rejection of paid clergy and the dismissal of the necessity of outward sacraments—I will only consider the former in depth here.

In a context where the clerical class was known for exercising a monopoly on religion and abusing their state-sponsored power, early Friends extended the New Testament idea of the priesthood of all believers to its extreme by rejecting the role of clergy all together (1 Pet 2:1–10). Rejecting the legitimacy of the established priesthood, early Quakerism had no ordination process, pastor or priest. What made a minister was not training nor lineage but an authentic transformation of the heart by the Inward Light of Christ and what he or she produced with their life. Fox referred to paid clergy as "hireling" ministers. A firebrand preacher, Fox challenged these "professors of faith" whose ministry came from academic credentials, which did not render them true ministers of the gospel:

> As I was walking in a field on a First-day morning, the Lord opened unto me that being bred at Oxford or Cambridge was not enough to fit and qualify men to be ministers of Christ; and I stranged at it because it was the common belief of people. But I saw clearly, as the Lord opened it to me, and was satisfied, and admired the goodness of the Lord who had opened this thing

unto me that morning, which struck at Priest Stephens's ministry, namely, that to be bred at Oxford or Cambridge was not enough to make a man fit to be a minister of Christ. So that which opened in me, I saw, struck at the priest's ministry. (Fox et al. 1985: 7)

Fox took it upon himself then to travel around to various churches and speak to Christians—whether from the front of a "steeplehouse" during a service or out in the field—and tell the people, "Did not the apostle say to believe that they needed no man to teach them, but as the anointing teacheth them?" and again, "I brought them Scriptures, and told them there was an anointing within man to teach him, and that the Lord would teach his people himself" (ibid., 7–8). This teaching cut to the heart of not just the teaching of the church, but its very power over people. As long as religion lay in the hands of the powerful, the people would always be at the mercy of a passive, consumptive faith.

In his *Apology* (1678), Robert Barclay chastises the clergy of the day, calling them "Greedy dogs which never have enough. Shepherds who feed themselves and not the flock, eating the fat and clothing themselves with the wool, making merchandise of souls" (Barclay 2002: 289). He outlines five main areas of criticism that early Friends had with ordained ministers:

(1) "[They] have no immediate call from Christ, to whom the leading and motion of the Spirit is not reckoned necessary. . ." but instead "were ordained by wicked and ungodly men;" (2) do not believe that the grace of God is necessary; (3) do not wait for the God's spirit but act in their own wisdom and natural strength from "what they have gathered and stolen from the letter of the Scripture and other books;" (4) "are such as strive and contend for superiority, and claim precedency over one another, affecting and ambitiously seeking after the forementioned things— such as being "distinguished from the rest by their garments and large phylacteries, . . . [seeking] greetings in the marketplaces . . . chief seats in the synagogues . . . [desiring] to be called of men Master. . ." (5) "are such as not having freely received, will not freely give, but are covetous, doing that which they ought not for filthy lucre's sake, as to preach for hire and divine for money, and look for their gain from their quarter, and prepare war against such as put not into their mouths." (Ibid., 287–89)

Barclay's challenge leveled against ordained clergy was scathing, but was motivated by a conviction that Quaker ministers be people who were immediately called and set forth by Christ, ministers of grace and love, ministers who were humble, who gave gospel ministry freely and under obvious guidance and direction of the Spirit (ibid., 287–89).

> We are for a holy, spiritual, pure and living ministry where the ministers are both called, qualified and ordered, acted and influenced in all the steps of their ministry by the Spirit of Good; which being wanting, we judge cease to be the ministers of Christ. Anything otherwise was to uphold a fruitless and dead ministry; of which (alas!) we have seen the fruits in the most part of their churches. (Ibid., 289)

Cutting away the tools of those in power reversed the role of faith in peoples' lives. Christendom in the hands of the empire was a ritualized and consumptive faith, one that was used to create classification and control the masses. By stripping priest and sacrament away, Quakers were able to counter with a more participatory experience of faith. Without clergy or sacrament the gathered Quaker community waited upon the Lord in silence—sometimes for hours—to speak through individuals present. If Jesus was to teach the people himself, then they would have to wait and listen until he did so. The rejection of ordained clergy allowed Quakerism to be fully theocentric, Jesus Christ was the head of the church, he was present among the gathered assembly, teaching and leading them. Communion and baptism were not outward affairs to be controlled by the hirelings but were inward experiences not limited to a church service. As Dandelion describes it:

> They were unnecessary and might indeed get in the way of people experiencing the inward sacramental state. For Fox, the injunction in 1 Corinthians 11:26 to break the bread until the Lord came again had been superseded by his coming. Indeed, Fox went on to say that Christians had already been called to a different supper, that of the inward marriage supper of the Lamb described in Revelation 3:23. (Dandelion 2007: 30)

Christians gathered in silence, with no clergy and no sacraments, waiting for Jesus to lead them to speak was truly a radical alternative worship, if somewhat austere. But for Friends, this stripped down practice of worship was not a new denominational style, nor was it "an alternative liturgy . . . [it was] the *end* of all worldly forms of worship" (Gwyn 2006: 124). Even the experience of worship was itself a resistance to the conventions of the day:

> The meetings were strongly emotional, filled with dread, punctuated at times with the inchoate sounds of sobbing, groaning, sighing, or impromptu "singing in the Spirit." These were "boundary experiences," events that stopped the world, interrupting one's sense of life's normality and the self-evidence of social conventions. (Ibid., 122–23)

Friends' understanding of ministry and worship reveals ways they reinterpreted Scripture that sought to resist the cultural practices of their day.

Finally, one last example demonstrates the Quaker stripping away of ordinations and ordinances could be called the Quaker "manner critique." If authentic resistance is a life without artifice or hypocrisy, that leads one to cut "through conventions of manners, norms, and communication" (Duncombe 1997: 32), then early Quakers did this by their refusal to doff their hats, take oaths, take titles, use the pagan names of the days of the week, and participate in religious ceremonies—this was also a result of their understanding of classism as well as Truth (Barbour and Frost 1988: 40–41). Early Friends challenged religious artifices and rituals as well as the manners, norms, and conventions of their society because they believed they either revealed a lack of authentic faith or led people to hypocrisy. As Fox wrote in his journal:

> Bring people off from Jewish ceremonies, and from heathenish fables, and from men's inventions and windy doctrines . . . and all their beggarly rudiments, with their schools and colleges for making ministers of Christ, who are indeed ministers of their own making but not of Christ's; and from all their *images and crosses*, and *sprinkling of infants*, with all their *holy days* (so called) and all their *vain traditions*, which they had gotten up since the apostle's days, which the Lord's power was against, and in the dread and authority thereof I was moved to declare against them all, and against all that preached and not freely [as in those who did not require tithes], as being such as had not received freely from Christ. (Fox et al. 1985: 36; italics added)

Here Fox points out things he believes need to be stripped away because of the inauthenticity they created within Christianity. He then repeats the same formula again, this time attacking images and vain traditions, which "the Lord's power was against." These worked against the entire movement of the Spirit, which Fox believed was to create free, unencumbered, and unmediated communion with Christ.

Following this same formula of manner-critique, Fox explains his initial reasoning behind refusing to remove his hat in public. This acts as a constructive critique and response for the authentic transformation Fox called for:

> Moreover when the Lord sent me forth into the world, he forbade me to put off my hat to any high or low; and I was required to "thee" and "thou" all men and women, without any respect to rich or poor, great or small. And as I travelled up and down, I was not to bid people "good morrow" or "good evening," neither might I bow or scrape with my leg to any one; and this made the sects and professions rage . . . they could not bear to hear it, and the hat-honour, because I could not put off my hat to them, it set them all into a rage. (Fox et al. 1985: 36)

Fox's manner-critique challenges the false-selves of his contemporaries and of society as a whole. He was convinced it was the Lord who "showed me that it was an honour below, which he would lay in the dust. . .an honour which proud flesh looked for, but sought not the honour which came from God only" (ibid., 37). In this way, not only does he reveal through a kind of public theater the hypocrisy of the professors, but discovers through their rage and anger, the evidence proving, "that they were not true believers" (ibid.). The goal for the early Quaker movement was to rebuild the church in a way that those within it were authentic resisters to passive, ritualistic Christianity.

Production: Publishers of Truth

The move from passivity to production can be seen not only in the convincement narratives and challenges to the manners of the time, but also in active production of new cultural artifacts. If participation entails the shift from consumption to production, then early Quaker practices of publication and traveling in ministry mirrors DIY communities of today. From the earliest beginnings of the movement, Quakers were, as they called themselves, Publishers of Truth. Friends harnessed the power of the printing press to produce a flurry of pamphlets, books, tracts, letters, and broadsheets. Some estimate that between when Quakerism began in 1652 and 1725, there were up to four million Quaker publications in print (Russell 1942: 166). In the early years, the practice of submitting all work to Fox prior to publication made him the unofficial censor, but in time he set up a committee to formally oversee this work: the Second-day Morning Meeting. The Second-day Morning Meeting met regularly to handle what they understood to be two interrelated things: the organization of traveling (local) missionaries—so they would not all travel to the same place—and supervising the various publications of Friends (1942: 137). The integration of these two aspects of early Quaker ministry demonstrates that, as Elbert Russell notes, "Their literature in all its forms remained by and large a part of their missionary effort, a part of their 'witness' and proclamation of religious truth" (ibid., 167).

Another salient feature of early Publishers of Truth was whose voices were heard through the printed page and what was written about. The first and earliest authors were those men and women in leadership; they used the presses to send their message both within England and beyond. They wrote epistles, addresses, and brief proclamations of their message; sent replies to their accusers; and made use of the ample time many of them had in prison to write even more feverishly (ibid., 80–81).[14] "They spread their message by religious exposition, theological argument and by accounts of personal experiences and reports of controversies" (ibid., 81).

These authors were typically, at least in the early part of the movement, of little education. Yet they wrote with their own missionary fervor. In the earlier years (1650s and 1660s) a loose, personal, and fiery zeal prevailed:

> In general they adopted the sharp controversial tone and denunciatory style common to churchmen, Puritans and many of the sects. They showed the same or even greater vigor, assurance and missionary zeal. They used mainly the theological and religious vocabulary of the Puritans and mystics, although the Friends often used it in a peculiar sense. . . . It was also in part redeemed by the vital experience and glowing earnestness behind the verbiage. (Ibid., 81)

Because their actions often circumvented the authoritative positions of the religious and political elite, production of this nature was often done to their own detriment and persecution (ibid., 59). Russell reports that, "In spite of some arrests for owning, circulating or selling Quaker

---

14. Russell remarks that their production from jail was so efficient that it became standard policy to refuse ink and paper to Quaker prisoners (Russell, *The History of Quakerism*, 81).

publications, and in a few cases the seizure or destruction of offending presses, there was a large output of printed matter."[15]

The Quaker journal was another genre of writing peculiar to Quakers that dominated Quaker publications. As Russell argues:

> The Quaker "journals," as their autobiographies are usually called, are the distinctive Quaker literary form. They almost created a new and distinctive type of literature. This is natural since the essence of Quakerism is the individual experience of God and spirit truth. It finds its highest expression in the personal life rather than in theologies or institutions. (Ibid., 172)

These journals were published in an evangelistic tone, meant to help draw the readers into their experiences and invite readers into their own personal transformation: "The motive of the writer of the autobiographies is usually evangelistic—to commend the Quaker faith by the story of the author's 'convincement,' experience, sufferings, providential deliverances, labors in the ministry, and attainment of inward power and peace" (ibid.).

Margaret Fell (1614–1702) not only used her wealth, home[16], and her social position in society for the benefit of the Friends, she was also a prototypical Publisher of Truth (Wallace 2006: 101). "She supported ministers on an international scale with everything from pamphlets and epistles, to advice, medications, funds, and moral support" (ibid.).[17] Fell was a prolific author, writing upwards of sixteen books and count-

---

15. In 1662, the Licensing Act was passed to control what was published and keep nonconformist works from being printed (ibid., 166). Offending publishers were open to severe penalties. "Often Quaker printers were arrested and their stocks and presses confiscated. To reduce the risk of total loss in this way a book was sometimes printed in sections by different printers. Usually the printer's name was omitted, although it is boldly given in a surprising number of cases" (ibid.).

16. Her home, Swarthmor Hall, was a central hub, clearing house, and coordinating center at the beginning of the Quaker movement (Fox and Glines, *Undaunted Zeal*, 5).

17. It should also be noted that Fell created the Kendal Fund, to support missionaries (ibid., 235–36). The Kendal Fund "was raised to . . . help the work, and it was disbursed through Swarthmoor. The expenses of the 'Publishers of Truth' were paid where necessary: they were furnished with clothes and Bibles; and food and bedding were supplied to those in prison. Quaker books were bought and distributed. The [missionary] campaigns in London and the south of England in 1654–1657 were largely financed by this fund" (Russell, *The History of Quakerism*, 74). See also "The 'Kendal Fund' For Air to Quaker Preachers Travelling or Jailed" (Barbour and Roberts, *Early Quaker Writings*, 474–76).

less epistles, political tracts, and theological pamphlets in her lifetime.[18] While she was the most prolific, Fell was not the only Quaker woman to show zeal in publishing truth. Bonnelyn Kunze reports that "Quaker women produced about 171 published documents between 1641–1700. Of this total, Margaret Fell's published output in this period represented thirteen percent" (Kunze 1994: 131).[19]

> Her prolific correspondence, often with complete strangers, gave pastoral support and theological insight to those working in isolation. It was Margaret Fell who in 1660 penned the first comprehensive outline of the Quaker "testimony" against bearing arms. (Dandelion 2007: 18)

In her writings Fell often showed a peculiar sensitivity to other groups of people[20] and she exemplified a unique invitational approach to individuals she often disagreed with. It is of interest to note what Fell included in these letters to strangers. Revealing her theology of mission, Fell constantly begins her letters quoting John 1:9, "The true light, which enlightens everyone, was coming into the world," in hopes to appeal to "that of God" in the person she corresponded with—surprisingly those she addressed this way are often her opponents. A good example of this is found in a letter to Oliver Cromwell, the military leader of the English Commonwealth and the one ultimately responsible for countless Quaker persecutions: "Friend above words I am moved of the Lord to write a warning to thee from the Lord God of Heaven and Earth that thou harken to the Light of God in thy conscience, which is the Light of Christ:

---

18. Glines suggests that more than five hundred of Fell's letters have gone unpublished (Fox and Glines, *Undaunted Zeal*, xvii).

19. Kunze offers a detailed breakdown of Fell's output: "of the 171 documents, thirty-one were calls to repentance, fifty-four were statements of religious doctrine, eighteen were polemical tracts against public officials and ministers, ten were epistles reporting on acting of women's meetings, and sixteen were complaints of persecution" (Kunze, *Margaret Fell*, 131–32). Garman suggests, in her introduction to "Hidden in Plain Sight," that the number publications by women was over two-hundred in the first fifty years (Garman, *Hidden in Plain Sight*, 3).

20. Another area of exploration for implication of mission is Fell's letters to the Jews. "She wrote five tracts addressed to them, the first in 1656, *For Maasseh Ben Israel, The Call of the Jews,* and the last in 1677, *The Daughter of Sion Awakened*. In her frequent scriptural references, she tactfully stays with the Old Testament" (Fox and Glines, *Undaunted Zeal*, 255). In these letters, she appeals to the "Universal Seed of God," (ibid., 391) and in a letter to Jewish Rabbis, she utilizes the Quaker practice of queries, which all draw on the Hebrew Bible (mainly Isaiah) and make no mention of Jesus Christ (ibid., 183).

who doth enlighten everyone that comes into the world, that by it thou may be guided, lead, and taught. And now is the mighty day of the Lord come and coming, wherein he is teaching his people himself, by his own immediate light and power which is eternal" (Fox and Glines 2003: 36).

This is not the exception to the rule for Fell's writings, it is one of the prominent ways in which she corresponded with people. For Fell, what was important was the invitation, the participative drawing out of the Light within people, which she believed to already to be at work in the world. She believed that the Light had come to enlighten even their greatest adversaries as well. Margaret Fell was a prime example of how early Friends refused to passively accept the terms of Christianity, instead they dismantled and rebuilt something new and authentic in its place.

Conclusion

Early Quakers were a participatory renewal movement in the church in the way they exhibited authentic resistance to consumerism by challenging professors of faith, rejecting practices that had become shrouded in legalism and prompted hypocrisy, and by setting forward a participative vision of Christianity by producing something new in its place.

Open Work: Inclusion, Discernment and Gospel Order

Open Work, informed by the elements of collective intelligence and decentralized authority, is the third and final element of the participatory rubric. In the Quaker community, knowledge and power operates under a decentralized paradigm. This kind of decentralization is seen in three ways: first, John Bellers' idea of a college of industry is investigated as a prototype of a utopian, participatory community of shared practice; second, the inclusive, many-voiced nature of Quakerism is considered with regards to the role of women in early Quakerism; and third, the concept of Gospel Order is considered as a theological framework for a decentralized paradigm of authority.

Creating a College of Industry

First, if Lévy is correct in thinking that knowledge is geared toward creating an "achievable utopia," and "collective intelligence communities are apprenticing communities, where adherents gain the skills necessary for the thriving of that community," then the second generation Friend John Bellars (1654–1725) was an early proponent of creating such a community. He called these communities "colleges of industry" or workhouses. He proposed forming communities that employed the poor and educated their children (Bellers and Fry 1935: 49).[21] He drew on biblical sources to find "patterns of moral authority" and based much of his ideas on passages such as Luke 16:19–31, Matthew 25:31–46, and Acts 17:23–28 (Abbott 2006: 24).[22] He also wrote on a broad array of topics such as "world government, vocational training, cooperative communities and heath" (ibid.).

The idea for his college of industry came out of a concern to create a community where the poor would gain the skills needed to thrive and keep the poor from being trapped in vice. When Bellars was twenty-five years old, he was appointed overseer of a Quaker fund that helped to employ the poor (Bellers and Fry 1935: 6), and it was most likely that experience that initially drew him to such work. While the yearly meeting and many of the Quakers who were exposed to Bellers ideas were impressed with his work, there was only one workhouse formed in his lifetime: the Clerkenwell workhouse in 1731. In that house approximately thirty inmates made their living, including the elderly, young boys, and pensioners (ibid., 9). They learned various occupations such as shoemaking and spinning cotton and wool, while the children were employed to make items such as mops and yarn out of what was produced elsewhere in the house (ibid., 10). Unfortunately, over time, conflict between the inmates and "inefficient organization militated against success" (ibid.).

While his views were never widely adopted, Bellers pressed on, trying to formulate in ever-clearer terms how this utopian vision could be realized.[23] He believed that "the Life of a Man is of greater Value with

---

21. From 1743 a list of queries from Philadelphia Yearly Meeting includes the question: "Are the poor taken care of, are their children put to school and the apprenticed out to Friends, and do Friends apprentice their children only to Friends?" (Barbour and Frost, *The Quakers*, 109).

22. Interestingly, he appeals to the Lord's Prayer for his ethics when he writes: "How sincerely can we say the Lord's Prayer, Forgive us our Trespasses as we forgive them which Trespass against us; when for the loss, possibly of less than 20 Shillings, we Prosecute a man to Death? Would it not be more natural and agreeable with our Prayers to God, to have Compassion on our deluded Fellow Creatures" (Bellers and Fry, *John Bellers*, 76).

23. Although Bellers was picked up by a number of socialists, including Karl Marx

God than many Pounds, and ought to be so with Men" (Palmer 1996: 65). Bellers believed these communities of shared practice could embody the Quaker "passion for the worth of every individual, putting into actual practice the Quaker doctrine of the divine light inspiring every human heart" (Bellers and Fry, 1935: 20). This is because the church had the responsibility to care for the poor and create opportunities for them to gain skills and employment so that they were "not demoralized by idleness" (1935: 21). He thought with the proper foresight and divine guidance, "Utopia could quite easily be made a reality, and earth be made a heaven" (ibid.). But in order to do this, the rich were going to have to take responsibility for their exploitation of the poor and so create opportunities for the poor to make a "plentiful living":

> As a good and plentiful Living must be the Poor's Encouragement; so their Increase, the Advantage of the Rich; Without them they cannot be Rich; for if one had a hundred thousand Acres of Land, and as many Pounds in Money, and as many Cattle, without a Labourer, what would the Rich-Man be, but a Labourer? As as the Labourers make Men rich, so the more Labourers, there will be the more rich Men (where there is Land to employ and provide for them.) Therefore, I think it is the Interest of the Rich to encourage the honest Labourers Marrying at full Age; but by the want of it, it seems to me the World is out of Frame, and not understanding its own Interest. The Labour of the Poor being the Mines of the Rich. (Bellers and Fry 1935: 38)

As Fry notes, Bellers clearly "believed in leveling up the poor and not leveling down the rich" (Bellers and Fry 1935: 18).

This vision of utopia was rooted in a biblical conviction that if both the rich and poor could work together out of a concern for one another, they could build a witness to society "as a *Pattern and Example* to the rest of the Nation, by which you may shew forth the more the Christianity of your Faith, by the Virtuous Works that come from it, of which Love and Charity is the Chief" (ibid., 34; emphasis added).[24] Bellers's utopian vision sought to create an alternative vision of society rooted in the teachings of Jesus. It was a participative vision that involved both the

---

who quoted him in the footnotes of *Das Kapital* calling him a "veritable phenomenon" (Palmer, "Religion and Ethics in the Thought of John Bellers," 61).

24. Note the overlap between what Bellars says here and George Fox's challenge to Friends to "Be patterns, be examples," and the "answering that of God."

rich and poor sharing knowledge, skill and power together. In the college of industry, dialogue and a mutual concern was fostered.

For Bellars, mission clearly meant creating communities that carried out God's work on earth and embodied primitive Christianity:[25] "What is prayed for of God above, men must be instrumental to accomplish here below, there being few, if any, who believe He will make His angels visible to do it" (ibid., 22). There is an underlying theology of participation in this utopian vision inasmuch as

> God, to Bellers, is the Creator; but man can play a role in helping to complete his creation. The work of making the lot of mankind more comfortable, for instance, "will be instrumental in God's hand in finishing his Creation (Man being the Head of It)." (Palmer 1996: 64)

This connects to knowledge as decentralized networks inasmuch as collective intelligence also fosters dialogue, apprenticeship and communities where mutuality of learning and teaching are bonded together.

Inclusion, Margaret Fell and Swarthmoor Hall

Within their male dominated Christian culture, Quakers resisted the status quo by forming an alternative leadership structure that created space for more than just educated white men to be in charge. By rejecting ordination and the role of clergy, and by arguing that what was central to Christianity was an inward encounter of the Inward Christ, early Quakers restructured how the church functioned. That restructuring became an "open work" that relied on the participation of the whole group, men and women, young and old, educated and uneducated, poor and rich. This was a movement that not only said it was non-hierarchical or rather followed under the headship of Jesus, but formed an architecture that necessitated that non-hierarchy.

Quaker women were publishers of truth, many argued for theological reasons why women should be able to speak in public, and their

---

25. "The Poor thus in a College, will be a Community something like the Example of Primitive Christianity, that lived in common [cf. Acts 2], and the Power that did attend it, bespeaks its Excellency; but considering the Constitution of Mankind that have Estates (but it's not so with the Poor) it was none of the least Miracles of that Age, and so abated as other Miracles did (Bellers and Fry, *John Bellars*, 47). This is point number seven in a series of eight points Bellers spells out as "Some of the Advantages the Poor Collegians will have" (ibid., 45–47).

writings today are seen as the beginnings of feminist theology (Garman 1996: xii). Women were at the forefront of shaping the Quaker movement and its leadership. George Fox met Elizabeth Hooten in 1647, who became the first women minister in the movement (ibid., 1). Hooten was a former Baptist preacher who became one of Fox's earliest allies and mentor's as an older and more experienced minister. Later in 1660, she was whipped out of Boston three times (Dandelion 2007:50), and died on a missionary journey to the Caribbean with Fox (Gwyn 2006: 130). A statue of Mary Dyer still stands in Boston, honoring one of the first four Quakers martyred in the Colonies (1659/60). Many other women were formidable missionaries and Publishers of Truth in early Quaker history.[26]

There are many things to be said about Margaret Fell's leadership within early Quakerism; she was and is still known as the Mother of Quakerism. However, Quaker decentralization is symbolized in the image of Margaret Fell's home, Swarthmoor Hall. Swarthmoor , in Ulverston in Northeast England, acted as a network of activity for early Quaker correspondence and support (Wallace 2006b: 277)—a manor, whose Lord, Judge Thomas Fell, Margaret's first husband, was not even a Quaker. It was his wife who single-handedly re-created Swarthmoor into the early Quaker hub that held records, put up traveling ministers, hosted worship, and was a general base of operation for those coming and going throughout the north of England. And while Swarthmoor was by no means the only hub of Quaker activity, it was an essential one, run by a powerful Quaker leader.[27]

A further example of women's leadership and the mutual apprenticing that goes hand in hand with collective intelligence is symbolized in women's meetings (Garman 1996: xiv). These meetings began in 1659 as a separate space where Quaker women could not only handle the business of caring for Friends under persecution, but also apprentice one another in the skills necessary for leadership. As Garman writes, while "The creation of these separate 'Women's Meetings' caused controversy among early Friends, [it] also provided women with opportunities to develop their skills in organization and administration" (ibid., 1).

26. Doug Gwyn remarks that there was great involvement of women and challenge of gender roles within the early movement (Gwyn, *Covenant Crucified*, 111).

27. For instance, Elbert Russell shows that as Friends moved into the southern part of England (1655) they set up a second base of operations in a tavern called the Bull and Mouth in the heart of London (Russell, *The History of Quakerism*, 35).

Gospel Order

In the section on Remix, I referred to Robert Barclay's articulation of a Quaker understanding of the Spirit's centrality to understanding and interpreting Scripture. By placing the authority of the church in the Spirit rather than in the biblical text, early Quakers were able to form a decentralized polity, one that did not rely on the authority of one biblical expert, but on a community of discernment. In another of Barclay's works, *The Anarchy of the Ranters* (1676), he set out to establish a vision for authority that rejected both the "unrestrained individualism of the Ranters and the absolute authoritarianism of the Roman church." In the book Barclay demonstrated the Quaker conviction that "the basis of church authority [is] in the manifest presence, leading and authority of the Holy Spirit, which was common ground for all Friends" (Russell 1942: 151). This basis, rooted in a community of discernment, under the guidance and leading of the Spirit was called Gospel Order.

Gospel Order names the architecture that structures the theocentric, participative organization that holds Quakerism together. Gospel Order is the ecclesiastical system, or polity, that George Fox, Margaret Fell, and Richard Farnworth (and a few others) constructed in the 1660s in response to a number of controversies that took place among Friends including the Nayler controversy (Dandelion 2007: 48).[28]

In 1667–68, Fox and Quaker leadership set about the work of establishing a networked style of leadership. It was then that they organized men and women's monthly meetings where business was conducted through a consensus model of decision-making. These meetings then connected to quarterly meetings, which represented a larger geographical area and took on business that affected their region. These meetings were overseen by a yearly meeting throughout England (Gwyn 2000: 352). Fox initiated a system that placed authority in the headship of Christ rather than in any one person, gender or group of people; it allowed the participative community to thrive without any experts. It fostered ownership over decisions made, inclusion of all who were present to voice their

---

28. Richard Farnsworth refers to it as *Gospel Liberty* in his 1664 tract, where he argues that God gives liberty to all of humanity to live in harmony with him—or to choose not to. But God also gives liberty to Christians who "stand fast in the liberating power of a conscience tender toward God" (Gwyn, *Covenant Crucified*, 259). As Gwyn argues, this view of Gospel Liberty is one that forms the very purpose of Quakerism: "So there is a teleology, a meaningful goal to human existence: to live in harmony, justice, righteousness, and peace, i.e, in a way that glorifies the Creator" (ibid., 259).

leadings on the subjects under consideration, and operated as networked paradigm in which knowledge was spread throughout the community and Christ was able to guide the group through a process of listening and corporate discernment. For Fox, "True government is the power of God working through visible, ordered bodies of those who wait upon the Lord for guidance" (ibid.).

Early Friends demonstrated the theology behind this regimen in a number of writings. First, George Fox:

> Then they act like spiritual holy men and women, and come to be members of the church of Christ. Then a spiritual care cometh upon the elders in Christ, that all the members walk in Christ, in his light, grace, spirit, and truth, that they may adorn the confession and profession of Christ, and see that all walk in the *order* of the holy spirit, and the everlasting *gospel* of peace, life, and salvation. This *order* keeps out of confusion; for the *gospel* of peace, the power of God, was before confusion was. All the heirs of the *gospel* are heirs of its *order*, and are in this *gospel* which brings life and immortality to light in them, by which all men and women may see their work and service in it, to look after the poor widows and fatherless, to see that nothing be lacking, and that all honour the Lord in their lives and conversations. (Fox et al. 1985: 365)

And from Isaac Pennington:

> The gospel is free; the grace and mercy thereof free; the spirit a free spirit (freely given of God, and freely ministering for God); the church a spiritual building, built in the freedom and liberty of the life of the spirit; the order and government of the church is from and in the same free spirit, guiding a people whom God makes willing in the day of his power; the maintenance of the ministry a free maintenance; the whole obedience and worship free, in the free spirit, and in the truth which is begotten in the heart by the free spirit. The head of this church is Christ, the living spirit, who hath appointed none to be head under him here on earth, nor hath given power to any to make any laws concerning his kingdom, or the government thereof; concerning his ministry, or the maintenance thereof. (Is it not thus? Doth not the least child of light see it to be thus?) But the church of England was a church built by force; settled by force; her ministers maintained by force; her order, unity, uniformity, and government, forcible; and the free pure spirit of life can have no scope in her, but according to the wills of her rulers, teachers,

> and people: if it move otherwise, if it appear otherwise, it is sure to be nick-named and persecuted. O England! England! can God always suffer these things? Will not his hand at length be stretched forth against thee?
>
> Sixthly, What kind of order was set up in this church? Was it the true gospel order? Was it the order of Christ's spirit, whereby the carnal wisdom of man might be quenched, and his spirit have scope? Or was it a carnal order, whereby the carnal wisdom, learning, knowledge, and arts of man might have scope, and the spirit in its motions be quenched? (Pennington 1681: 337)

What we find in these passages and others like them is an appeal to a new ordering of life for those who come under the guidance of the Holy Spirit. It marks a shift from a life rooted in the old order, under the first Adam, to life re-ordered under the reality of Jesus' resurrection. This re-ordering of life under what Paul calls the new creation holds implications, as we will see below, from women in leadership, to Quaker nonviolence, to the very ordering of Christ's church as Pennington argues. Pennington draws a contrast between the ordering of a church that finds its basis in the free Gospel and a church that is based on experts, uniformity and force. Quakers saw Gospel Order in contrast to this kind polity and instead set out to organize a church rooted in the wisdom of the Spirit.

What was put in place was an alternative model, one that by its very existence was a witness and a critique of other models of church organization. In contrast to expert driven, top-down models of church, this decentralized community of discernment operated on mutual accountability, regular meetings, and waiting upon the Lord for guidance. In this model, no priests, bishops, or presbyters are needed, only a participative community practicing discernment. In other words, instead of doing away with priests altogether, Quakerism insists that the entire community takes on the function of priests:

> The church is a royal priesthood . . . the priestly function of Christ is manifested among Friend, not with any priestly liturgical office (since the outward celebration of the sacraments had been superseded by the strong prophetic listening as a pattern of worship), but in the everyday life of the community. The church offered spiritual sacrifices to God through its holy and righteous living. On the human level, the community was both priest and sacrifice. In Fox's mind the priestly dimension of Christ's

present work was incarnated (in part) by the community living Gospel Order. (Cronk 1991: 19)

The very structure of the church, operating out of Gospel Order, was to be itself a witness to the world about the alternative possibilities inherent within a life under the order of the Spirit.

Quakers exhibited knowledge as an open work in the way they sought to form communities of shared skill and knowledge, as seen in John Bellars College of Industry, in their inclusion of many voices, and by their organizing under the power of God's Spirit as represented by Gospel Order. Finally, by practicing the alternative practices mentioned above, but specifically Gospel Order, early Quakers embodied an "achievable utopia" within their context. These practices of resistance and possibility set Friends a part as a participatory movement.

CONCLUSION

Because of the way early Quakerism practiced remix, productive resistance, building an open work, in ways that embodied Gospel Order, early Quakers exhibited the qualities of a convergent and participatory community. Early Quakerism was not unlike many fan movements of today, breathing new life into the traditional texts and practices of Christianity in ways that challenged the "authorized" interpretations and powers of their time. Early Quakerism was a realizable utopia, a prototype, or as Jenkins says, "dress rehearsal for the way culture might operate in the future." It may not have stayed that way, as is often the case. But at its core, early Quakerism is best understood in light of my convergent model, demonstrating that it was a vibrant participatory renewal movement of the seventeenth century.

CHAPTER 6

The Convergent Model and Freedom Friends Church

IN 2008 AND 2009, I undertook the project of researching Quaker meetings that could be compared to emerging churches as outlined by Eddie Gibbs and Ryan Bolger (2005). In my research process, I used snowball sampling, a form of convenience sampling used in qualitative research that is based upon having contact with a small group of people who help form the basis of the initial study (Bryman 2008: 184–185). This ultimately led to researching one small Quaker meeting in Salem, Oregon in greater detail. Freedom Friends Church was an attractive option because of their reputation and uniqueness in the Quaker world and willingness to work with me. There are both strengths and weaknesses involved in using just one congregation. The key strength of focusing on one meeting is the ability to go deep into the research process with Freedom Friends allowing time for face-to-face interviews with people, investigating their website and founding documents, corresponding with congregants over email, and reading through their Faith and Practice.

The main weakness in using one meeting is that the research is based on a non-probability sample (ibid., 168), thus, generalizability of this case study is not an option. However, this is not a problem within the context of this book. The point of drawing on the research provided below is not so much to generalize findings about Freedom Friends Church as it is to demonstrate the usefulness of the model of participatory convergence. In this chapter, I argue that Freedom Friends Church is an example of Quakers putting the texts and practices of their tradition in dialogue with their context in ways that remix, resist and decentralize authority, thus creating an alternative social community that seeks to bring renewal within the Quaker tradition.

TRADITION AND CONTEXT

The rise of postmodernity in the West poses both problems and possibilities for the Friends church. Friends of every branch face challenges associated with epistemological foundationalism, fragmented identities, and the effects of consumerism on faith. Quaker theologian John Punshon, in *Reasons for Hope*, describes the future of Quakerism as being connected to the retrieval and reinterpretation of its tradition within this new postmodern setting:

> A postmodern church will not relinquish its claims to truth, but it will be able to lead its members to it by means of experience and tradition, rather than argument. It may well have more in common with the early Church than it has with the Church of more recent times. (Punshon 2001: 351)

Punshon's central argument is that the practices and theology of the Friends Church are well suited for the postmodern condition. The Quaker distinctives offer the church reasons for hope,

> the declining numbers of Friends Church can be explained by its failure to find and occupy a distinct niche; [and] a powerful and accessible niche is waiting to be found in the historic character and practices that make Friends distinctive. (Ibid.)

Freedom Friends Church is a Quaker meeting that demonstrates Punshon's point. Started in 2004 by three women—Peggy Morrison,[1] Alivia Biko and Jane Wheeler—Freedom Friends Church intentionally began as an attempt to create a new expression within Quakerism, one that "highlighted [their] deep resonances with traditional Quakerism and [their] unique interpretation of how those traditions could be lived out in a post-modern age" (Freedom Friends Church 2009: 1). Eight years later, Freedom Friends has garnered attention from Quakers around the world and established itself as one of the first meetings to label itself "convergent" (Daniels 2012: 136).

---

1. During the editing of this book, Peggy Senger Morrison's name was changed to Peggy Morrison. The main text will reflect this change.

Using the model of participatory convergence, I demonstrate how Freedom Friends Church in Salem, Oregon is a Quaker meeting seeking to bring about renewal by drawing on its tradition in dialogue with its postmodern context in ways that remix, resist and decentralize while creating a participatory and newly formed expression of community within Quakerism. First, a short history and description of Freedom Friends is put forward to put them in their Quaker and cultural context. Second, I will apply the participatory rubric to Freedom Friends and investigate whether or not they could be labeled a participatory renewal movement within Quakerism.

The Birth of Freedom Friends Church

Two Quaker women, Peggy Morrison and Alivia Biko, met in 1997. Morrison, a recorded Quaker minister, and Biko a well-respected and very active member in her local and yearly meetings, had similar dreams for starting a church that was Quaker, Christ-centered, and welcoming of sexual diversity. Their dreams predated their meeting, and it was not until 1999—when they began traveling in ministry together—that they realized their shared dream. They knew that they were to do the project together, but considerable time passed before they felt clarity to move forward.

Everything changed in the fall of 2002 when the vision was solidified for Morrison during a trip to Northern California. While there, Morrison visited a worship service at Glide United Methodist Church, a predominately African American church located in the Skid Row of San Francisco, with her friends Pam Calvert and Helen Haug. Glide was originally a small, socially minded congregation that now has an operating budget in the millions and uses their resources to serve the poor. Calvert described Glide as being

> A very enthusiastic, music based, welcoming ministry. The founding pastor is Cecil Williams. . . . He's really sort of created a church for all people. It's a big, enthusiastic, music-based, gay-friendly . . . praise church without a whole lot of heavy theology, and there's no alter call. (Calvert 2009)

On their way back from the service, while riding the BART, Morrison heard God speak to her. Calvert recalled the experience, "On the way back, on BART, Jesus talked to her and said, 'Okay, your job is to go back to Salem and do that as a Friends church in Salem.'" Morrison explained, "I 'slipped away' from our conversation and asked Christ why we couldn't have a Quaker Glide. He said, 'Go ahead.' I said, 'When?' He said, 'Get started'" (Morrison 2009a). Interestingly, Biko had a similar experience at the same time that day:

> [Alivia] was in meeting [for worship] at Salem Friends Meeting in Salem that day. She received in the silence: 'Be prepared to do settled ministry. You aren't going to be traveling anymore.' We talked on the phone within an hour of the messages that occurred at approximately the same time. We started praying, thinking, and planning then. (2009a)

The point was not to make an exact replica of Glide; given their tradition and context, this was not the desired path, but what Morrison saw that day was an example of how a church could be faithful to both its Christian tradition and open to reinterpretations of that tradition in new contexts:

> Obviously we weren't trying to replicate Glide. We could never get a band that rocking, and bands have to be all or nothing. What we were trying to replicate was the Christianity and inclusion—that I think we have done, but with less dancing—[that's] the pity. (Morrison 2009a)

There were still roadblocks to pursuing the vision. On one hand, in 2003, Morrison was scheduled to be on a mission trip to Africa, while on the other hand, Biko still served on an executive committee for the Northwest Yearly Meeting (NWYM)—an Evangelical Friends denominational head in the Pacific Northwest—which she needed to first resign from before putting her attention into the new church plant. It was after Morrison returned from Africa that she and Biko decided to share their vision with another close friend and Quaker, Jane Wheeler. "She not only wanted to be on board, but she had a vision of her own, and she is not a woman prone to the mystical. She saw a large room full of people gathered, and I was there, and it was a church, and she knew it was going to happen" (Morrison 2009). These three women realized they "had all felt for a new expression of Quakerism in their community" (2009). Now that everything had fallen into place these women began to discern how to move their leading forward so they "started to meet for informal worship and discussion; they seasoned their desire and came to feel very clear in the call. They were to bring into being a Christ-centered, inclusive, semi-programmed, lightly pastoral friends Church" (Freedom Friends Church 2004).

Seeking an Inclusive Christ-Centered Quakerism

One of the main obstacles to proceeding was the inclusive vision behind Freedom Friends Church. A Quaker meeting that was inclusive of sexual diversity was out of harmony with the Northwest Yearly Meeting *Faith and Practice*.[2] Under the sub-heading "Friends Faith: What We Believe" in the section "Human Sexuality," the NWYM *Faith and Practice* states:

> We hold that only marriage is conducive to godly fulfillment in sexual relationships for the purposes of reproduction and enrichment of life. We consider sexual intimacy outside marriage as sinful because it distorts God's purposes for human sexuality. We denounce, as contrary to the moral laws of God, acts of homosexuality, sexual abuse, and any other form of sexual perversion (see "Human Sexuality," p. 80). The church, however, as a community of forgiven persons, remains loving and sensitive to those we consider in error. Because God's grace can deliver from sins of any kind, we are called to forgive those who have repented and to free them for participation in the church. (Ibid.)

---

2. The *Faith and Practice* is a "book of discipline" put together by the local Quaker churches that make up the denomination called Northwest Yearly Meeting. The NWYM *Faith and Practice* is used as a description of the common life and identity of these churches: "As the Friends of NWYM, our common life is described by our Faith and Practice. Together, we seek to live in obedience to the same Life and Power that called early Friends to courageous evangelism, compassionate service, community, integrity, simplicity, equality and peacemaking in ways that speak to the present culture" (NWYM, *Faith and Practice*, 2). The "polity is connectional, rather than congregational or episcopal" (23), therefore it is the Yearly Meeting (the annual gathering of members and representatives from local churches) and its clerk that function as the final "court of appeals" in matters pertaining to interpretation of the *Faith and Practice* (23, 39). This means that "Local churches and ministry points within NWYM are joined together in a covenantal relationship. Spiritually, we are connected to each other in the common bond of fellowship and united by the Presence of the Holy Spirit. Organizationally, we agree to be united in purpose, through our joint identity and mission, and by our willingness to affirm and be guided by our Faith and Practice. We are committed to mutual support, accountability, and to being a people who love one another as we have been commanded by Jesus. In doing so, we witness to the world that we are, indeed, His people" (33). Finally, as the *Faith and Practice* confers, it is Christ Jesus who is the head of the church. Therefore, every connection, interpretation and issue for discernment is subject to Christ's present leadership (1, 23).

This statement, coupled with a more in depth statement found in the appendix labeled "Earlier Interpretations of Christian Faith," which was added in 1982 states:

> Friends believe that the practice of sexual perversion in any form is sinful and contrary to the God-ordained purposes in sexual relationships. These perversions include sexual violence, homosexual acts, transvestism, incest, and sex acts with animals. The sin nature is capable of vile affections when humankind rejects the moral laws of God. (2011: 80)

Both these statements meant that there was no easy way to form a fully-inclusive church in partnership with Northwest Yearly Meeting.

Further, same-sex orientation has increasingly become a hotly disputed issue among most Christians, and Friends are no different. In 2012, George Fox University and NWYM, rooted in Gurneyite evangelicalism, underwent internal debates over the rise of two University groups supporting and affirming gay rights: OneGeorgeFox and Common Ground.[3] Northwest Yearly Meeting is not the only group of Quakers wrestling with questions of sexual diversity. Recently, Indiana Yearly Meeting struggled to hold its 191-year-old association of Quaker meetings together through tumultuous discussion:

> The roots of this momentous decision lay in a minute, approved in June of 2008, in which West Richmond Friends Meeting found unity to "affirm and welcome all persons whatever their . . . sexual orientation." (Sexual orientation was only one of eight categories of persons that they explicitly welcomed and affirmed, and it is the only one of those eight categories to prove controversial.). (Angell 2012: 11)

One woman, a member of Indian Yearly Meeting, expresses the sensitivity of this issue well:

> My faith community is . . . in the midst of a great loss, a loss that has turned life upside down for many of us. My faith community decided that we have a problem and the only solution is to

---

3. OneGeorgeFox, a group of George Fox University alum, wrote an open letter to the university because they felt the need for the university to change its policy's dealing with LGBTQ students. OneGeorgeFox exists because "Our hope is that we can be part of creating change within our community, so that LGBTQ students can come to George Fox to study, to worship and to serve, in a safe and affirming environment" (http://www.onegeorgefox.org/). Today there are more than four hundred signatures on their letter.

> quit being a community, to quit working together, to quit worshipping together, and to end a 191 year relationship as a Yearly Meeting and fellowship of Friends. . . . This problem changes my faith community for everyone. (Ibid., 22)

Thus, just a few years prior in 2004, Morrison, Biko and Wheeler approached the creation of Freedom Friends with fear and trepidation. They faced serious questions: (a) is there room in the Quaker world for a meeting like this; (b) if so, how should they proceed, and (c) is it possible to avoid beginning on a schismatic note? Calvert posed this last question to the three women:

> We were doing daily emails as friends will, saying "are you going to be a Ranter?" Are you going to be completely unaffiliated and unaccountable? To me, having done this research around what happens in the Hicksite separation and beyond . . . [there is] this urge to schism. [It] is something that is very very problematic within Quakerism, this easy schisming. We didn't start out that way. We started out as a body, the body of the church, and every meeting that separated out was set off by another meeting until what happened in Joel Bean's time. (Calvert 2009)[4]

There was a concern from all parties invested in the vision of Freedom Friends that any new expression of Quakerism not begin in the same way that many other meetings have begun. One evangelical Friend explained to me in an interview her initial feelings when she learned about the possibility of Freedom Friends, "My feeling was more one of concern . . . I have such a sense of Christians solving their problems by disowning and separating from each other that I [thought], 'that sounds like a bad repetition of Christian history to me.'" Morrison and Biko, feeling this concern, struggled with whether or not they should willingly lay down their memberships at their Friends Church in Portland and whether Morrison would be willing to lay down her recording as a Friends minister in Northwest Yearly Meeting.

---

4. Calvert refers to her historical research related to what is known as the Pacific Northwest Quaker Women's Theological Conference, a bi-annual gathering of Evangelical and Liberal Quaker women in the Northwest who come together to dialogue about their differences and similarities (Calvert, "How Blessed It Is," 2003). The friendships that emerged out of this conference are represented by many of the women who came together in support of Freedom Friends early on.

Adding to the Fabric of Quakerism

Not wanting to be out of step with the Holy Spirit, the three women called on a group of Quaker women to hold a meeting for clearness on February 6, 2004. The goal was to seek clarity on starting Freedom Friends and how this new church would affect their relationships with their yearly and monthly meetings (Calvert 2009). Among the women represented, there were Quakers from Northwest Yearly Meeting (evangelical), Pacific Yearly Meeting (liberal) and North Pacific Yearly meeting (liberal). While not officially representing their yearly meeting, they had to have a reputation of being "deeply rooted in Quaker practice and Gospel Order" (Freedom Friends Church 2008). They gathered for the weekend at Shalom Center of the Queen of Angels Monastery in Mt. Angel Oregon. Over the weekend they worshipped, prayed and listened together, waiting for guidance from the "Present Christ." Clearness emerged in the meeting, and this group of women affirmed that:

> The three Friends seemed to have a clear call. The meeting also affirmed that this expression of Quakerism was not a good fit for either local Yearly Meeting, and might cause dissension. There was no clear sense to challenge either Yearly Meeting; in fact, the sense seemed to be to set the meeting up in an independent fashion, maintain the best relations possible, and be a testimony to both Yearly Meetings. (FFC 2008)

In its creation, Freedom Friends borrowed from both liberal and evangelical Quakerism and created something new in the process. For one, they have a pastor but she does not preach and does not receive a salary. And while they worship is silence for forty-five minutes they also sing and say prayers together as a congregation. The diversity represented in this meeting for clearness and their final desire to see Freedom Friends be independent while "[Maintaining] the best relations possible, and be a testimony to both Yearly Meetings" points to a deep desire to remain rooted within the Quaker tradition while carefully moving in a new direction. Morrison said these early deliberations demonstrated how FFC was not meant to be "a criticism of anything else." Instead, "We add to the fabric; we're not a breach in the fabric" (Morrison 2009).

Morrison and Biko returned from the monastery to a meeting with the pastor of Reedwood Friends Church where both their memberships and Morrison' recording were held. A meeting was arranged with the pastor, the presiding clerk of NWYM, and both Morrison and Biko.

The clerk agreed that "a church that was inclusive along lines of sexual orientation in membership and ministry would not fit within the Yearly Meeting" (FFC 2008). The meeting would determine, "Whether [our church] could support us, take us under their care, or gently walk us out of the building . . . there was a lot of options out on the table" (Morrison 2009). The meeting with the elders could have gone in many directions, but Morrison and Biko experienced an atmosphere, as they described it, of support and surrender.

It was clear to the elders that Christ had placed a call on these women, but it was not clear to them that they could bless it. One elder referenced the Biblical figure Gamaliel, and his wisdom in refusing to condemn the leadings of the Apostles. The Biblical advice was: "If this is from man, it will falter, but if it is from God, we do not want to stand in its way" (Acts 5:33–39). The elders affirmed this as their stance (Freedom Friends Church 2008).

For all parties involved, it "was a long and a tender and a broken meeting." Biko and Morrison were highly valued members in good standing. While the elders could not take the new church under their formal care, they made space to recognize it as a meeting once it was established. They "decided to hold our memberships until we had it up and functioning when they felt clear to transfer our memberships, giving it its first 'we recognize you'" (Morrison 2009).

One of the most difficult aspects of this final break was that Morrison, as a recorded minister in NWYM, was now out of harmony with its *Faith and Practice*.[5] Consequently, she had to surrender her recording to the church elders. This surrender was very difficult for her to do because she took her recording very seriously (Calvert 2009). However, this difficult surrender is indicative of how difficult it is to bring about something new within a tradition. Freedom Friends wanted to present a reinterpretation of Quakerism, but they were not willing to burn their bridges doing so.

In Salem, Oregon in March 2004, the first business meeting was held; Freedom Friends Church (FFC) was born. Here was the beginning

---

5. This is how it is worded in Freedom Friends' *Faith and Practice*: "Friends do not 'ordain' ministers as other Christian denominations do. It is our contention that God calls and ordains—names and equips—ministers. Friends record this gifting when they see it. Some Friends record ministers essentially for life, others for specific task. Some Meetings will 'release' ministers but not record them. It is always considered an observation of what God is doing in and through that person, not a special status or elevated position" (Freedom Friends Church, *Faith and Practice: First Edition*, 58).

of a new testimony, an alternative community within the Quaker world. In the first six months, FFC reported that there were fourteen semi-regular attendees, all ranging from age ten to sixty. It was, and still is, a place other Friends felt welcome to visit as well. Thirteen people visited within the first six months, eight of whom were from other Quaker meetings. In keeping with a trend that has continued to this day, six of these attendees were new to Quakerism. Not only were the theology and age range diverse, but so were other issues represented in the church: "Some of us struggle with physical problems like depression, sleep disorders, developmental, neurological or other major health challenges. Some of us are unemployed or under-employed. Yet all of us are valuable to the community" (Freedom Friends Church 2004).

Conclusion

Postmodernity, among many other cultural shifts, has challenged Quakers to reinterpret their tradition in a new context. Freedom Friends is one Quaker church that seeks to remain rooted in Quaker practices and theology while dialoguing with its present context in a way that creates an alternative social community within contemporary Quakerism. In the following section, I look more in-depth at the practices that make FFC stand out as a Quaker community, showing how they demonstrate the three characteristics of renewal through participatory convergence.

RESPONSE: THE ELEMENTS OF PARTICIPATION

In this section, I demonstrate how Freedom Friends has put their Quaker tradition in dialogue with their context in ways that exhibit remix, resistance and decentralization.

Remix

In *Textual Poachers*, Henry Jenkins argues that alternative social communities found in fandom are not always ideologically consistent, because they transgress traditional boundaries in order to form something new. "A poached culture, a nomadic culture, is also a patchwork culture, an impure culture" (Jenkins 1992: 283). Gibbs and Bolger, found in emerging churches there is a blending together of ancient and contemporary spiritual practices where the use of liturgies, labyrinths, stations, lectio divina, and monastic-oriented practices helped frame the world in their worship (Gibbs and Bolger 2005: 225–27). These communities "[Draw] from a variety of traditions to produce a newly created mix is the liturgical equivalent of DJs working with a mix of songs to produce fresh expressions and moods" (ibid., 222).

Freedom Friends exhibits this kind of patchwork, or remix, culture within the Quaker world. It draws together an understanding of Quakerism that transgresses the traditional boundaries and challenges sanctioned readings or interpretations often taken as "copyright" within the tradition. Three places that this is evident is in their relationship to the rest of the Quaker world, their empathetic view of the Bible, and their practice of Quaker worship.

Freedom Friends as Convergent Friends

The word "convergent" within Quakerism signals both the intended meaning of the word where two elements are brought together to eventually meet, and a more symbolic use in that it describes Quakers who are committed to conserving the tradition within emergent cultures through the ongoing practice of remix. Freedom Friends exhibits both aspects of convergent.

Freedom Friends understands itself to be a "uniting meeting," drawing Quakers from liberal and evangelical yearly meetings. Their *Faith and Practice* states:

> We are a uniting meeting, having received members by transfer from Friends General Conference, Friends United Meeting and Evangelical Friends International. But equally important to our call is the fact that a majority of our members are new to Quakerism. Teaching the ways of Friends is an important part of our mission. (Freedom Friends Church 2009: 1)

This is true in Freedom Friends founding members. Morrison and Biko were both members of Northwest Yearly Meeting, the evangelical yearly meeting in the pacific Northwest which includes programmed Quaker meetings in Oregon, Washington, and Idaho. Wheeler was a member of North Pacific Yearly Meeting (NPYM), which is the unprogrammed, liberal Quaker yearly meeting covering Washington, Oregon, Idaho, Montana, and northern Wyoming. T. Vail Palmer Jr., lifelong

Quaker and theologian, is not only a member of Freedom Friends but a recorded minister there with recordings in four different yearly meetings—programmed and unprogrammed. A number of other members in the meeting have travelled in ministry visiting Quakers around the world in Europe, Great Britain, Africa, and South America. Others have served on various committees and Quaker boards. For a meeting of about thirty people, its footprint in the Quaker world is large. This is because as a blended and "united meeting" they are not locked into one particular tradition, which enables them to be conversant with all of the various Quaker streams and comfortable dialoging with others of differing viewpoints.

FFC is the result of another "uniting" group in the Northwest known as Multwood which is a gathering of Quaker women initially formed by members of two Portland area Quaker meetings: Multnomah Monthly Meeting (liberal-unprogammed, NPYM) and Reedwood Friends Church (evangelical-programmed, NWYM) in 1985. The goal "was to encourage each other in our individual ministries and leadership roles within the Society of Friends" (Abbott 2006).[6] This group continues to meet with the hopes of helping each other grow in leadership and ministry, and building friendships and creating a safe space for dialogue across yearly meeting lines (ibid.). Morrison, Biko, and Wheeler have all been a part of Multwood.

The support they found in this group was essential to their early discernment, and the group's ethos of bringing different groups together in dialogue is an important part of what makes Freedom Friends unique. Pam Calvert, author of "How Blessed It Is for the Sisters to Meet: Historical Roots of the Pacific Northwest Quaker Women's Theology Conference" (2003), an article detailing the history of "convergent" Quaker women's meetings in Pacific Northwest, views Multwood as a fertile field for this kind of dialogical work, "a space for these conversations to take place that allowed creative theology to begin." This creative theology, where both liberal and evangelical groups are brought together in a new remix, is evident at the very heart of Freedom Friends.

As with most remixes, Freedom Friends does not fit easily into one category of Quakerism or another. Theirs is a paradoxical relationship with the two pre-existing Yearly Meetings in the Northwest. Both have supplied inspiration and substance to Freedom Friends, but Freedom

6. Quaker historian Margery Post Abbott has a more in-depth history of Multwood in *An Experiment in Faith*.

Friends is independent of both groups. It is both "old" and "new" in many ways:

> Freedom Friends Church ... is a very unusual, but not completely unique hybrid in the Quaker world, falling somewhere between Liberal and Pastoral Friends. We were founded by Friends from Northwest Yearly Meeting, Evangelical Friends International, but have come to include Friends from Friends General Conference and Friends United Meeting. We are Christocentric, semi-programmed, pastoral, socially progressive, and pacifist. Our outreach is focused on justice, relief and peace work. There are presently no Yearly Meetings within easy geographic reach that are a good fit for us. Consequently, we are an independent Monthly Meeting. (Freedom Friends Church 2009: 14)

While Freedom Friends is independent, they do not see themselves as completely unique. This is important for a true remix; the "original artwork" should always be recognizable and distinct, while being changed and incorporated in creative and new ways. For Morrison, this means that Freedom Friends is not a break with the old, nor is it a criticism of liberal or evangelical Friends, it is a new addition to what is already there.

While it is clear that Freedom Friends works to maintain good relationships with other Quaker groups and remain in dialogue with any willing to engage with them, it has been shown in previous chapters that alternative communities who remix texts and practices often stand as witnesses against the more dominant systems of which they are a part. The mere existence of Freedom Friends as an inclusive, Christ-centered Quaker community is not meant to critique other Quaker meetings, but is a witness to an alternative way of being a faith community together. It challenges previous models to consider new interpretations, practices, and formulations of the Quaker tradition.

Worship, Lightly-Pastoral

FFC remixes not only the groups they pull together through dialogue and engagement, but also Quaker practices. As their literature says, "We are semi-programmed, lightly pastoral and socially progressive. We believe in continuing revelation." To a seasoned Quaker, these adjectives signal something new in the Quaker world. Elton Trueblood explains the original vision behind Quaker worship well when he says,

> Worship, according to the ancient practice of the Religious Society of Friends, is entirely without any human direction or supervision. A group of devout persons come together and sit down quietly with no prearrangement, each seeking to have an immediate sense of divine leading and to know at first hand the presence of the Living Christ. It is not wholly accurate to say such a Meeting is held on the basis of silence; it is more accurate to say that it is held on the basis of "Holy Obedience." Those who enter such a Meeting can harm it in two specific ways: first, by an advance determination to speak; and second, by advance determination to keep silent. The only way in which a worshipper can help such a Meeting is by an advance determination to try and be responsive in listening to the still small voice and doing whatever may be commanded. (Trueblood 1966: 86)

In the mid-1800s, Quakerism split into two main groups: those who adopted the role of pastors in their meetings (Gurneyite) and those who kept to the tradition of refusing to have paid clergy (Hicksite and Wilburite). Those with pastors are referred to as "programmed" meetings, those without as "unprogrammed." Dandelion explains the shift from unprogrammed to programmed that happened within Gurneyite meetings and the role of the Quaker minister:

> Pastors were not priests; everyone was still spiritual equal. Rather, a pastor was someone serving the Meeting to help enhance and lead worship. Very quickly, those Meetings with pastors changed from the 'unprogrammed' silent format to what can be called programmed worship. In other words, there are a number of different elements to worship, such as singing and preaching, praise and prayer, which are pre-programmed before the event, as opposed to the single activity of silent waiting. Both are programmed in one way but the pastor or pastoral team needs to make a decision about content and order. (Dandelion 2008: 35)

Freedom Friends blends both unprogrammed and programmed elements together into a "semi-programmed" liturgy. The basic order of service is: (a) gratitude, asking and listening which comes in the form of worship through singing, (b) congregational prayer or what they call "gratitudes and petitions," and (c) about forty-five minutes of "expectant" worship in silence.[7] One church member's e-mail, forwarded to me, stated:

7. Other ways they incorporate spirituality into the life of the meeting are through a twelve-step group and a healing circle, which they practice occasionally, "where

> The way Sunday services are done at Freedom Friends I think attracts me in such a way as to make it so I anticipate services all week. Sharing gratefulness and petitions does not promote "over share" or "too much information," but an ongoing narrative has been created where people know basically what is going on with others. The narrative might be a bit like an addictive soap opera, but with real people, less pathology, and not so much money in clothes. People are well enabled at Freedom Friends whether visitors or long time attenders to participate in the narrative right off, or wait a while. It is like a play where everyone has lines offered them if they want to participate. The stage is real life. The expectation that God works primarily in and through the day-to-day lives of people seems quite normal at Freedom Friends. The silence part allows people to mentally review what others said during the first two parts of the service if they want to. I tend to think of God as love and creative energy. These kinds of things are themselves potentially numinous or experiences of the extraordinary.

While there is no sermon by the pastor on a typical Sunday morning, there is often someone who stands and shares during the silent or expectant worship, offering "vocal ministry" to the group. At the beginning of 2012, Freedom Friends began experimenting with what they do on fifth Sundays. On these Sundays they invite guests to offer music and sermons.

Expectant worship in a Quaker meeting is equivalent in priority to taking communion in other churches. Each part of the meeting points towards the expectant worship at the end where the meeting gathers, listens and communes in silence with Jesus who is present in their gathering. Each person anticipates the Holy Spirit within them, prompting them to stand and offer a short, personal message about something God leads them to share. This expectant worship and "vocal ministry" is something common in almost all Quaker meetings: programmed meetings often have a short period of silence (1–5 minutes) in their worship, while the unprogrammed meetings are silent for their entire meeting for worship.

One of the elements that sets FFC apart from other meetings, especially unprogrammed ones, is that they "set the bar low for what counts as vocal ministry." It is not uncommon in unprogrammed meetings for there to be no vocal ministry or only one or two people who share in the

---

Friends with deep wounds can talk about their burdens and pray for each other" (Freedom Friends Church, "First Annual Report," 2005).

whole hour. In these meetings there is often a fear that one might share out of one's own wisdom and strength, rather than led by the Spirit. In other meetings, the fear is around what a person might share about God, disrupting the delicate balance that many of the more pluralistic meetings struggle to maintain. However, for FFC "All God's children are given gifts for the use of the body of Christ, and the world, therefore all can be ministers. The church should encourage the use of these gifts in and out of meeting" (Freedom Friends Church 2009: 7).

Therefore, FFC has intentionally created an environment where people feel free to offer vocal ministry because the emphasis is on learning how to listen to God's Spirit and participate together in that ministry, rather than getting it right or maintaining acceptability. Instead of treating God as ineffable or that which we cannot speak of, FFC reverses this modern tendency. "Peggy once told me that she would rather have people give ministry that was not Spirit-led than the other way around, and it is really like, if you think this may be for the group, share it. People are very supportive of that" (Wilcox 2009).

FFC maintains a culture where people are encouraged to offer "spoken ministry" as a means of practicing how to listen to a God who still speaks. By encouraging participation in this way, FFC is not only returning to the roots of Quakerism but also creating a contemporary response to the non-participatory deadlock that many older meetings now face. By helping people to "recognize the signs" and lowering expectations for what gets shared in meeting for worship, newer members are more willing to participate in this essential part of Quaker worship:

> Freedom Friends was the first place where I felt led to vocal ministry. And so that was really meaningful for me and just having the space and being able to recognize the signs in me in such a small group, in such a supportive place, and I find that do speak more when I'm there than other places . . . so that is really special and unusual I think. To have a place that kind of cultivates that. (Ibid.)

What helps in this process is that the pastor guides people along, explaining each step that happens in worship, the petitions, the thanksgiving and the expectant worship that they practice weekly. This facilitates understanding and gives language to what they are doing so that newcomers can also participate.

One last way that FFC is "lightly pastoral" is in their understanding of their liturgy. They have created a "mobile" rhythm of worship that is meant to shape the community not just on Sunday morning, but for the rest of life as well. In other words, Freedom Friends sees worship as being something that congregants can practice or replicate outside of Sunday morning without the need of the pastor present:

> We are intentionally trying to create a spirituality that can be replicated on any day and on any moment. [We] have discovered that "thank you," "please help" and "please shut up and listen" does it. . . . People can learn it and they can learn to do a daily spiritual practice based on what they do on Sunday morning without the need for a worship band. Or a sermon or anything else. Just them and the Spirit. (Morrison 2009)

Therefore, a central goal of worship, and thus the reason for its mobility, is aiding the participants to listen to God in silence amidst the chaos of their lives. Morrison tells a story about an old Quaker meeting in Pennsylvania that underscores this idea:

> 15th Street Meeting in New York in the 1800s used to go out and put straw down on the cobblestone so that the horses going by, so that the clip-clop noise, would not disrupt the beautiful silence of the meeting. Attempting to put straw down on the cobblestone of the world won't work. You need to be able to worship in the presence of sound so everything we do, so our customary practices, what we tolerate, I don't think we've eldered anyone for much of anything in the meeting. But we regularly speak to that which helps you listen and that which doesn't help you listen. We have to educate all the time. We have to tell people what we think is going on in the silence and what they should be looking for and expecting and hoping for. (Ibid.)

The point is not to have beautiful silence, but to learn how to listen, what to listen for, and how to respond. This can be done in a variety of ways and Freedom Friends allows for a diversity of expression. This is why they consider themselves "fidgetter friendly." "You can get up and walk around in meeting. You can knit, you can read. You can paint at the art table. We don't try and get better and better at silence we try and get better at centering in the midst of noise." As with all remixes, Freedom Friends has adapted older Quaker practices in new ways by bringing them into conversation with today's context.

Reenactment and a Healing Community

One further aspect of remix is the participants' reenactment of core stories or key texts. Quakers such as James Nayler offer an early example of how Friends participated in "reenactment" in a way that aligned closely with what has been called an empathetic reading of the Bible. A faith community remixing Scripture today will exhibit empathetic qualities through the way they read, interpret and act on their understanding of the Bible. Empathetic reading suggests both verbal and non-verbal cues by practitioners:

> Empathetic exegesis is attempting to put ourselves inside the skin of the people we are seeking to understand and explain. We seek to enter into the concrete life-situation out of which the writing has come, to understand what the writer was saying to his/her time, and to enter with sympathy and imagination into that ancient community and to relive its sacred history. We attempt together to stand within the Bible and look out at the world through the window of biblical faith. We listen to the biblical narrative and by means of historical memory and identification we participate in the original events. We think along with Isaiah, Paul, or Luke. Empathetic exegesis is the use of our imagination and "near sympathy" to identify ourselves as closely as possible with the original writer and the community to which he/she was writing. (Palmer 2012)

While Freedom Friends does not have a ministry of walking naked through Salem, as Nayler did in Bristol, they do exhibit qualities of reenactment in at least two ways: living out the Sermon on the Mount and seeking healing as a community. First, the most important way they practice reenactment is by seeking to embody the way of Jesus by living the Sermon on the Mount:

> Like the early founders of the Religious Society of Friends we seek a renewal of Gospel Order. Believing that the Present Christ will come and teach His people, we return not to an apostolic church, but to the very feet of the Master. Because of this, our faith is centered on living out the Sermon on the Mount; which incorporates our testimonies of peace, integrity, equality and simplicity. . .We attempt to live out our testimonies in our community in ways that are a witness. (Morrison 2005)

How this looks for FFC is different from your average Quaker meeting. It leads them to being, as they call it, "ditch walkers," or people who are similar to the Good Samaritan and pull the misfits of society out of ditches. Morrison put it this way, "There are multiple people who would be dead if it were not for this meeting. We're ditch walkers. We've gotta save lives and we let God save souls. We're not really worried about saving souls, that's His job." They see it as part of their ministry to reach out to those often turned away or rejected by other churches. This is where they push the inclusive part of their meeting further than simply welcoming and affirming LGBTQ people: they seek to literally be inclusive of everyone, including the poor, the sick, and people who are disabled.

Second, they strive to be a healing community. From holding "healing circles," to supporting one another in recovery and sitting with those at risk for suicide, they embody the healing ministry of Jesus:

> A good meeting for worship depends not on if there is good silence or good ministry, but if lives are transformed by the Spirit in meeting. People are dying out there in ditches for the lack of what we carry in our back pockets. We consider it our job to find them and try and help them live. There are people in this meeting who might literally be dead if it were not for this meeting. We think that is a mission. (Biko and Morrison 2009)

When asked whether she thought Freedom Friends was "missional," Morrison said, "The Sermon on the Mount is our mission statement, if we have one." They talk about, practice and have had classes on it. The Sermon on the Mount for them is a key text that they seek to understand empathetically. Outsiders notice the centrality of this for Freedom Friends as well. Calvert sees at the heart of FFC this Quaker vision of following Christ in a deeply embodied way: "I think it is a Quaker distinctive. . .we are walking in the kingdom now, right now. And that is our call to fully embody that. And I believe that FFC is a witness to that specific Quaker distinctive" (Calvert 2009). By taking the Sermon on the Mount as more than a Read-Only text, Freedom Friends demonstrates new ways of being Quakers while embodying the way of Jesus in their context.

Drawing on various practices from within the Quaker tradition, Freedom Friends takes what has often been considered Read-Only culture and remixes it into something new. They do this as convergent Friends who seek to be a uniting meeting, drawing together various strands of Quakerism in new ways. They transform Quaker understanding and practice of worship by being semi-programmed, lightly pastoral, and practicing worship in ways that are contextual. Finally, they embody an empathetic reading of the Bible by living out the Sermon on the Mount as a community that reaches out for and seeks to bring healing to those often cast off by society and the church.

Conclusion

Freedom Friends practices remix by bringing together Quakers and non-Quakers into a space where dialogue can begin to shape a new expression of Quakerism. They also remix through the worshipping practices and understanding of pastoral leadership they engage in. Finally, they remix through reenactment as a healing community.[8]

Authentic Resistance

In the previous chapter, building on Fox's convincement narrative, I argued that the Quaker tradition demonstrated authentic resistance in at least three ways: first, Fox's despairing spiritual pilgrimage revealed the depth to which early Friends were disillusioned by the inauthenticity of those professing to be Christians among the mainstream and dissenting crowds. Second, Fox's convincement sealed a conviction of resistance to all outward symbols and authorities because neither could bring about an authentic experience—only communion with the Inward Light of Christ could bring true transformation. Finally, Fox's statement "Jesus is come to teach the people himself," signifies an authentic resistance that rejects the "trickle down" theology and passive faith of Christendom. Instead, as "Publishers of Truth," early Quakers challenged the ritualization of religious consumption by becoming active producers. Similarly, Freedom Friends demonstrates what a faith community looks like that is rooted in authentic experiences, resisting top down spirituality and passive faith. They do this in at least three ways as they: strip away obstacles to encountering God, "make new Quakers" through convincement narratives, and by their DIY-styled production of their *Faith and Practice*.

---

8. Peggy Morrison's book of sermons *Messages to a Refugee Planet* (2010) is another good example of remix and Scripture.

Stripping Away Creedalism

Central to fandom is the practice of stripping away all that encumbers individuals from re-imaging a world that they wish to inhabit, fostering deeply authentic experiences and raising their emotional investment within their communities. Similarly, Freedom Friends fosters authenticity by stripping away the parts of Christianity that obstruct people from encountering God.

Freedom Friends exists as an alternative space within Christianity where those who have found themselves outside the church are welcomed to be a part of the body of Christ. To create this space they not only form an approachable and contemporary Quakerism, they work to strip away the obstacles that keep people from expressing and growing in their faith. They do this by rejecting a creedal Christianity, one that is based on strict or exclusive beliefs. Instead, they nurture a non-creedal community. Their *Faith and Practice* states:

> The first three sections [of the faith and practice] are a clear expression of a progressive Christian faith. It is a Quaker flavor of Christianity focusing on the leading of the Spirit of Christ in our lives. We hope that it reflects what others have called a "generous orthodoxy." This document is a call to Gospel Order, not a creed. The distinction is one of function. Members interpret this faith as they are led. No one is required to assent to it. We have great theological diversity in our meeting and this expression of faith is a center for us—a campfire to sit around, each at their own comfortable place and distance. (Freedom Friends Church 2009: 1)

As with all of early Quakerism and at least some Quaker groups today, Freedom Friends functions as a non-creedal community, critical of the "formulaic and inauthentic theology" espoused within a majority of Christian circles (Dandelion 2008: 76). In this way, they fit the description of 'b' baptist churches that McClendon described as having, "no authoritative creeds; no single set of doctrines marks them off from all others; no fine spun theory particularizes their way of life; no private 'revelation' separates them from other Christians" (McClendon 2002: 26). One concern for early Friends was that creeds represented a top-down, one-sided, formulaic, and inauthentic element of Christianity. Just because one knew the creeds, recited them, even believed them, did not mean that one had come to know the inward Christ or experienced the "Day of the Lord" in which everything was inwardly and outwardly changed for an individual. To draw one's faith on creeds was to gather "yesterday's manna," a sentiment expressed in Quaker Poet John Greenleaf Whittier's poem "The Meeting" (1870):

> But God is near us now as then;
> His force of love is still unspent,
> His hate of sin as imminent;
> And still the measure of our needs,
> Outgrows the cramping bounds of creeds;
> The manna gathered yesterday
> Already savors of decay...

Freedom Friends similarly rejects creedal Christianity in favor of creating a community of faith that allows for diversity of belief, grounded in the discernment of the community:

> Most groups of Friends have what is called a Faith and Practice, this may be a collection of testimonies, advices and queries, or it may be an explicit declaration of Faith. At Freedom Friends we think that the distinctive thing about our Faith and Practice is how it is used and how it is not used. This is not a creed, it is not written in stone, it can be changed by the discernment of the meeting for worship business. It is not used as a test of acceptability. You do not have to agree with everything in this document in order to participate in the community. But it is the best articulation of the beliefs of the Friends who felt called to start this church. We use it to call to people, and as a starting point for discussion and study. We are orthodox in our Christianity, but we are not fundamentalist.... We believe we are still learning. (Freedom Friends Church 2013)

As a non-creedal community they remain open to dialogue and new ways of thinking that may call into question earlier articulations of their faith. Being open to new revelation means that they see their understanding of truth as progressive and open to change. Thus, they are truly an "open" community, both in terms of their inclusivity of all people, and in their theological approach. On the cover of Freedom Friends' *Faith and Practice* there is an image of a neon sign that says "open." That same sign sits at the front door to their meetinghouse. It has become for them a logo that describes a key feature to their community.

As early Quakers demonstrated, truth that is coercive and absolute not only is non-participative, but also creates obstacles to accessibility.

Quakerism has defined itself in large part by the stripping away of such obstacles, creating a more authentic Christianity. Freedom Friends Church demonstrates this stripping away in what they "renounce:"

> We renounce slavery in all its forms. Free people must always be vigilant, guarding against creeping bondage. Physical slavery is still a scourge on our planet in many places, and many are enslaved in poverty. In our lives more insidious forms often replace the old forms of this evil: the slavery of addictions; to food, drugs, tobacco, sex, alcohol, spending and many more. Pride can become a slavemaster and so can power. We acknowledge only one safe master, and that is our God and Redeemer. We see complete surrender to God as the most effective prevention to slavery. (Freedom Friends 2009: 11)

In this statement it could be said that Freedom Friends seeks to embody the theme of freedom in their community. Both of these statements in their *Faith and Practice* are unique within the Quaker world and sets them apart as a truly unique participatory Quaker meeting. Their rejection of "slavery" shows how stripping away can foster deeper authenticity. Because of their attention to "creeping bondage," they work to be a healing community by using healing circles in which attend to one another's "deep needs" (Freedom Friends 2005). They also do this by praying openly for one another during worship, using their email list for prayer concerns throughout the week, and by hosting AA meetings and incorporating insights from the twelve-step tradition:

> We have found that the best treatment for active addictions and slaveries is a spiritually based 12-step group, such as Alcoholics Anonymous. We find the precepts of AA to be harmonious with the gospel and with holy living. We incorporate these precepts into the life of the church in every way we can. (Freedom Friends 2009: 11)

As a Quaker meeting, they are able to not only strip away that which inhibits people from experiencing the inward Christ, they are able to form a community of healing and friendship that aids one another in coming to authentic freedom in Christ.

Convincement Narratives

In fandom, we have seen that participants display high levels of emotional investment towards their fan object; this reveals the importance of the subjective experience in building authentic communities. One of the ways that early Quakers helped move Christianity towards the subjective was through their convincement narratives, often written about in their journals. Below, I offer one convincement narrative from an important member of Freedom Friends Church, Jaye Kysmet.

Jaye Kysmet sought an authentic experience with God and a community that was free from the creeds and fundamentalisms that barred her—as a transgender woman—from experiencing Christ. In the mid-90s Kysmet, a male who had not yet transitioned to female, began seeking God through Buddhism. Buddhism offered a reflective and non-judgmental space for Kysmet and a good place to begin exploring spirituality, but looking back in 2009 she felt that the Buddhist search for God ultimately left her still searching because it was not focused enough: "The problem I had with Buddhism was that . . . as a general rule they don't believe there is any God, but they also leave out the possibility that if there is a God you're never going to be able to figure it out or understand it."

Kysmet wanted more. Back then she was an intern and social work student, who was drinking and using with the clients she was to supposed to be supervising. The sense of despair combined with spiritual seeking mirrors the desperation that many Quakers, like George Fox, experienced. Her first "God Shot," as she called it, came when reading the Big Book from Alcoholics Anonymous and she began wrestling with whether or not she was an alcoholic. She denied it for a long time, thinking she could not be because as far as she knew her estranged father was not. Through a series of events, she tracked down her biological father, only to discover that he had died only weeks before at the age of 48 from alcoholism. This led her on the road to recovery.

Then there was the second "God Shot," known to her as the "Billy conversion experience." In 2007, shortly after her transition, she was going through a very rough time at work, where her co-workers were resistant to her and treated her very poorly. One night she had come to the end of her rope: "I was literally making out a balance sheet, trying to figure out if my kids would be better off with me alive or dead." She tried contacting the Human Resources department at the mental health hospital she worked in to find out what kind of benefits she had, but there was no response.

Just then a co-worker named Billy came in from the day shift looking visibly shook. Billy said, "I've got to talk to you before you leave." He pulled Kysmet aside and told her that he woke up in the middle of the night from a nightmare about Kysmet committing suicide. Billy invited her to his church. This marked a serious turning point in her life. This first church she went to for about a month but she left feeling deceived:

> I went there the first time and the pastor invited me to a woman's Bible study and they seemed really accepting. They had to lend me a Bible, I didn't even own one. They let me do that for about a month or so and then all of a sudden they pulled me into the pastor's office and said, "You can't go to women's groups, you can't use the women's restroom" . . . and all this other stuff, and normally I probably would have just chucked the Bible and said, "Okay, screw this." But the experience with Billy was profound enough that I literally went home and started opening the phone book and calling different churches randomly and saying "I'm trans, I'm in recovery and I've had a fairly powerful experience, I don't know if I believe wholesale in this or not but I need some place to grow and learn more, at least." (Kysmet 2009)

The experience she had reflects the first stage of convincement, a "powerful in-breaking of God" that leads to a changed life (Dandelion 2007: 23). She knew she had had a powerful experience, this drove her to pursue an authentic relationship with God by searching out new communities that would make space for her to do so. Her search led to another church which she attended for a year. It was there that she was baptized by the pastor of the church. Eventually, however, that began to unravel for similar reasons as the last church.

The next place Kysmet found was FFC. She took a quiz on www.belief.net called the "Belief-o-Matic," which quiz matches a person to a particular faith tradition. Kysmet's resulting matches were Unitarian Universalist, Buddhist and Quaker. Since she was familiar with the former two, she decided to start looking up Quaker churches. She came upon Freedom Friends website which caught her attention:

> When I found their website it said, passionately Christ-centered, passionately inclusive, and passionately Quaker. And so I started reading stuff online, from their website, to see what they meant by those terms. I ran across a thing on there that talked about

gender identity and stuff like that, and so I knew that I would be safe here. And that was probably the key selling point.

That was enough to get Kysmet in the door. Her experience of Freedom Friends lined up with what she read about it. "When I got here . . . not only was I accepted, but I was invited to the [Pacific Northwest] Quaker Woman's Theology Conference."[9] She was happy to find an accepting community that made space for her to connect with God: "I ended up here mainly because of the rejection from the other churches."

Her first meeting at Freedom Friends was another powerful experience. Later, she had tattooed on her arm the words to one of the hymns they sung on her first Sunday there:

> The very first song that I ever heard when I walked in was "All Thy Names" and we sing it very regularly. It talks about how, "why must all thy children dwell in separate rooms when all thy names are one" and "why must one man's heaven be another man's hell?" [That was] the very first song I heard, the very first time I ever came. . . . It's just been reinforced ever since.

That first meeting left an impression with Jaye; not only was she welcomed by the people, but the songs they sung and the other practices they participated in all left her with a feeling that she was finally in the right place. It was only a matter of time before Jaye became a member of the church and began work for the planning committee of the Pacific Northwest Quaker Women's Theology Conference.

Tattoos play a big role in Kysmet's spirituality. They help tell the narrative of her life, including her "God Shots" and her becoming a Quaker. As a student of religion she was impacted by Tibetan Buddhish, Hare Krishna and Quakerism to name only a few. "Anything that's had meaning or been some kind of impact on my life I've ended up inking." After being at FFC awhile she began reading Quaker books and "remixed" a number of Quaker sayings into a new tattoo: "Let thy life speak as way opens to that of God in everyone." When she was asked by people what Quakerism was, or why she believed it, this was what she would point to as an explanation:

---

9. The PNQWTC was born out of Multwood, which desired to bring people cross-branch dialogue to Quaker women from the liberal and evangelical yearly meetings in the Pacific Northwest. This was the same group of women who had supported the birth of Freedom Friends as an inclusive, Christ-centered, Quaker community.

> So I tell them: Let thy life speak is basically walk your talk. As way opens is trusting that things happen in the right time, the right reason, the right season. . . . To that of God in everyone is, whatever God is, it's in everyone and therefore we have the peace testimony and the social justice and the trying to help other people and live simply.

For Kysmet, her ink was sacramental, an outward sign of deep internal reality. Where early Friends stripped away all that encumbered in order to experience true convincement, Kysmet produced permanent expressions of creativity on her body to signify the same. Her arms tell her life story. And her life story was one of seeking and finding. One that began with a couple powerful experiences of God and ended at Freedom Friends Church, becoming a convinced Quaker, finding a space where she could have an authentic experience of God and find belonging.

Producing a New Faith and Practice

Finally, in the same way that early Friends were Publishers of Truth, Freedom Friends are cultural producers. Creating as a consequence of their authentic transformation in Christ, they resist consumer culture and "participate as producers" (Gibbs and Bolger 2005: 155). If the church in modernity succumbed to the influence of consumerism, the postmodern church intends to reverse this waywardness (ibid., 157). Consumerism has created worshippers who are passive recipients, "thereby filling religious expression with materialistic desire" (ibid.). Instead, emerging communities, such as Freedom Friends Church, "are contributors to rather than recipients of worship" (ibid., 158). At Freedom Friends, participation is woven into the very fiber of the community, rejecting the commoditization of faith that leads to both individualism and a rejection of tradition. Of the many ways they participate as producers, their *Faith and Practice* is a major contribution to Quaker culture.

The *Faith and Practice* is the result of five years of hard work and discernment. The goal was to use it to call people to a new expression of Quakerism. They started with its creation before anything else took place. The initial ideas for the first three sections were laid out by Morrison before the formation of Freedom Friends. Much of the document was formed while she was staying at a monastery for a retreat:

> Our Faith and Practice is the expression of the way we already live in community. We wrote it to give the church continuance through time, as a guideline for those yet to come. They can use it as long as it speaks to them though we also know it will be changed and altered as new truths come to light. We also hope it will encourage other people who love God. We want others who hold our values to know they are not alone, to help give them language for what they have not been able to speak. We want people to know that all different types of people with various economic statuses, sexualities, educations, theologies, and temperaments, really can form one community and love God together. (Morrison 2009b)

Even as the *Faith and Practice*, was being put together prior to the existence of FFC, many outside voices were invited into the process. Once the church was formed, everyone in the community became involved in the writing and revising. Having everyone involved in the process of creation allows them room to express their gifts accordingly. Once FFC began to have business meetings, the members approved—through the practice of Quaker discernment—the sections that had been written, and a task force was formed to help bring the rest of the project to completion. One member of the church is a freelance publisher, copy-editor and type-setter. She joined the *Faith and Practice* task force once she began attending FFC. Here is how she explained some of the process:

> Each section was in the process of being written and approved. Every time we met, each task force member chose a section to write before our next meeting. These sections were often discussed at length. At our next meeting, we would go over what was written and then new assign new sections. There was serious discussion, laughter and good work at every meeting. I thought the writing of it went pretty smoothly. At the first business meeting for a section, we would read it out loud, for the second it would go online on the forum, for the third, we would read it again and discuss any changes to be made, we would then [move] to approve it. (Hoggatt 2009)

Each addition to the *Faith and Practice* went through these three stages so that everyone in the entire meeting could edit, add, discuss, and join in the process of creating the theological document that reflects and shapes their community. Morrison remarked that Biko was able to use her gifts and experience as she made revisions and watched "for errors, and especially for clarifications and asking us to define terms and make sure we are using the terms consistently. She is a great copy editor." Remarkably, the entire book was approved through taking the sense of the meeting—meaning that there was a Spirit-driven consensus among the group (Morrison 2009b).

This high level of participation from the entire community put in service for the creation of a document of this nature has not gone unnoticed by outsiders. "Our Faith and Practice has been read online tens of thousands of times. Many people who visit FFC for the first time have already read our Faith and Practice. It is an outreach tool." Three years after its first printing, their *Faith and Practice* is still available for sale online and is in its fifth printing.

Besides the outside attention the *Faith and Practice* has generated, it has also acted in a similar way to fan fiction within participatory culture, creating high levels of activity within the meeting. Often church communities have a difficult time getting people to join in the collective work of the meeting. One outsider to Freedom Friends saw the high levels of participation as building emotional attachments to what was created:

> to hear about their process, having written it on their own, and they were so excited to see this book, they were overjoyed. People in my [Friends] church could give a care about the faith and practice. Half of them probably don't know what it is. So they have this really intimate relationship with this document. And that's awesome. I think [my meeting] would be a stronger Quaker meeting if we worked with our faith and practice that way. Part of the reason we don't is because it's so old and it's easier to just blow it off. (Peterson 2009)

Because what they are doing is both contextual and rooted in their commitment to the Quaker tradition while being wrapped in creativity, Freedom Friends' *Faith and Practice* is an example of how a tradition can be honored through the participation and innovation of fresh creativity.

Freedom Friends demonstrates how a Quaker meeting can embody an authentic resistance to consumer culture and in the process create a participatory community by stripping away the obstacles that stand in the way of people participating in a worshipping community. This is seen in their desire to welcome all people, be non-creedal, set a low bar for vocal ministry, and seek to recognize the gifts of everyone. Secondly, we have seen through the convincement narrative of one member of their community how this stripping away makes space for authentic convincement, especially for those on the fringes of society. Finally, the Freedom Friends

Faith and Practice is an open work that supports their participative community and demonstrates how authentic transformations leads to new cultural productions. Not only does the *Faith and Practice* describe the life of their community, it is open to new interpretations and revisions by that same community.

Conclusion

Freedom Friends practices authentic resistance in the way they seek to dismantle the obstacles that keep people from encountering God, by "stripping away creedalisms," challenging fundamentalism and slavery. Because of this they are able to create a space where authenticity takes place as is seen in the convincement narratives of members of their community. Finally, their *Faith and Practice* is an example of a new work that is produced out of a desire to create something that is authentic to who they are.

Open Work

In early Quakerism, knowledge operated along the lines of a decentralized network. In this model, knowledge as a decentralized network is a synthesis between collective intelligence and the architecture or structure one uses to pass knowledge along. This form of knowledge is based in consensus models of decision-making where many voices come together to make decisions. Therefore it espouses a holistic epistemology, and a leveled ecclesiology. Knowledge as a decentralized network is an "open work" inasmuch as it is "hackable" and open to revision, reinterpretation and expansion. In the previous chapter, I identified a number of practices that early Friends engaged in that show they were a decentralized, holistic and many-voiced movement. These same qualities are evident within the life of Freedom Friends Church in three ways: its practice of being a many-voiced community, commitment to dialogue and commitment to and practice of Gospel Order.

Many Voices and Theological Hospitality

Part and parcel of Freedom Friends non-creedal approach to theology is their renunciation of religious fundamentalism and intolerance in every form (Freedom Friends Church 2009: 11). Fundamentalism, as they describe it is "asserting the absolute truth and completeness of one's own beliefs and practices to the deliberate exclusion of possible truth in other beliefs and practices" (ibid., 11–12).[10] Fundamentalism—and what we can rightfully call foundationalism—is, according to the *Faith and Practice*, a "sin," "incompatible with holy living and grace" (ibid., 12). Instead, Freedom Friends asserts a holistic understanding of truth:

> We believe that God calls human souls in more ways than we can imagine, and that God abides with anyone who seeks God in spirit and in truth, regardless of how they name God. We can and will make clear the truth and power that has been given to us, our Gospel path, but in no way do we think that we possess the whole, or only, truth. We prefer to live in relationship to the truth. We believe it to be blasphemous for a human, or human group, to claim to hold the whole truth. (Ibid., 11)

By rejecting fundamentalism as they understand it, Freedom Friends demonstrates what a faith community looks like that truly embodies a holistic and decentralized approach to authority. Their *Faith and Practice* demonstrates "theological hospitality,"[11] which is a way of being both Christ-centered, while remaining open and welcoming to those who hold different views:[12]

---

10. This is an extended definition of fundamentalism that is provided in the glossary of the *Faith and Practice*: "This can refer to a particular set of beliefs, or to a way of practicing those beliefs. In religious fundamentalism adherents are called to a literal interpretation of their sacred text, strict adherence to its rules and guidelines, submission to religious authority, and often an intolerance to other belief systems. In our experience, fundamentalism asserts the absolute truth and completeness of its own beliefs and practices to the deliberate exclusion of the possibility of truth in other beliefs and practices. Some use this word exclusively for Christian fundamentalism, especially 20th century American fundamentalism, but we think that the broader definition of the process rather than a particular set of beliefs is most useful. This definition makes it easier to see the connections between the Christian Inquisition and the attack on the World Trade Center" (Freedom Friends Church, *Faith and Practice: First Edition*, 48).

11. This is a term Quaker author and convergent Friend Brent Bill has often used to describe the work of the church as well as convergent Friends more specifically. Diana Butler Bass says, "Part of universal hospitality is in the practice of befriending other religion traditions and practices, while remaining deeply grounded. Brent Bill thinks Christians need to engage in "theological hospitality," that we "should be open and welcoming...instead of starting with theological differences that divide us" (Bass, *A People's History of Christianity*, 303).

12. For Freedom Friends, true inclusivity is grounded in the person of Jesus.

> You do not have to agree with everything in the document in order to participate in the community or be a member. We recognize that parts of it can be believed in different ways: whether truth is metaphorical or literal, it is still truth. We recognize that there can be agreement in principle, but divergence in application. This is the best articulation of the beliefs and intentions of the Friends who felt called to start this church. We use it to inspire, and as a starting point for discussion and study; it is our organizational guideline. It is the campfire that we sit around. (Freedom Friends Church 2009: 19)

What is important to Freedom Friends Church is that people participate and come and sit around the "campfire." Agreements and divergences will all be worked out around the fire through dialogue, listening and discernment.

This practice has created an environment in which the "stranger is welcome," a practice Gibbs and Bolger found essential to other emerging communities (Gibbs and Bolger 2005: 117ff). Freedom Friends is committed to being open to everyone and creating a hospitable community for those seeking God. While other emerging churches in today's context are committed to being hospitable to the poor and those often hurt by the church, there is little mentioned about these communities welcoming people who struggle with mental illness, psychological disorders, or who are queer. All these people are not only welcome in worship but find their voices and value within the community (FFC 2008). There is an overwhelming sense that FFC is made up of people who identify with being "misfits" in one way or another and that this safe space is what they needed from the church. As Kysmet put it:

> We're church on the island of misfit toys because most of us that come to this particular church have been pretty damaged by organized religion. And have a lot of baggage, a lot of us have mental illness pieces and things like that going on. So they're pretty loose. They don't try to force us into anything.

"Friends use the word Christ to refer both to the historical Jesus and the present Spirit that 'has come to teach His people Himself.' In many ways the Friends movement is an attempt to return not to the Apostolic Church but to the very feet of the itinerant Rabbi. Many Friends see their worship as community with the Present Christ . . . you cannot make an inclusive Friends statement without reference to Him" (Freedom Friends Church, *Faith and Practice: First Edition*, 43).

Another woman who was a student while attending FFC said, "It felt like a really good cleansing space for me from school. I was pretty unhappy and so I'd just go and decompress. It was nice to have the outside community and everyone there is so different that it feels like a really safe space" (Wilcox 2009). Part of this attraction both for her and other members of the church is that the people there are "[n]ot really like churchy people." FFC sees church not as a place for the healthy, but for people who are sick, who need to be there: "The Work of the church present is to preach the Good News of Freedom, to bind the wounds of the brokenhearted, and to open the prison doors of the enslaved" (Freedom Friends Church 2009: 5).

One member, Ashley Wilcox, sees FFC as "the statue of liberty for the Quaker meetings: 'give me your poor, huddled masses'" (Wilcox 2009), hinting at the level of issues people struggle with. In this way, they create a community that welcomes "strangers" of all kinds: people dealing with depression, recovering from alcoholism and drug use, and who have struggled with suicide. Morrison sees their community as being able to point to people who have experienced transformation in their lives because of the church: "I consider our corporate outreach [to be making] Quakers by process of resurrection."

FFC exists to welcome people who cannot go anywhere else. Their practice of radical hospitality means that they cannot worry about being seen as "acceptable" in the eyes of others:

> We have lost people, I believe because people in meeting can feel free to say if I wasn't here this morning, I'd have a needle hanging out of my arm. And some people don't want their children to hear that, sometimes it's a bit much, but there's lots of churches for those folks to go to. . . . It does not hurt my feelings that people come and look at the [meeting] and go "Wow, this is just so not for me." It's gotta be accessible; I'm not worried about acceptable. (Morrison and Biko 2009)

In all of these ways, Freedom Friends is a many-voiced community that puts into practice an inclusivity rooted in radical hospitality and welcome of the stranger.

A Networked Community

Another way that Freedom Friends practices community in a decentralized way is by seeing itself as a loose-knit family that is connected through various mediums beyond Sunday morning worship. Even with its wide-ranging diversity, there is a deep level of commitment to one another: "A church is a family not just in terms of communal identity but also in terms of the support it provides among its members" (Gibbs and Bolger, 98). Because they are on the margins of the Quaker tradition and are made up of people on the margins of faith and society, FFC tends to protect each other like family:

> There are some people who are very explicitly Christian in the meeting and some people who are really not. But I feel like people there are really good at translating for themselves or taking away what they need . . . it's a lot of people who don't fit in anywhere else and so everybody kind of protects each other. (Wilcox 2009)

One of the ways that this family is being lived out is very similar to other communities found within participatory culture. Freedom Friends has created a networked community by building on the technology available through the internet, social networks, blogs and other "networked" technologies.

One way Freedom Friends exhibits networked styles of community is by their use of websites such as Facebook. Their Facebook group is highly active and is used by the members of the church to stay in contact throughout the week, share prayer requests, pictures from gatherings, minutes from business meetings and even ask for financial donations. Even though the community itself is around thirty people, their Facebook group has 169 followers, suggesting that there are many more who feel drawn to support this community's work. In October 2012, there were sixteen posts by five members of the group and twenty-four comments by responders. September had even higher interactions with twenty-two posts by four members and thirty-five comments. In general, the majority of posts to the group come from Alivia Biko, who is now the pastor of the church, Peggy Morrison, and Ashley Wilcox, the meeting's presiding clerk. But it is open for anyone to post, and many do.

Another way that they operate as a networked community is how they understand and use their website: www.freedomfriends.org.[13] Their website is home to an online version of their Faith and Practice, art and poetry created during meeting for worship, a page for frequently asked questions, an online forum, and other resources for the meeting. They feel that their website gives cohesion to their public identity more than a meetinghouse does and is an integral part of their community life:

> You'd almost be better to have a website and no meetinghouse. I remember the young people early on saying, there's only one thing worse than having no website and that's having a lame website. (Morrison 2009)

Some may be critical of this perspective on community, arguing that the internet is supplemental to "real" community, but for Freedom Friends this interconnectivity through the web is essential. Mirroring practices demonstrated in participatory culture, this level of connectivity is an assumed part of what it means for them to be community:

> I think they would say that it is part of how we get together . . . [some people from FFC] have consequently spent a lot of time disabled, unemployed, students, whatever, and they spend a lot of time online because that's their connection with the world. We [also] have people who have way too much to do and haven't been successful in setting up a lot of weeknight meetings with extra stuff. (Ibid.)

The internet creates a space where both of these groups, those disconnected and those too busy, stay in touch with one another.

At Freedom Friends, there are at least two categories of people: those who are students, disabled, unemployed and are more available to connect online or find it as their main way of connecting to others, and those who have too much happening in their lives to attend weekly

---

13. Their website, www.freedomfriends.org, is one of the main ways people find to the meeting for the first time. At least half of the people who attend Freedom Friends have come because they found out about the meeting online (Morrison, "Response to Friends World Committee," 2005). All of their annual reports mentioned the activity of their website, how many visitors their site received that year, and how many people came because of their website. In their first annual report they wrote on their development as a virtual community: "The wider world continues to watch our progress through our website which is updated often. We have had 8700 page hits since we put it up late last spring. Pastor Peggy wrote a post-election hangover cure [online] that was widely read and well received" (Freedom Friends Church, "First Annual Report," 2005).

meetings or miss worship on Sunday morning. One sojourning member who lived in another state for a few years said she stayed in close contact with members of the church throughout the week through Google Chat and the church forums. Even when she could not occupy the same physical place with her community, she was able to remain connected through virtual space (Wilcox 2009).

This way of connecting as a community removes some of the emphasis from Sunday as the only time the community connects. In the current pace of our world, people have—or make—less and less time to connect. The Internet helps to serve as a vehicle that people can use in order to maintain a web of friendships. They seek to be "a people rather than a place, a community rather than a meeting" (Gibbs and Bolger 99) in a way that makes sense of who they are as people, and they have a strong sense of community and camaraderie. For Biko:

> Nothing replaces actual face-to-face events and discussions, and time hanging out for relationship making. Nothing. That said, all the other tools are tools to prolong, refine, or hone the relationship/s. So yes, I think they do build community, but in a secondary manner, not a primary manner, unless of course, someone . . . finds us on the internet and comes in our actual door because of it. So I consider the impetus for getting face-to-face time and actual face time as primary. All else, internet, phone, texting, are secondary and are tools to encourage and grow the primary relationship/s face-to-face. (Biko)

Morrison reinforces this strong integration between community life at Freedom Friends' meetings and what takes place online. Thinking about it as "supplemental would be even too separate. I think they would say that it is part of how we get together" (Morrison 2009). The Internet provides a vehicle for checking in and remaining connected as a networked community throughout the week.

Gospel Order: An Open Framework

One last way that Freedom Friends creates a decentralized structure that allows for many voices to participate in their meeting is through their emphasis on Gospel Order. Gospel Order is the theological framing of the communal practice of group discernment, providing an architecture that, "broadly defined by its participants," entails a "hackability," while also fostering dialogue.

In the previous chapter, the nature of Gospel Order was discussed. There I described it as "The architecture that structures the theocentric, participative organization that holds Quakerism together." Contemporary Quaker theologian Lloyd Lee Wilson understands Gospel Order as the conviction that the mission of the church is to join with Christ in the restoration of creation (Wilson 2001: 8–9):

> The new order of the Kingdom of God, restoring the divine intent for the cosmos from its brokenness and sin, was (and is) gospel order. This order was present and available already, not postponed to some future date when Christ would return to an outward rulership over creation" (Ibid., 9).

Therefore, Gospel Order is the act of the community of Jesus working for redemption within the created order, and the embodiment of that redemption rooted in an understanding of how the world was meant to look.

> Gospel Order is the order established by God that exists in every part of creation, transcending the chaos that seems so often prevalent. It is the right relationship of every part of creation, however small, to every other part and to the creator. Gospel Order is the harmony and order which God established at the moment of creation, and which enables the individual aspects of creation to achieve that quality of being which God intended from the start, about which God could say that "it was very good." ... It is an organizing principle by which Friends come to a clearer understanding of our relationship to God in all of the divine manifestations and the responsibilities of that relationship. An attention to Gospel Order enables the meeting faith community [the church] to perceive and accept the spiritual gifts which God offers, as well as to develop and exercise those gifts as God desires. Finally, Gospel Order is both a distinctive aspect of Quaker witness and testimony and the means by which Friends come to understand how they are to witness to the world. (Ibid., 3–4)

Quakers historically have accepted that Christ's work inaugurated Gospel Order in the world, and the community that lives under that reordering of society will not only live in the world differently, they perceive all of life in a new way:

> Quakerism is more than a way of life in the world, a particular path one choose to follow through this time and space we inhabit, as one chooses to be Republican or Democrat, pro-union or not. Quakerism is really a new way of perceiving and understanding the world itself; a different way of integrating, interpreting, and responding to the data and stimuli of the world. To become a Quaker—a convinced Friend (and I hope that all Friends are convinced, whether birthright or not)—is to come into a new and different understanding of what is true and what is not, which will lead one into very different patterns of belief and action. (Ibid., 15)

As we saw in John Bellar's vision, Gospel Order names a theological vision, and ecclesial structure that seeks a "realizable utopia" under the reign of Christ. Not only does Gospel Order pave the way for a decentralized, many-voiced community, but it also establishes the possibility for a highly alternative social community to form within potentially any given context.

Freedom Friends draws heavily on a theology and practice that mirrors Wilson's understanding of Gospel Order. Their usage reflects a traditional Quaker understanding, as well as Wilson's framing of new creation. Their general definition of Gospel Order is:

> This term was first used by George Fox to describe the way Friends viewed the cosmos and humanity's place within it. This view presumed a God designed orderliness that was seen in all of creation. They viewed creation as good and designed for goodness. Sin and evil is a dis-ordered state. Jesus Christ demonstrated perfect Gospel Order and made a connection for us that empowers us to live in Gospel Order. Among Friends you will often hear this term used to describe Quaker practices, which if done well are harmonious with Gospel Order. (Freedom Friends Church 2009: 49)

There are at least three ways that Freedom Friends refers to Gospel Order in their Faith and Practice: as a reality inaugurated by Christ, a way of living and perceiving the world, and a way of structuring the organizing of the church and conducting business as Friends.

When discussing their beliefs about Christ FFC argues Jesus inaugurated Gospel Order with his life and remains present to teach his people how to live it out now:

> He was, and is, the perfect teacher of Gospel Order—living as we are intended to live. Through the agency of the Holy Spirit He is present, now, to the believer as teacher and guide. We believe that He is both come, and coming—that His kingdom is among us, and that we can live as citizens of that kingdom in this life. (Ibid., 3)

In their discussion of heaven they refer to it as a way of life for the community:

> Christ also prayed for, and promised, that by His presence and through the transformational work of the Spirit, that His kingdom could be experienced now. This is why we dedicate ourselves to the life of Gospel Order and freedom—to build and enjoy the Kingdom present and to anticipate, and be made fit for, the kingdom to come. (Ibid., 5)

Third, under "fundamentalism," Gospel Order is used as a theological lens compatible with an inclusive approach to community:

> We renounce the intolerance of religious fundamentalism in all its forms. Free Christians need only to live according to Gospel Order and hold up Christ, in order to fulfill The Great Commission. We believe that God calls human souls in more ways than we can imagine, and that God abides with anyone who seeks God in spirit and in truth, regardless of how they name God. (Ibid., 11)

And finally, central to being a decentralized community, Gospel Order names the open work nature, or architecture, of the church,

> It is our intention to keep the structure of Freedom Friends Church as simple and light as possible while maintaining functionality and Gospel Order. We want the members of our community to spend the bulk of their ministry time outside of the meeting; living out, rather than maintaining, Quakerism. (Ibid., 21)

Freedom Friends builds on a theology of Gospel Order that draws first on the present reality of Jesus, showing that those who follow Jesus will work to enact the reality that he brought about through his own life, death and resurrection, and finally this has deep implications for the kind of community that emerges and how that community is structured as a body. Gospel Order is able to remain open because it is not based simply on the past, or a conservation of tradition, but is rooted in the resurrected reality of Jesus Christ present now with his people, guiding them in truth. A community that is transformed by Gospel Order is able to remix, authentically resist and remain open as a many-voiced movement through the discernment of God's spirit.

Practically speaking this is "lightly pastoral," meaning that even the leader is not seen as the expert in all things. Beyond this, however, they have a completely participative process for making decisions together as a community:

> Though the presiding clerk facilitates the proceedings, there is no expression of hierarchical power. We believe that every person, whether a member, attendee, or first-time visitor, may have a message or an opinion to bring to the group that we need to hear and we hold each message with respect and openness. We strive to honor each person and the unique gifts they bring. We do not micromanage the committees and task forces; we trust them even as they are accountable to the Monthly Meeting.
>
> Every piece of business goes through the Monthly Meeting and it is the final decision making body. We desire to be transparent and have no closed doors or secrets. Even though this can sometimes mean waiting until the next monthly meeting for a piece of business, we believe this is crucial for gospel order. In meeting, we hold each item for business before God, trying to sense the movement of the Spirit and the sense of the meeting. (Ibid., 21)

This consensus-based process of group discernment that Quakers use is known as "the sense of the meeting." It is a process that is neither democratic nor simply oriented around finding consensus. The practice stresses that all participants come together and listen to God, the goal is to find "clearness" together as a community around what God is leading them to do.

> We use our hearts and minds and ears to listen to each other and sometimes decisions are obvious and easy to reach. When there is difficulty we slow down and listen, to that of God in each other, and also in expectant silence and prayer to what God would say to us. (Ibid., 61)

It is the role of the presiding clerk—not the pastor—to guide the group through the process of seeking clearness, maintaining Gospel Order (15), listening to people as they share, making use of queries—or open-ended questions—to help draw out what the group collectively hears. If the group is able to come to clearness around a specific question, "the clerk articulates that sense of the meeting, and a decision and action is put forward from that sense" (ibid., 62). Freedom Friends' practice of Gospel Order in this way ensures that all within the community are able to participate, drawing on the collective intelligence of the group:

> We believe that the Spirit is available to everyone regardless of age, experience or membership status...What we call the sense of the meeting is not the collected wisdom of our members and attenders, but a collective discernment of God's will. (Ibid., 17)

This is due to the non-expert culture that is a part of Freedom Friends. Reflecting on this in 2009 when Peggy Morrison was pastoring Freedom Friends, she said:

> The clerk of the meeting is the CEO of the meeting and ministry and oversight holds me [. . .] responsible. I don't have any set responsibilities. I'm kind of clerk of pastoral care. I don't do all the pastoral care; I mean these people provide pastoral care to each other all the time and they know they're doing it. . . . And nobody thinks that that's my domain and my domain only. (Morrison 2009)

Because of this there is feeling that Freedom Friends is a safe space for many to participate and take part in all levels of the church, and guide its direction. "Business sessions should be a safe and constructive place to learn. We can learn when to speak courageously, and when to hold our tongue. We get to practice listening and making ourselves understood" (Freedom Friends Church 2009: 15ff).

Lastly, this decentralized feature is also found in the very understanding of their *Faith and Practice* as an open document. Not only was it written collectively through a process of discernment, but it is open to revisions: "We expect this to be a living document. We expect that future incarnations of Freedom Friends will continue to hear revealed Truth, and will be bold to speak it, and so will need to revise this document" (ibid., 2). Elsewhere they write, "The Faith and Practice of Freedom Friends Church is intended to be a stable but dynamic document. If the meeting feels that additions or changes need to be made, the Ministry and Oversight Committee will appoint a Faith and Practice Task force to work on the concerns of the meeting." In this way, Freedom Friends operates under what Peggy Morrison calls an open source model:

> A way of producing and developing material with the intent that others will have access to the end product's source material. Inviting the participatory culture. A philosophy. This way of thinking presumes differing needs and contexts and agendas, anticipating that others will change the source of the best functionally in their environment. (Morrison 2011: 30)

A decentralized structure that remains open to revisions like this may appear to encourage an anything goes attitude, but Freedom Friends strongly rejects this position as well. Instead, they recognize that there are "weighty friends" within the community who "carry considerable spiritual weight" (Freedom Friends Church 2009: 15) and are careful to explain the process for how their group can work together to make discussions as a community. Besides listening carefully, following the process of Quaker discernment as laid out in their Faith and Practice, and the guidance of weighty Friends, the only way a community knows if something works is by trying it out:

> What does go? You've got to embody it to find out. You have to do that with engaged tolerance. You have to give it flesh and blood. Notions are just notions until you give them flesh and blood. So you put body and voice and time and energy and money into engaging with people. And then what is embodied will bear fruit. Or it won't. (Morrison 2011: 22)

The only way that a decentralized community can ultimately know if it is on the right track is to practice embodying what they say they believe. It is in the act of this embodiment that remix, active resistance and a decentralized community will either birth a new social community or it will fail to bring about something new in the world.

Freedom Friends remains a many-voiced community, constantly working to include all those who want to be a part, valuing each person's voice and contribution. They are tech-savvy, building a strong web presence and fostering a networked community that remains in conversation through time and across space. Finally, rooted in an understanding of Gospel Order, Freedom Friends Church is an open work. Based in consensus decision-making, guided by a clearly defined process, weighty Friends, and the Holy Spirit, they are able to remain open to revisions, adaptions and new revelations.

Freedom Friends is an open work inasmuch as they are made of many voices, all of which are free to contribute to the collective identity of the group due to the "Gospel Order" framework of the church. They exhibit theological hospitality, creating space for a diversity of belief and practice within the group. Because of their use of social media, they are able to operate as a networked community that does not rely solely on physical space to build connections and relationships with one another. Finally, because they are committed to Gospel Order they allow themselves, their community and their *Faith and Practice* to remain open-ended and expandable based on the discernment of the community.

CONCLUSION

Only eight years old, Freedom Friends is still relatively young for a Quaker meeting, and yet, in a short time they have achieved a status within the Quaker world that sets a precedence for other Quaker meetings seeking participatory renewal to follow. They demonstrate how as apprentices within the Quaker tradition, they have put their tradition, its key texts and practices in dialogue with their contemporary setting in ways that foster a new contextual theology through the use of remix, authentic resistance and decentralized authority. They remix Quakerism as convergent Friends, pulling together the best that Quakerism has to offer and synthesizing it in new ways. They embody an authentic resistance in the way that they strip away the practices of fundamentalism and creedalism, creating space for people to encounter God in powerful ways. Finally, they are a decentralized community that draws upon the open structure of Gospel Order, forming a many voiced, discerning community.

Conclusion

IN THIS THESIS, I have developed a convergent model of renewal that is based on central ideas from Alasdair MacIntyre, Stephen Bevans, and Henry Jenkins. The model can be used to investigate both new and old renewal movements and can determine whether the renewal fostered convergence and participation. The model can illuminate how renewal movements that are both convergent and participatory remix texts, resist through production and authenticity, through creating open works. Where we find tradition and context put in dialogue by insiders in these ways we will find renewed participatory communities. The model can also reveal renewal movements that fail to be faithful to their tradition, context, and usher in a renewed participatory community.

The convergent model of renewal draws on MacIntyre's understanding of tradition as historically extended arguments that are socially embodied within community, Bevans' understanding that mission is always embedded within the church's context, and Jenkins' understanding of participatory culture as a community of fans that resist, subvert, and challenge authorized meanings and dominant structures by embodying alternative social practices within culture. By way of conclusion, I will summarize key points from these three thinkers and then suggest questions that can lead to further study.

MACINTYRE AND TRADITION

Alasdair MacIntyre's thorough account of what a tradition is, the challenges posed to traditions by modernity, and how traditions overcome epistemological crises forms the philosophical basis of the model developed here. For traditions to overcome crises, apprentices not only learn the language, virtues and the practices of their own tradition, but also another's tradition and context as a "second first" language. The convergent model argues, along with MacIntyre, that change within a tradition comes about by insiders to the tradition who are able to put their tradition in dialogue with the challenges of competing traditions and contexts. Successful apprentices will not only be able to guide their traditions to reformulations but will do so by drawing on their tradition as the ground for further innovation and creativity. Both MacIntyre and the convergent model treat tradition as an open work, capable of being extended, adapted, and changed over time in ways that remain faithful to the past, while contextually congruent.

The model draws heavily on tradition because, following MacIntyre, it accepts that there is no place to stand outside tradition. In the same way that Stephen Bevans argues that everything is contextual, one of MacIntyre's major insights is that tradition is unavoidable. While modernity has argued to the contrary, MacIntyre demonstrates that there is no neutral or objective space where apprentices can stand to adjudicate rival claims. For instance, within the church there is no gospel as such, but instead many interpretations of the gospel. Therefore the work of apprentices within a tradition is to constantly to overcome the challenges and crisis their tradition face in changing times. Tradition, as it has been described, is not a deterministic force but rather an evolving, adaptive and open work. Rather than being seen as a liability or albatross, tradition provides the material, resources and skills necessary for renewal. As I have stated, tradition is the only grounds for innovation. MacIntyrean understanding of renewal necessarily involves drawing on the resources within one's own historical interpretive community.

The model developed here demonstrates how early Quakers and Freedom Friends Church are both examples of apprentices within their tradition, reformulating their tradition in ways that help their communities overcome the challenges of their time. As I demonstrated in Chapter 6, early Quakers were both a convergent and participatory renewal movement within Christianity. Through a variety of tactics they worked within Christianity—as apprentices of their tradition—in ways that sought to release Christianity from the shackles of hypocrisy, apostasy and inauthenticity and build something new in its place. Similarly, Freedom Friends is a contemporary example of what reconstruction of a tradition looks like. They demonstrate that the trusted Quaker forms can be sustained when adapted in new ways. Freedom Friends has managed to create a participatory church that redefines Christ-centered Quakerism by appropriating it within today's context in ways that are clearly faithful to both tradition and context.

BEVANS CONTEXTUAL THEOLOGY

Bevans' contextual theology is a helpful missiological companion to MacIntrye's philosophy inasmuch as Bevans accepts the inevitability of tradition. He demonstrates the essential role of context within the development of a new theology. From Bevans' perspective, context is the impetus for change and renewal within the mission of the church. Modernity has not been kind to the church's understanding of tradition and context, which divided mission between the practice of evangelism and the practice of social action. This helps to explain a great deal of the fractures Quakers have experienced in history. However, since the advent of contextual theology, other approaches have been developed that do not rely on these dualisms.

Contextual theology overcomes issues of modernity by recognizing that there is no theology but contextual theology. All theology is derivative. Even early Quakerism was itself a contextual theology, one that—as Everett Cattell alludes to in the introduction—sought to draw on where God was already at work within human culture. If this is central to the Quaker narrative, then this is an aspect that can be retrieved and re-contextualized in today's context. I argued that the synthetic model is the most fitting for developing a robust model of how this might look for Friends or any faith tradition seeking renewal.

Contextual theology, again similar to MacIntyre, shows that it is the participants within the culture who do contextual theology. MacIntyre calls them apprentices, contextual theology refers to them as insiders or participants of a particular tradition and context. Each participant has something to contribute, and those using the synthetic model believe that "true human growth" stems from being in dialogue with others. As David Tracy puts it, "the self finds itself by risking an interpretation of all the signs, symbols, and texts of its own and other cultures" (quoted in Bevans 2002: 91). They will be the ones who learn how to empathize with their tradition in ways that allow them to create and innovate, building on the resources they have at the ready.

Synthesis draws on four sources: tradition, culture, dialogue and praxis. The process of synthesis is composite, complex, open and always on the go. Yet, it must involve these four features. Synthesis demonstrates how a new theology can borrow from the surrounding culture and incorporate it into its own textures. "This composite makeup of every culture means that every culture can borrow and learn from every other culture and still remain unique" (ibid., 90). This is true for politics, technology, theology and other differences within culture. Aspects of any context from this perspective are ambivalent; what matters is how these things are used and developed (ibid., 90–91).

Early Quakers practiced synthesis in the ways that they drew on Jesus' teachings and the biblical narrative in new ways, fostered communities of authentic convincement that challenged Christendom, dialogued with dissenters and learned from them, and sought to produce an alternative Christian vision through their worship practices, their missionary activity, and the vast amounts of self-publishing they engaged in. Freedom Friends is an example of a new synthesis arising within the Quaker world today. They, too, have sought to allow context to shape their outlook, interpretations of their tradition and practices. Freedom Friends is in dialogue with their tradition, context and others who may not believe what they believe. In the process they have demonstrated what a contextually appropriate Quakerism can look like.

JENKINS AND PARTICIPATORY CULTURE

The first two chapters covered the theory behind understanding tradition and context. Chapter 3 on Jenkins and participatory culture developed key insights into understanding what participatory culture is and the elements that make it up. Participatory culture is both a specific name for today's context and a set of strategies and tactics for challenging the individualism and the passivity of consumerism found within that context. Fan studies demonstrate that fans within today's context use "tactics" to create meaning and resist popular culture. Fans construct meaning and produce new cultural artifacts based on pre-existing texts. While these texts are unauthorized by sanctioned interpretations, they enable new communities to be established as liberating spaces.

Three keywords arise from Jenkins' understanding of participatory culture: poaching, convergence and production. Each of these three words describes what it takes to create a new, alternative and participatory community. Poaching describes the process of "active reading" where texts are read and appropriated within an individual's life. Poaching is the process of taking original texts and reintroducing them into new contexts. Convergence names a bringing together of old and new mediums, where only the "delivery technologies change." Convergence is a collective, communal process that is ad-hoc and unstable, while constantly working toward a new consensus. Because of the many voices involved in the process, convergence names the essential nature of participatory culture as an "open work." Finally, participatory culture is productive rather than consumptive. Production happens as fans create the kind of objects they would like to consume. Fans may practice dismantling one aspect of culture, a text, or a practice in order to remix it for a new purpose. D.I.Y. represents this kind of ethos. Production critiques what is available by offering an alternative space.

As suggested above, participatory culture reflects a predominant ethos within the West. As such, it not only names the cultural milieu in which dialogue with tradition will take place, but the kinds of practices that those within the culture may find resonance with. I named six elements of participatory culture: authentic resistance, remix, cultural production, collective intelligence, decentralized authority and alternative social community. Authentic resistance is seen in zine culture and the D.I.Y. movement. Both resist the passive act of consumption, moving to create and produce something that is authentic to the individual or community it represents. Authentic resistance seeks to return to an authentic self and reality as it really is. Closely aligned with authentic resistance is cultural production. Those who practice cultural production do so in order to create a liberating space within consumerism.

One example of how cultural production creates an alternative space is YouTube. When the division between consumer and producer, writer and author is circumvented, that community is practicing cultural production. *Remix* is a central practice to participatory culture. Remix names the ability to read and write, to consume and produce. Remix poaches cultural artifacts, texts, symbols, images, etc. and builds on the previously established meanings while subverting them in ways that create new meaning. Remix demonstrates how tradition is given credit within an emerging creative class of practitioners. *Decentralized Authority* is the structure through which participatory culture works. It downplays expert systems and instead builds on the assumption that everyone has something to contribute. These systems are open-ended, expandable and display "hackability." *Collective intelligence* describes the participatory and mutuality of knowledge. It shows how apprentices can gain skills, understanding and knowledge through a "circuit of exchange." This is something that does not happen naturally but must be fought for, built to nourish a sociability of knowledge and a mutuality of learning. Thus it projects, in the words of Pierre Lévy, an *achievable utopia*. Therefore, the final element of participatory culture is an alternative social community. This community is an achievable utopia, a group of people who are creative resisters, cultural producers who establish a liberated space that projects images of a better world.

A CONVERGENT MODEL OF RENEWAL

Woven together in the manner of synthesis MacIntyre, Bevans, and Jenkins reflect the theoretical core to my convergent model of participatory renewal. It is convergent because it contains the old and new "media," both tradition and context. It is participatory because it identifies the practices central to the cultural dialogue that the model nourishes. It follows synthesis because it takes seriously the dialogue between tradition and context and builds on the praxis within participatory culture. Given this as background, the model can be summarized: convergent, participative renewal takes place when apprentices or participants are in dialogue with the original texts, practices and interpretations of their tradition and current context identifying both same-saying, concept borrowing, as well as "exorcisms" through a process that (1) remixes the original texts of the tradition with new texts and interpretations, (2) fosters authentic resistance through the participants authentic expressions of their subjective experiences and (3) is structured as an open work where many voices can participate, power is shared, and the work is open-ended and expandable. In doing so they will (4) create a renewed participatory community that is both rooted in their tradition and in their contemporary context and done in a way that draws on the contributions of all of those within the apprenticing community.

USING THE MODEL

This convergent model can be used to determine renewal movements that are both *convergent* and *participative*, which I demonstrated through two examples: early Quakers and Freedom Friends Church in Salem, Oregon.

Early Quakerism

The early Quaker movement was a renewal movement within Christianity. Applying the convergent model as a lens to understand early Quakerism reveals that it was not only a renewal movement, it was also highly participative. Early Friends were apprentices of the Christian tradition, deeply invested in the biblical narrative and Christian practice. They were also fluent in seventeenth-century British culture, which was under great upheaval. Through much dialogue with their context, other dissenting religious groups and the Christian tradition, Quakers were able to identify places in their culture where God was at work, and places within their culture that needed to be resisted. They embodied *remix* through both an empathetic reading of Scripture and reenacting the biblical story. They fostered a community of *authentic resistance* by their massive amounts of publishing, their response to the hypocrisy and inauthenticity of those around them, and by creating a socially embodied community that sought to live out authentic spirituality in the midst of worldly practices they disapproved of. They established their movement as an *open work* based on their mutuality of knowledge, models of discernment, inclusion of many voices and their understanding of Gospel Order. These factors led early Quakers to being a renewed participatory community within the seventeenth-century.

Freedom Friends Church

Freedom Friends Church in Salem Oregon is a Quaker meeting that demonstrates what a convergent and participatory Quaker meeting looks like within today's context. Applying the convergent model to Freedom Friends reveals how they are not only apprentices within the Quaker tradition, but also bring together disparate threads of a divided Quaker tradition. They seek to embrace their own culture as participants within late modernity. Freedom Friends as apprentices of their tradition and context *remix* their tradition as a uniting meeting, bringing together insights from different Quaker sub-traditions. They also remix new and old practices within their worship setting and through the reenactment of the Sermon on the Mount as a healing community of "ditch walkers." They foster *authentic resistance* in the way that they seek to strip away creedalism, instead encouraging authentic encounter with God. Because of their resistance to creedalism, as well as a number of other features that dominate within Evangelical Christianity, they create a liberating space where convincement narratives from unlikely sources are able to emerge. Finally, the production of their *Faith and Practice* is a clear example of producing something new as a means of resisting the present order. Finally, they have created an *open work* inasmuch as they are an inclusive community that amplifies many voices and builds on consensus of the group. Theological hospitality is central to who they are as a community. Gospel Order structures what they do as a community that practices discernment together. Their *Faith and Practice* is always up for revisions, new insights and changes. All of these factors put together reveal how Freedom Friends is not only convergent but also a renewed participatory Quaker community. Freedom Friends demonstrates not only how the model works, but what Quaker renewal looks like in the twenty-first century.

TAKING THIS BEYOND

There are many tests that have yet to be done with the convergent model. First, it needs to be applied to other religious traditions: are there renewal movements within Judaism or Islam that match these characteristics? What insights can be gleaned from these case studies? Second, the model needs to be tested alongside more social movements such as the civil rights or Occupy Wall Street. Is the model broad enough to cover renewal movements of all kinds? What are its limitations? Third, if the model proves to reveal key insights into change and renewal, can it help facilitate participative renewal within local congregations, or other movements that are in a state of crisis? Fourth, what are examples of groups that have failed to follow through the steps the model outlines? What are negative examples of this model in use? Finally, other questions abound: where do apprentices come from? How can apprentices be nurtured in today's world in a way that they might be able to walk through this model with their own tradition? How often does a group need to go through a process like this? Is it every generation? Does this model help overcome all crises or only certain kinds?

There are many questions left to be answered and much work still to be done, but the groundwork has been laid for a model that can facilitate renewal that does not need to let go of the richness of its tradition in order to create something new. Early Quakers and Freedom Friends Church demonstrate that there is a way to be faithful to one's tradition, while enabling it to move forward and enter new contexts in creative ways. Renewal of tradition is not only possible and desirable; it is necessary for our future life together.

Afterword

> I was a-trembling, because I'd got to decide, forever, betwixt two things, and I knowed it. I studied a minute, sort of holding my breath, and then says to myself: "All right then, I'll go to hell"
>
> —HUCK FINN

WITH THESE WORDS, HUCKLEBERRY Finn courageously decides to do the wrong thing for the right reason. His friend Jim, a runaway slave has been captured and sold by a couple of scoundrels. Huck is considering doing the correct thing by writing to Jim's owner. Instead, he decides to help Jim escape -again. He turns his back on everything he has been taught is real, things he mostly believes, to follow what his own experience tells him is true. Huck's decision is based in love. He believes he will be damned for the choice. He goes with love, anyway.

Lawrence Kohlberg would call this the highest level of moral development. It is the ability to see beyond rules and social norms and apply principles that are both underlying and transcendent. Wess Daniels has carefully described a way for Quakers to remain true to the underlying principles laid down by Fox and Fell while applying those principles in a transcendent fashion for the twenty-first-century. This path starts with honoring our tradition and then releasing it from the bonds of accumulated baggage and freeing it to respond to the needs of the day. In doing to so we call others to participate in a Spirit lead re-creation. This will only work if we, like Huck Finn, ground our decisions in Love. Unlike Huck, I do not think that we need to fear damnation. Yet a certain question keeps rising in me.

What fresh hells do we need to visit? What denizens thereof are in need of liberation? Elizabeth Fry entered the very real hell of Newgate prison to defy the rules of class and apply both love and practical help. Love is always practical. If we choose to take up Wess's challenge and participate in the application of love, and the re-creation of Quakerism, where will we be called to go? What comfortable tools will we need to lay down to have free hands? What would happen if...

- we declared a complete and total armistice in the battle over what the Bible says?
- we entirely stopped the activity of deciding who is fit for ministry, while recognizing, nurturing and even honoring good ministry when we see it?
- we slowed back on the reflection, the defining, the processing, and the writing of beautifully worded minutes, and just each one did what Love tells us to do, not so much for ourselves, but for others?
- we cranked down the weirdness factor, and just joined our culture as full participants?

Then, when we had forsaken the bickering and peculiarity we could throw the word Quaker around a bit and surprise people. In a good way.

We are supposed to be a city on the hill. You see the hill and the city on it far off. If it looks good you might decide to stop there, only then do you ask, "What city it this?" What if we were like that?

I don't know. I'm just asking good questions—it's a Quaker thing. But you want to know another Quaker thing? Finding the answers and shouting them from the rooftops. Good practical answers—like "the foods right here and the toilets are right over there." And when the questions change the answers change, but what is underlying and transcendent does not. That's the shine.

Now, the ending of every good piece of worship—and that's what this book has been, a mighty fine piece of worship—needs a benediction. I'm gonna let Huck take care of that as well.

> *So there ain't nothing more to write about, and I am rotten glad of it, because if I'd a knowed what a trouble it was to make a book I wouldn't a tackled it, and ain't a-going to no more.*

Peggy Senger Morrison
Chemeketa Community College

Bibliography

Abbott, Margery Post. 1995. *An Experiment in Faith: Quaker Women Transcending Differences*. Philadelphia: Pendle Hill Pamphlet.
———. 2006. "Bellars, John." In *The A to Z of the Friends (Quakers)*, edited by Margery Post Abbott, Mary Ellen Chijioke, Ben Pink Dandelion, and John William Oliver Jr., 35–58. Lanham, MD: Scarecrow.
———. 2008. "A Brief History of the Evolution of the Pacific Northwest Quaker Women's Theology Conference." No pages. Online: http://pnwquakerwomen.org/Site/OurHistory-673.html (accessed October 17, 2012).
Angell, Stephen. 2012. "The Impending Split in Indiana Yearly Meeting." *Quaker Theology* 11:20 (2012) 11–32.
Bakhtin, Mikhail. 1965. "Rabelais and His World." In *Cultural Resistance Reader*, edited by Stephen Duncombe, 82–88. London: Verso.
Baldwin, Rosecrans. 2008. "Machinery Nostalgia." *New York Times*, June 19, 2008. http://tmagazine.blogs.nytimes.com/2008/06/19/the-digital-ramble-machinery-nostalgia/ (accessed September 12, 2012).
Barbour, Hugh, and Arthur O. Roberts. 1973. *Early Quaker Writings, 1650–1700*. Grand Rapids: Eerdmans.
———. 1988. "James Nayler, 1618–1660: The Quaker Indicted by Parliament." *Church History* 57:3 (1988) 240.
Barbour, Hugh, and J. William Frost. 1988. *The Quakers*. New York: Greenwood.
Barclay, Robert. 2002. *An Apology for the True Christian Divinity*. Glenside, PA: Quaker Heritage.
Barker, Chris. 2003. *Cultural Studies: Theory and Practice*. 2nd ed. London: Sage.
Bass, D. B. 2009. *A People's History of Christianity: The Other Side of the Story*: New York: HarperCollins.
Bassett, Caroline. 2007. *The Arc and the Machine: Narrative and New Media*. Manchester, UK: Manchester University Press.
Bellers, John, and A. Ruth Fry. 1935. *John Bellers, 1654–1725: Quaker, Economist and Social Reformer: His Writings*. London: Cassel.
Benson, Lewis. 1983. *Catholic Quakerism*. Philadelphia: Religious Society of Friends.
Bevans, Stephen B. 2002. *Models of Contextual Theology*. Revised and expanded edition. Faith and Culture Series. Maryknoll, NY: Orbis.
Bevans, Stephen, and Roger Schroeder. 2004. *Constants in Context: A Theology of Mission for Today*. American Society of Missiology Series. Maryknoll, NY: Orbis.
Biko, Alivia, and Peggy Morrison, interview with author, February 12, 2009.

Bolger, Ryan K. 2007. "Practice Movements in Global Information Culture: Looking Back to McGavran and Finding a Way Forward." *Missiology* 35:2 (2007) 181–94.

Bosch, David J. 2005. *Transforming Mission: Paradigm Shifts in Theology of Mission*. American Society of Missiology 16. Maryknoll, NY: Orbis.

Branson, Mark L. 2004. *Memories, Hopes, and Conversations: Appreciative Inquiry and Congregational Change*. Herdon, VA: Alban Institute.

Brewin, Kester. 2007. *Signs of Emergence: A Vision for Church that is Organic/Networked/Decentralized/Bottom-Up/Communal/Flexible/Always Evolving*. Grand Rapids: Baker.

Britain Yearly Meeting (Society of Friends). 2012. "Introducing Quakers." http://www.quaker.org.uk/intro-quakers (accessed May 21, 2012).

Bryman, Alan. 2008. *Social Research Methods*. 3rd ed. New York: Oxford University Press.

Burgess, Jean, and Joshua Green. 2009. *YouTube: Online Video and Participatory Culture*. Malden, MA: Polity.

Calvert, Pamela. 2003. "'How Blessed It Is for Sisters to Meet': Historical Roots of the Pacific Northwest Quaker Women's Theological Conference." *Quaker History* 92:2 (2003) 19–51.

———. 2009. Interview with author.

Cattell, Everett L. 1970. "The Future for Friends?" *Quaker Religious Thought* 12:3 (1970) 1–5.

———. 1971. "A New Approach for Friends." In *In What Future for Friends*, edited by Friends World Committee for Consultation, n.p. Ithaca, NY: Snow Lion, 1971.

Chafkin, Max. 2012. "Revolution Number 99: An Oral History of Occupy Wall Street." http://www.vanityfair.com/politics/2012/02/occupy-wall-street-201202 (accessed September 14, 2012).

"Consensus Decision Making." Last modified May 24, 2012. http://99.0ccupymediawiki.org/wiki/Consensus_decision_making.

Cooper, Wilmer A. 2001. *A Living Faith: An Historical and Comparative Study of Quaker Beliefs*. 2nd ed. Richmond, IN: Friends United.

Creasey, Maurice A., and David L. Johns. 2011. *Collected Essays of Maurice Creasey, 1912–2004: The Social Thought of a Quaker Thinker*. Quaker Studies 8. Lewiston, NY: Edwin Mellen.

Cronk, Sandra Lee. 1991. *Gospel Order: A Quaker Understanding of Faithful Church Community*. Pendle Hill Pamphlet 297. Wallingford, PA: Pendle Hill.

Damrosch, Leopold. 1996. *The Sorrows of the Quaker Jesus: James Nayler and the Puritan Crackdown on the Free Spirit*. Cambridge, MA: Harvard University Press.

Dandelion, Ben Pink. 2005. *The Liturgies of Quakerism, Liturgy, Worship and Society*. Aldershot: Ashgate.

———. 2006. *The Friend. James Nayler and the Unity of Covenant Quakerism*. London, UK: Britain Yearly Meeting.

———. 2007a. *An Introduction to Quakerism*. New York: Cambridge University Press.

———. 2007b. "Testimony as Consequence, Not Value." *Friends Quarterly* 35 (2007) 189–95.

———. 2008. *The Quakers: A Very Short Introduction*. New York: Oxford University Press.

———. 2009. "Quaking with Confidence." *Friends Journal*, December 1, 2009. Philadelphia: Friends.

Daniels, C. Wess. 2008a. "New Quakers: A Faithful Betrayal?" *Quaker Life* (January/February 2010) 27–29. Richmond, IN: Friends United Meeting.

———. 2010b. "Convergent Friends: The Emergence of Postmodern Quakerism." *Quaker Studies* 14:2 (2010) 236–250.

———. 2011. "Convergent Friends." In *Historical Dictionary of the Friends (Quakers)*, edited by Margery Abbott, 87–88. Lanham, MD: Scarecrow.

———. 2012. "Freedom Friends Church." In *Historical Dictionary of the Friends (Quakers)*, edited by Mary Ellen Chijioke, Margery Post Abbott, Pink Dandelion, and John William Oliver, Jr., 136. Lanham, MD: Scarecrow.

De Certeau, Michel. 1984. *The Practice of Everyday Life*. Berkeley, CA: University of California Press.

Duncombe, Stephen. 1997. *Notes from Underground: Zines and the Politics of Alternative Culture*. London; New York: Verso.

———. 2002. *Cultural Resistance Reader*. London: Verso.

———. 2007. *Dream: Re-Imagining Progressive Politics in an Age of Fantasy*. New York: New Press.

Eastern Region, Evangelical Friends Church. 2007. *Faith and Practice*. Canton, OH: Eastern Region.

Fell, Margaret. 1980. *Women's Speaking Justified*. Amherst, MA: Mosher.

———. 1995. "The Testimony of Margaret Fox Concerning her Late Husband George Fox: Together with a Brief Account of Some of His Travels, Sufferings, and Hardships for the Truth's Sake." In *Hidden in Plain Sight: Quaker Women's Writings 1650–1700*, edited by Judith Benefield, Margaret Applegate, Mary Garman, and Dortha Meredith, 233–43. Pennsylvannia, PA: Pendle Hill.

Fox, George. 1959. "Letter of George Fox and other Friends to the Governor of Barbadoes." Philadelphia: Tract Association of Friends.

———. 1975. *A Journal or Historical Account of the Life, Travels, Sufferings, Christian Experiences, and Labour of Love in the Work of the Ministry, of that Ancient, Eminent, and Faithful Servant of Jesus Christ, George Fox*. 2 vols. The Works of George Fox. New York: AMS.

Fox, George, John L. Nickalls, Henry Joel Cadbury, and Geoffrey Fillingham Nuttall. 1985. *The Journal of George Fox*. A revised edition by John L. Nickall; with an epilogue by Henry J. Cadbury and an entroduction by Geoffrey F. Nuttall. Philadelphia: Religious Society of Friends.

Fox, Margaret Askew Fell, and Elsa F. Glines. 2003. *Undaunted Zeal: The Letters of Margaret Fell*. Richmond, IN: Friends United Press.

Freedom Friends Church. 2004. "Six Month Report." Salem, OR.

———. 2005. "First Annual Report of Freedom Friends Church." Salem, OR.

———. 2008a. "Fourth Annual Report." Salem, OR.

———. 2008b. "History of Freedom Friends Church." Salem, OR.

———. 2009. *Faith and Practice*. Salem, OR.

———. 2013. *Faith and Practice*. Updated Edition. http://freedomfriends.org/FF-What.htm (accessed March 28, 2013).

Friedman, Edwin H., Margaret M. Treadwell, and Edward W. Beal. 2007. *A Failure of Nerve: Leadership in the Age of the Quick Fix*. New York: Seabury.

Friesen, Dwight. 2009. *Thy Kingdom Connected: What the Church Can Learn from Facebook, the Internet, and Other Networks*. ēmersion: Emergent Village Resources for Communities of Faith. Grand Rapids: Baker.

Garman, Mary. 1996. *Hidden in Plain Sight: Quaker Women's Writings, 1650–1700*. Wallingford, PA: Pendle Hill.

Gibbs, Eddie, and Ryan K. Bolger. 2005. *Emerging Churches: Creating Christian Community in Postmodern Cultures*. Grand Rapids: Baker Academic.

Giddens, Anthony. 1990. *The Consequences of Modernity*. Palo Alto: Stanford University Press.

Guiton, Gerard. 2005. *The Growth and Development of Quaker Testimony, 1652–1661 and 1960–1994: Conflict, Non-Violence, and Conciliation*. Quaker Studies 7. Lewiston, NY: Mellen.

Gwyn, Douglas. 1986. *Apocalypse of the Word: The Life and Message of George Fox (1624–1691)*. Richmond, IN: Friends United.

———. 2000. *Seekers Found: Atonement in Early Quaker Experience*. Wallingford, PA: Pendle Hill.

———. 2006. *The Covenant Crucified: Quakers and the Rise of Capitalism*. London: Quaker.

Hamm, Thomas D. 1992. *The Transformation of American Quakerism: Orthodox Friends, 1800–1907*. Religion in North America MB718. Bloomington, IN: Indiana University Press.

———. 2004. "George Fox and the Politics of Late Nineteenth-Century Quaker Historiography." In *The Creation of Quaker Theory*, edited by Ben Pink Dandelion, 11–18. England: Ashgate.

Harkin, Michael Eugene. 2004. *Reassessing Revitalization Movements Perspectives from North America and the Pacific Islands*. Lincoln, NE: University of Nebraska Press.

Higgins, Dalton. 2009. *Hip Hop World: A Groundwork Guide*. Groundwork Guides. Toronto: House of Anansi.

Hoggatt, Sarah, interview with author, 2009.

Holman, Peggy, Tom Deyane, and Steven Cady. 2007. *The Change Handbook: The Definitive Resource on Today's Best Methods for Engaging Whole Systems*. San Francisco: Berrett-Koehler.

Jay-Z. 2010. *Decoded*. New York: Spiegel and Grau.

———. 2010. Interview by Terry Gross, *Fresh Air*, NPR, November 16.

Jenkins, Henry. 1992. *Textual Poachers: Television Fans and Participatory Culture*. Studies in Culture and Communication. New York: Routledge.

———. 2006a. *Convergence Culture: Where Old and New Media Collide*. New York: New York University Press.

———. 2006b. *Fans, Bloggers, and Gamers: Exploring Participatory Culture*. New York: New York University Press.

Johnson, Richard, Deborah Chambers, Parvati Raghuram, and Estella Tincknell. 2004. *The Practice of Cultural Studies*. Thousand Oaks, CA: Sage.

Jones, T. Canby. 1971. *Quaker Understanding of Christ and of Authority*. Philadelphia: Faith and Life Movement.

Kallenberg, Brad J., Nancey C. Murphy, and Mark Nation. 1997. *Virtues and Practices in the Christian Tradition: Christian Ethics after MacIntyre*. Harrisburg, PA: Trinity.

Kreps, Daniel. 2008. "Radiohead Launch 'Nude' Remix Contest." *Rolling Stone*, April 1, 2008. http://www.rollingstone.com/music/news/radiohead-launch-nude-remix-contest-20080401 (accessed September 12, 2012).

Kunze, Bonnelyn Young. 1994. *Margaret Fell and the Rise of Quakerism*. Houndmills Basingstoke, UK: Macmillan.

Kysmet, Jaye, interview with the author, 2009.
Lasn, Kalle. *Culture Jam*. 2000. New York: Quill.
Lessig, Lawrence. 2008. *Remix: Making Art and Commerce Thrive in the Hybrid Economy*. New York: Penguin.
Lévy, Pierre. 1997. *Collective Intelligence: Mankind's Emerging World in Cyberspace*. Cambridge, MA: Perseus.
MacIntyre, Alasdair C. 1980. "Epistemological Crises, Dramatic Narrative, and the Philosophy of Science." In *Paradigms and Revolutions*, edited by Gary Gutting, 55–75. Notre Dame, IN: University of Notre Dame Press.
———. 1984. *After Virtue: A Study in Moral Theory*. 2nd ed. Notre Dame, IN: University of Notre Dame Press.
———. 1988. *Whose Justice? Which Rationality?* Notre Dame, IN: University of Notre Dame Press.
———. 1990. *Three Rival Versions of Moral Enquiry: Encyclopaedia, Genealogy, and Tradition*. Notre Dame, IN: University of Notre Dame Press.
———. 1999. *Dependent Rational Animals: Why Human Beings Need the Virtues*. Chicago: Open Court.
Marsden, George. 1991. *Understanding Fundamentalism and Evangelicalism*. Grand Rapids: Eerdmans.
Maslin Nir, Sarah. 2011. "Wall Street Protesters Broadcast Arrests on Social Media." *New York Times*, September 24.
McClendon, James William. 2002. *Ethics*. Systematic Theology 1. Nashville: Abingdon.
Mohr, Robin. 2006. "Robinopedia: Convergent Friends." http://robinmsf.blogspot.com/2006/01/robinopedia-convergent-friends.html (accessed April 26).
———. 2013. "Changes in Worldwide Friends Since 2007." *Friends Journal* 59:5 (May) 28.
Moore, Rosemary Anne. 2000. *The Light in their Consciences: Early Quakers in Britain, 1646–1666*. University Park, PA: Pennsylvania State University Press.
Moulitsas Zuniga, Markos. 2008. *Taking on the System: Rules for Radical Change in a Digital Era*. New York: Celebra.
Murphy, Nancey C. 1996. *Beyond Liberalism and Fundamentalism: How Modern and Postmodern Philosophy Set the Theological Agenda*. The Rockwell Lecture Series. Valley Forge, PA: Trinity.
Murphy, Nancey C., and James Wm. McClendon, Jr. 1989. "Distinguishing Modern and Postmodern Theologies." *Modern Theology* 5:3 (1989) 191–214.
Neelon, David. 2009. *James Nayler: Revolutionary to Prophet*. Becket, MA: Leadings.
Noll, Mark A. 1994. *The Scandal of the Evangelical Mind*. Grand Rapids: Eerdmans.
———. 2002. *America's God: From Jonathan Edwards to Abraham Lincoln*. New York: Oxford University Press.
"Northwest Yearly Meeting: A Book of Christian Discipline." 2011. *Faith and Practice*. Newberg, OR: NWYM.
"Occupy Movement." Wikipedia, http://en.wikipedia.org/wiki/Occupy_movement (accessed September 14, 2012).
Oliver, John W., Charles L. Cherry, and Caroline L. Cherry. 2007. *Founded by Friends: The Quaker Heritage of Fifteen American Colleges and Universities*. Lanham, MD: Scarecrow.

Olofson Thickstun, Margaret. 1995. "Writing the Spirit: Margaret Fell's Feminist Critique of Pauline Theology." *Journal of the American Academy of Religion* 63:2 (1995) 269–79.

Palmer, T. Vail Jr. 1993. "Early Friends and the Bible: Some Observations." *Quaker Religious Thought* 26:2 (1993) 40–55.

———. 1996. "Religion and Ethics in the Thought of John Bellers." In *Truth's Bright Embrace: Essays and Poems in Honor of Arthur O. Roberts*, edited by Arthur O. Roberts, Paul N. Anderson and Howard R. Macy, 61–74. Newberg, OR: George Fox University Press.

———. 2010. *Friends and the Bible: Later Seventeenth Century and Early 18th Century*. Unpublished manuscript.

———. 2012. E-mail message to author, October 17.

———. 2013. Palmer Jr., T. Vail. "Friends, God and the Bible." Forthcoming.

Parsons Morrison, Peggy. 2005. Response to Friends World Committee for Consultation's International Meeting Advisory Committee. Salem, OR.

———. 2009. Interview with the author, February 12.

———. 2010. *Messages to a Refugee Planet*. Salem, OR: Unction.

———. 2011. *Freedom Friends Church and the Remixing of Quakerism*. Boston: Beacon Hill Friends House.

Pelikan, Jaroslav. 1971. *The Christian Tradition: A History of the Development of Doctrine, Volume 1*. Chicago: University of Chicago.

———. 1984. *The Vindication of Tradition*. New Haven, CT: Yale University Press.

Pennington, Isaac. 1681. *The works of the long-mournful and sorely-distressed Isaac Pennington, whom the Lord in His tender mercy, at length visited and relieved by the ministry of that despised people, called Quakers; and in the springings of that light, life and holy power in him, which they had truly and faithfully testified of, and directed his mind to, were these things written, and are now published as a thankful testimony of the goodness of the Lord unto him, and for the benefit of others*. London: Benjamin Clark.

Peterson, Sarah. 2009. Interview with the author, March 25.

Pryce, Elizabeth. 2010. "'Upon the Quakers and the Quietists': Quietism, Power and Authority in Late Seventeenth-Century France, and its relation to Quaker history and Theology." *Quaker Studies* 14(2): 212–23.

Punshon, John. 1987. *Encounter with Silence: Reflections from the Quaker Tradition*. Richmond, IN: Friends United Press.

———. 2001. *Reasons For Hope: The Faith and Future of the Friends Church*. Richmond, IN: Friends United Press.

Quart, Alissa. 2003. *Branded: The Buying and Selling of Teenagers*. Cambridge, MA: Perseus.

Radiohead. 2008. "Radiohead Remix." http://radioheadremix.com/ (accessed September 12, 2012).

Richardson, Mark. 2012. "Radiohead: 'Nude RE/MIX.'" *Pitchfork*. http://pitchfork.com/features/articles/6846-radiohead-nude-remix/ (accessed September 12, 2012).

Russell, Elbert. 1942. *The History of Quakerism*. New York: Macmillan.

Schneider, Nathan. 2011. "From Occupy Wall Street to Occupy Everywhere." *The Nation*, October 11, 2011. http://www.thenation.com/article/163924/occupy-wall-street-occupy-everywhere (accessed March 25, 2012).

Shenk, Wilbert R. 1999. *Changing Frontiers of Mission*. American Society of Missiology Series 28. Maryknoll, NY: Orbis.
Silverman, Jacob. 2009. "The Ironic Metaphysics of Stephen Colbert's Mash-up Style." *Virginia Quartelry Magazine*, January 9, 2009. http://www.vqronline.org/culture/ironic-metaphysics-stephen-colberts-mash-style (accessed January 22, 2013).
Smith, Jez. 2012."Occupy Quakers Call for Worship in the World." March 5, 2013. http://www.nayler.org/?p=519 (accessed May 30, 2013).
Snow, David A., Sarah Anne Soule, and Hanspeter Kriesi. 2004. *The Blackwell Companion to Social Movements*. Malden, MA: Blackwell.
Spencer, Carole. 2001. "James Nayler: Antinomian or Perfectionist?" *Quaker Studies* 6 (September) 106–117.
Stansell, Ron. 2009. *Missions by the Spirit: Learning from Quaker Examples*. Newberg, OR: Barclay.
Stott, John R. W. 2008. *Christian Mission in the Modern World*. IVP Classics. Downers Grove, IL: InterVarsity.
Tallack, William. 1868. *George Fox, the Friends, and the Early Baptists*. London: SW Partridge.
Tapscott, D., A. D. and Williams. 2008. *Wikinomics: How Mass Collaboration Changes Everything*. New York: Penguin.
Taylor, Barry. 2008. *Entertainment Theology: New-Edge Spirituality in a Digital Democracy*. Cultural Exegesis Series. Grand Rapids: Baker Academic.
Terranova, Tiziana. 2004. *Network Culture: Politics for the Information Age*. Ann Arbor, MI: Pluto.
Trueblood, Elton. 1966. *The People Called Quakers*. New York: Harper and Row.
———. 1974. *While It Is Day: An Autobiography*. New York: Harper and Row.
Verkyl, Johannes. 1978. *Contemporary Missiology: An Introduction*. Grand Rapids: Eerdmans.
Wallace, T. H. S. 2006a. "Margaret Askew Fell." In *The A to Z of the Friends (Quakers)*, edited by Margery Post Abbott, Mary Ellen Chijioke, Ben Pink Dandelion and John William Oliver Jr., 101–2. Lanham, MD: Scarecrow.
———. 2006b. "Swarthmoor Hall." In *The A to Z of the Friends (Quakers)*, edited by Margery Post Abbott, Mary Ellen Chijioke, Ben Pink Dandelion and John William Oliver Jr. Lanham, 277. Maryland: Scarecrow.
West, Cornell. 2011. "Dr. Cornel West Brings It to Occupy L.A." October 7, 2011, http://www.cornelwest.com/occupy_la_100711.html (accessed September 14, 2012).
Wilcox, Ashley, interview with the author, February 12, 2009.
Williams, Walter R., and Paul N. Anderson. 1987. *The Rich Heritage of Quakerism*. Newberg, OR: Barclay.
Wilson, Lloyd Lee. 2001. *Essays on the Quaker Vision of Gospel Order*. Philadelphia: Quaker Press of Friends General Conference.
Yoder, John Howard, Ted Koontz, and Andy Alexis-Baker. 2009. *Christian Attitudes to War, Peace, and Revolution*. Grand Rapids: Brazos.

www.ingramcontent.com/pod-product-compliance
Lightning Source LLC
Chambersburg PA
CBHW051640230426
43669CB00013B/2374